Journ
my way

An offbeat life in the media

For John, in
token of our
40-year friendship
— Cardiff, Manila,
Worthing

Cedric
5/11/12

Also from Cedric Pulford and Ituri

Two Kingdoms of Uganda (history)

Byliners: 101 Ways to be a Freelance Journalist

JournoLISTS: 201 Ways to Improve Your Journalism

Air Madness: Road's Mistakes Repeated (environment)

Siren Society (politics)

Casualty of Empire (history)

Eating Uganda (history/religion)

Coming Second Doesn't Count (memories) *co-author*

Our Vanishing Freedoms (politics) *pamphlet*

ABOUT THE AUTHOR

Cedric Pulford is an acclaimed UK-based editor, writer and training consultant with wide overseas experience. He has carried out more than 30 major training projects around the world. He was on the staff of three British national newspapers and a major US daily. As a freelance journalist since 1978, he has had a long association with the Guardian newspaper group. Cedric has two university degrees in political subjects. His previous journalism books are the long-running *JournoLISTS: 201 Ways to Improve Your Journalism* (2001) and *Byliners: 101 Ways to be a Freelance Journalist* (2009).

FRONT COVER: The author climbs to a longhouse in Sarawak, mid-Eighties. A carved tree trunk serves as vertiginous steps

BACK COVER: Here's to the project! The author and Thomson Foundation colleagues, China 1981

Journalism my way

An offbeat life in the media

Cedric Pulford

ITURI

© Cedric Pulford, 2012, 2013

The moral rights of the author have been asserted

Journalism My Way published 2013 by
Ituri Publications
4 Chestnut Close
Woodford Halse
Northants NN11 3NB (UK)

(Shortened ebook edition 2012)

ISBN 9780957147942

www.ituri.co.uk

Text set in 10 on 12pt **Palatino**
by Book Production Services, London

Printed and bound in the UK by 4edge Ltd
www.4edge.co.uk

A CIP catalogue record for this book is available from the British
Library

FSC Mixed Sources
SA-COC-001695
© 1996 FSC A.C.

CONTENTS

ILLUSTRATIONS BETWEEN PAGES 152 AND 153:

ACKNOWLEDGEMENTS

Very many thanks to Chris Howe, until lately of the Daily Telegraph and my fellow tutor on training courses, for meticulously editing the manuscript of this book and for valuable additions to the appendix on e-journalism. Thanks too for checking various sections: my colleague Roderick Thomson and former workmates Bernard Dineen (Yorkshire Post), John Cardownie (Thomson Foundation), Paul Hopkins (National Council for the Training of Journalists) and Ashari Manis (Sarawak). Over so many countries and so many years, mistakes are almost inevitable. I've done my best to eliminate them, but those that remain are entirely my fault.

It has generally been impossible to discover the authorship of most of the archive pictures. We have therefore been unable to acknowledge them as we would have liked, but the publisher and author gratefully recognise all those photographers whose work has added so much to this book.

Chris Milner compiled the index and Ian Longthorne scanned most of the pictures in the book to produce digital files (jpegs). I'm very grateful also to Steve Fenner for sparing me the huge labour of retyping extracts from my articles over the years through the magic of optical character recognition. These extracts, limited in quantity, are as follows:

The section on Jean Seberg (Chapter One) is adapted from a contribution to the festival in her honour at Marshalltown, Iowa, November 2011. Chapter Five (America) is largely drawn from material in my book, *Siren Society* (2005). It includes material about US-style shopping malls and anti-Vietnam War protests that was first published in the Yorkshire Post. Some material in Chapter Nine (Global Heyday – Africa) previously appeared in the CPU Quarterly and Times of Zambia. Chapter 10 (Bamboo Curtain) has material from my articles in Media Reporter. Chapter 11 (Global Heyday – Asia and Caribbean) includes extracts from my articles in the Guardian, CPU Quarterly, Media Reporter, Times of Oman and Bangladesh Times. Parts of Chapter 13 (Abroad Again) are from my articles in Gemini News Service and Observer News Service, with additional research (street kids) by Mervin Syafunko and Andrew Matimba. Chapter 14 (On the Road) includes material (waffly writing) from

Byliners: 101 Ways to be a Freelance Journalist (2009). Chapter 15 (Entrepreneur) has content (Imber section) first appearing variously in the Observer News Service and the Ecumenical News International agency service. Chapter 16 (Author) has extracts on cultural relativism from *Casualty of Empire* (2007) and Lydd airport from *Air Madness* 3rd edition (2008). The good news/bad news issue in Chapter 17 (Back to Borneo) is adapted from my letter in UK Press Gazette.

PROLOGUE

It was the famously severe winter that anyone who lived through it remembers – 1962-63. It will live on for a generation or two in the folk memory of those who weren't. And in the height of the snow and fog I was to attend in Leeds for an interview with the editor of the Yorkshire Post.

It never occurred to me not to go despite warnings of severe travel disruption (some things don't change). The newspaper was the most famous regional daily in England, given that by then the Manchester Guardian had become a quasi-national. 'God the Father, God the Son and God the Yorkshire Post' was the tag that summed up its influence in that most patriotic of counties.

The proposition was even simpler than this great job opportunity. I had said I would come, and come I would. That was how we were taught.

'Oh, are you coming?' said the editor's secretary, sounding surprised, when I reached her by phone. 'Then we'll see you when we see you.'

It was as well that daily newspaper editors don't usually follow a 9 to 5 routine. I was incommunicado – long before mobile phones – as the train inched its way over the 200 miles from London to Leeds. I reached the Yorkshire Post in the early evening to find the editor, Kenneth Young, still in his office.

I was warmly welcomed by his secretary, who I now discovered was Marcia. She seemed impossibly glamorous – willowy and blonde. Perhaps she was; perhaps she was an averagely pretty, averagely well turned out young professional woman. Maybe she was of average height, even a brunette. (Forgive me, Marcia, if you happen to read this.) Who's to say? I can't. After a joyless stint in periodicals, for me everything about daily journalism was bathed in a golden light.

Kenneth Young was equally welcoming. 'We didn't expect to see you,' he said, echoing Marcia.

There was no personnel officer, aka human resources; no aptitude tests of any sort. Newspaper interviews could be quite soft then, or so it seems from today's standpoint. Yet perhaps the paraphernalia of the modern HR industry muddies the water and conceals more than it reveals. The old-time editors had a way of finding the right people for the right spots.

The interviewer who asks just one question – 'When can you start?' – isn't apocryphal. That's how it was with Mr Young. All my prepared and rehearsed answers weren't needed.

He went on: 'I see you've done some subbing [copy editing and headline writing]. The vacancy I have is for a sub. It's evening work, and it can be tedious ...'

He certainly wasn't overselling it.

' ... Would you be all right about that?'

Although I had some experience of reporting, it was not much at that stage. Later, I came to feel that everyone should have his or her fill of 'the road' before turning to the subtler pleasures of subbing, but for now I told Mr Young that I was very all right about subbing. The job was mine.

I was faced with the return journey to London. To stay at a hotel would have been the sensible course. With true Yorkshire frugality the newspaper didn't offer it, and in my innocence it never crossed my mind to suggest or hint at it. This was before credit cards. I had no way of paying for a hotel. And so began the crawl back to London. We reached King's Cross after midnight, my connecting train long gone.

There was nothing for it but to sleep rough, if a bench under cover in a railway terminus can be dramatised like that. It didn't matter. I was on my way in newspapers.

ONE
STARTING EARLY – TO 1960

There was never any doubt what I would do for a living. My school and university days were littered with attempts at journalism – editing publications as much as writing for them. More mysterious to me now is what drew me to journalism. It was not a hunger for news and gossip. They have never been in the centre of my radar. An interest in *issues* – the stuff of feature articles – yes.

My facility with the English language declared itself early, as did my interest in being an author. Perhaps I saw journalism as a way-station for authorship, not knowing the appalling hit rate of journalists in producing published books. I was in love with the *idea* of being an author: think of the Villa Mauresque and Somerset Maugham writing in elegant surroundings before abandoning the day's work for drinks on the terrace.

Or maybe the matter was more Freudian: a desire to reduce the chaos of everyday activities to the order and finality of columns of type neatly arranged in the printed page. I was at least as interested in how newspapers were made as in what went into them.

My school was in the same leafy London suburb where I was born in 1938. In the fine grading of the English social system, the independent Highgate School (founded 1565) occupied a niche between the grammar schools that drew the brightest from the working and lower middle classes, and major public schools for the wealthiest and the most landed like Eton, Harrow and Winchester or, one rung down, Malvern, Repton and Oundle.

Highgate was a good example of a well established species across the nation, the locally rooted public school. The parents were typically middle middle class doctors, lawyers, accountants, small business people and armed services officers living in North London, although a minority of pupils came from further afield and lived in one of the four boarding houses. Needless to say, there were no girls. A cluster of these strange creatures was to be found down the road at Channing School, but there was little interaction official or otherwise. (Highgate later abolished its boarding houses and admitted girls.)

I tasted both sides of school like when my father won promotion in his job as a senior insurance manager at his company's City head office. The family moved from comfortable Friern Barnet to glossy Ascot, some 30 miles to the west of London. This meant that in 1952, aged 14, I ceased to be a day boy and became a boarder. It was a traumatic lifestyle change at a difficult age. I was unhappy for the rest of my schooldays – but that's another story.

For a few months I found myself in a limbo called Waiting House. This, as the name proclaims, was for boys while they waited for space to become available in one of the regular boarding houses. Here I wrote and produced my first newspaper, called Waiting House Weekly. This was a hand-written affair about which I can remember nothing. I'd bet, however, that it wasn't a weekly – I fell in love early with alliteration – or if it was, the publication schedule didn't last for more than two or three issues.

My next effort, when installed in my boarding house, was The Lodge Clarion. (The Lodge was the name of the house.) This was an upgrade in professionalism – it was typewritten. It ran to three issues. Copies survive among the memorabilia of my friends from those days – their secret weapon if we fall out!

I was in the supporting cast of the next effort, a magazine for the Fourth Form. This class was known as Shell, and the magazine rather contrivedly was call the Conchologist, this being a student of shells. The editor and driving force was 'Ducky' Peers. It was a typical schoolboy nickname. Donald Peers was *the* singer of the day, and everyone knew Donald Duck. Peers = Donald = Ducky ... voila! Ducky's father had his own business, which meant not only that the issues were professionally typed but also that the second issue was produced by lithography. It was a revelation in polished appearance compared with the output from a duplicator (the precursor of photocopiers).

Not for the first or last time in media, however, the technology outran the content. Our inspiration soon failed us. The slog of finding content for issue after issue was beyond us. The Conchologist also ran to just two issues.

In those days I had acting ambitions. Trouble was, I was no good at it. I was unable to be anyone but me: I couldn't submerge myself in a part. I was cast as one of three riotous drunks in a tavern scene in Goldsmith's *She Stoops to Conquer*.

'If you insist on being miserable, you'd better play a morose drunk!' exclaimed Jeffrey Moorhouse, the drama teacher, in exasperation.

I was put out, although I shouldn't have been, when one of my close and as it turned out lifelong friends, Roderick Thomson, was cast in Shaw's *Arms and the Man*, with nothing for me. He had the plum role of Catherine. The obvious course of drafting in the girls from Channing for the female parts wasn't taken in those days.

The play was to be reviewed by the local newspaper, the famous 'Ham and High' (Hampstead and Highgate Gazette). I discovered there was a second local paper (name forgotten). My offer to cover the play for them was accepted. My review was, of course, hostile. I was especially pleased with the line 'his wife Catherine (Roderick Thomson), a throaty baritone ...'

The review was anonymous, which was just as well. Mr Moorhouse presented both reviews to a class. He concluded that one writer was determined to like the production and the other writer was determined to dislike it. He was right in the latter part; he might have added, if he knew, that in local papers everyone always likes am-dram! Well, almost always. At least I was a pioneer in that regard.

This little episode has been the only occasion in my journalistic career when I pursued a hidden agenda to pay off a personal score.

After the fourth-form effort, the Conchologist, some of us became involved with the two school magazines, the Cholmeleian and Forum. These were more business-like affairs.

The Cholmeleian – taking its name from Highgate's 16th century founder, Sir Roger Cholmeley – was the official school magazine. It had news of clubs and sports as well as literary contributions. It was edited by boys although it must have been under heavy guidance and control by the school authorities.

I, however, was co-opted onto Forum on the basis of a jokey article I'd written about marathon running. It was headlined, although not by me, Look What Pheidippedes Started. He was the legendary hero who ran to Athens with the news of the Greek victory at Marathon – the precise distance of the modern marathon – before dropping dead, unlike most of his successors.

The literary reference was typical of the editor, Lewis Rudd, a particularly clever boy who caused a sensation by appearing, and shining, on the radio programme Brain of Britain while still at school. He went on to a successful career in television, ending up with a gong although not having reached the highest peaks that might have been predicted.

Forum was the school's literary and artistic magazine. It was a proper production, quarto size (forerunner of A4) with thicker front and back covers and local advertisements. These would have been of dubious value for the advertisers, but were paid for from their 'goodwill' budgets.

The editorial contents were contrived and derivative, but they were all our own. I suppose the school authorities were keeping an eye open for problems, yet as editor I don't recall any vetoes or suppressions. This was before the great *evenements* of the Sixties so the authorities had little to worry about from student troublemakers.

Closer scrutiny could have headed off four lines of mine that embarrassed my father:

> *Whisky made my father tight.*
> *He staggered home the heck knows how,*
> *For he had swallowed Black and White*
> *And looked just like a Friesian cow.*

Black and White was a popular brand of whisky. In fact, my father scarcely touched whisky and was an abstemious drinker generally. Aside from the cringe-making and jejune association of Black and White whisky with Friesian cows, the whole matter would have been avoided by changing just one word – *his* instead of *my*.

The verse got into my father's office somehow. He endured a lot of ribbing. It was a measure of the man that he accepted it in good part and didn't take it out on me.

One of my heroes was P.G. Wodehouse. I resolved to seek a contribution from the Master, then in his upper eighties, so I wrote to him care of his publishers. The answer when it came was short, it was corny but it was from him. Authors used to pride themselves about answering fan mail. I'm not so sure that they do now.

The Master told a joke about a snobby woman who got on a New York bus and declaimed: 'I haven't been in a bus for years.' 'You don't know how much we've missed you,' came the reply.

He signed off with the joke couplet:

> *You like my little stories, do ya?*
> *Well, glory, glory, hallelujah!*

It was slender material, but I knew enough to know that in journalism it's often the name, not the content, that matters. We made the most of it.

I was spared National Service, that two-year period of conscription between school and university (or less typically after completing higher education). The examining doctor marked me as Grade 3 on account of severe acne of the face and back. Only Grades 1 and 2 were being called up. Conscription was abolished soon afterwards and, in tacit recognition that most 18-year-olds are too green to get full benefit from university, the institution of the 'gap year' took its place.

The doctor asked me whether I wanted to do National Service. He must have been giving me the choice. I said, not particularly. Afterwards, I thought I'd dodged the column and felt bad about it for years. The feeling was needless, as I think now. He'd asked and I'd answered truthfully. I suppose this small incident illustrates the force of public school ethics at the time.

I was doing well enough at school to be earmarked for Oxbridge. As an example of the educational escalator, the teachers never mentioned anywhere else. The absurd notion was put about, although not by them, that if you couldn't get into Oxford or Cambridge you went to Trinity College, Dublin. As if places like London, Durham, Manchester and Bristol didn't exist.

For a time it looked as if I was Dublin-bound. I failed to get into Cambridge. Later, despite by then being armed with a rare state scholarship awarded on the basis of excellent A level results, I failed again, this time at Oxford. These A levels were set by the universities themselves (the Oxford and Cambridge Joint Board), adding insult to injury.

By now I'd left school. Not for me the 'seventh term' in the Sixth. I hated school too much for that. In theory, I was preparing for the college entrance exams through private study. My approach was desultory. I had no access to an academic library, and I've no memory of reading anything much. I was fortunate in the circumstances, at the third assault on Oxbridge, to be accepted at Hertford College, Oxford, to read philosophy, politics and economics.

I found myself with several months to spare, and became one of the first to enjoy gap year travel. Through business contacts of my father, a job was found for me at the Montreal Star newspaper in Canada.

This was the tail end of the era of the transatlantic liners. I had passage on a Greek boat called the New York. The name was its only touch of modernity. My mother said afterwards that her heart sank at the sight of this ancient rustbucket. It was an immigrant ship. Since these travellers were by definition one-way, the management and crew had little incentive to maintain high standards.

I was met at Quebec City, where the sight of French language posters surprised me. In Montreal, I was put up at the YMCA – and, aged 19, was on my own in a vast, new continent.

The Montreal Star was the leading English-language newspaper in that bilingual city. My job got me nowhere near the editorial department. It was in accounts, where I processed classified advertising forms for invoicing. At least I could tell myself that I was working in a newspaper. At the time it was enough. I also worked for a few weeks in insurance offices in Toronto and New York. These offices were connected with my father's company. No doubt the clerical jobs were manufactured as a courtesy to him.

This working visit fired an interest in North America that a decade later led me to work in the United States as an immigrant.

It was time to return to England in time for the 1957-58 university year. The Queen Elizabeth was far removed in style and comfort from the SS New York. I was surprised that the three classes were kept apart with locked doors. First-class passengers could no more move downwards to where the action was than others could slip upwards for a bit of luxury.

Hertford in those days was an undistinguished and obscure Oxford college – 'the one you always thought was in Cambridge'. It was headed by Neville Murphy, an elderly don who had written a book years before, and who had the enviable skill of being able to land his Player's Weights fag-ends into a spittoon from a distance.

Christ Church or Balliol it wasn't, but it was still Oxford. I wasted no time in not applying to the main student publications, the newspaper Cherwell and the magazine Isis. They were well known routes to Fleet Street. Instead, I did everything else. I joined the Conservative, Labour and Liberal societies at the same time. I took up rowing with a college eight. I tried out for the table tennis club with visions of a half-blue before my eyes, to be set right with a flurry of forehand drives and backhand flicks that I hardly saw. If there had been a half-blue in bar billiards, I'd have made it.

I took long walks in the surrounding countryside as a way of avoiding my books. I was unhappy with study and with the idea of study. I wanted to be practical, to be doing a job. I couldn't see any connection between the arid process of study and success in a job later.

Still I resisted offering myself to Cherwell or Isis. Finally, well into my university three years, I was co-opted onto the staff of a magazine called Oxford Opinion by David Bell, a friend from school who was already on board.

This magazine, which had been running for several years, appeared three times a term. It considered itself an intellectual journal, with its design modelled on the severe look of the New Statesman and the Spectator. The contents were eclectic rather than ideologically or politically partisan.

Oxford Opinion must have been a rarity among student publications anywhere in Britain in living within its means without grants or subsidies. It was solvent and secure – a state that eluded Isis and Cherwell (Isis eventually being sold to its printer as a way of meeting its printing bills). The circulation was respectable within the university, with a network of distribution agents in the colleges; local traders placed advertisements; and end-of-term surpluses had been put into a reserve fund for emergencies.

All in all, unstudentlike, and a tribute to those who created it and continued it.

The magazine was printed for an unknown reason by Kings of Lymington, Hampshire, more than 100 miles away. It was exciting to pile into a car to visit the printworks in order to sign off the pages. It was less exciting to be stranded by the roadside when the car's big end went, which was quite a common occurrence in those days.

That was the only trip to Lymington in my time. Subsequently and sensibly, we dealt with Kings by post. The magazine looked just the same.

Each editor held office for a term. I moved along the conveyor belt to become editor at the start of my third and final year. I wrote an article about classical 19th century liberalism which an unknown fellow student quoted in a tutorial, but my interest was chiefly on the production side. I had little in the way of an agenda, and no political position beyond a romantic attachment to rural life and small-scale businesses. I was frightened of Labour red in tooth and claw.

I spotted ways of developing Oxford Opinion within the existing, careful parameters. My biggest idea was to bring out an extra issue during the term. Oxford terms were just eight weeks. The magazine appeared at the end of the second, fourth and sixth weeks. Clearly there was an opportunity to bring it out at the end of the first, third, fifth and seventh weeks. The innovation worked. It proved financially viable.

The magazine's front page was unexciting, to put it mildly. It was a solid block of text (as with the New Statesman and the Spectator in those days). I thought we could venture something more interesting without detracting from the serious feel. I put on a cover, with superior paper and two huge and balanced Os for Oxford Opinion. It wasn't going to win any design prizes, but it was a step forward and received as such.

Another school friend, Christopher Garner, by then at Cambridge, was persuaded to be Oxford Opinion's sales agent. He managed to build up a small circulation in the other place.

At this time, my path crossed with that of the beautiful young American actress Jean Seberg. It was towards the start of her life in Paris that I encountered not Jean the actress but Jean the writer. With another turn of fate's wheel, she might have become a fine writer instead of a consistently and unfairly underrated film star.

In Max Beerbohm's novel *Zuleika Dobson*, the entire male student body of the university fell in love with the beautiful Zuleika. I won't say that Jean had that high a profile, but she was pretty big in Oxford at that time after the huge publicity surrounding *Saint Joan* – the film she made for Otto Preminger after winning a worldwide contest for the name role!

And so, remembering my success with P.G. Wodehouse, I had the idea of making a big splash for Oxford Opinion by inviting this beautiful but unlikely movie star, this girl from Marshall-town, Iowa, a little place in the middle of nowhere (quote, unquote), who bobs up in Paris speaking what a newspaper at the time described as 'fluent but ungrammatical French', to write an article.

I sent a letter via Columbia Pictures in London without any great expectations. But I underestimated both Columbia and Jean. Soon I had a reply: yes, she'd be delighted. Such a letter these days would be most unlikely to get through the public relations barricades.

The article that Jean wrote for Oxford Opinion was produced without any fuss or complications. There was no press officer intervening in the process. We spoke comfortably on the phone. No fee was mentioned by either side, which was just as well because the magazine had no money to spare. The manuscript when it arrived was clearly genuine: no professional ghost writer would work on a beat-up old typewriter!

In her article, Jean sensitively and maturely for one so young describes the pros and cons of acting. The article also provides several pointers to her interest in writing. She gives 'inability to express oneself in one's own words' as one of the several reasons for wanting to be an actress. She complains that while a writer has a manuscript rejected for reasons to do with the book, an actor loses a part because of himself.

Jean shows a journalist's awareness of a strong ending when she concludes the article: 'There is always, even in the crowd artists, the bit players, the character actors, that secret hope that when the sheriff gallops up to ask which way he went, the answer will be "He went that-a-way", pointing right on up.' As a journalism teacher, I'd be happy to commend that ending to my students.

The circulation of Oxford Opinion increased at a bound.

My invitation to write the article evidently played directly to Jean's literary ambitions. Garry McGee's 2007 biography, *Jean Seberg – Breathless,* makes it clear that Jean wanted to be a writer. Furthermore, she was in love with one of France's biggest literary lions, Romain Gary, whose fame must have seemed the real deal. Who knows what might have been without the distractions of her later life; who knows what we've missed with the disappearance of her literary papers after she died.

Fast forward 50 years, and I was astonished to find that the Oxford Opinion article is quoted in McGee's biography. It's also in *Played Out: The Jean Seberg Story,* David Richards' 1981 biography (which I somehow missed at the time). Old articles never die, it seems. How this one got into these books shows the afterlife that pieces even in the obscurest publications can enjoy.

McGee and his research associate, Michael Coates-Smith, were aware of it from Richards and set about finding the article for themselves. Coates-Smith drew a blank at the Bodleian Library in Oxford, but found a copy of the magazine on file at the University Library, Cambridge. One up for Cambridge in the rivalry between these historic varsities!

David Richards, a drama critic at the time, told me he had forgotten where he got the article from, although the answer lies locked in his brother's barn in Massachusetts. It seems that Jean or someone else must have sent it to him. That makes me proud. Richards wrote in his book: 'When the article appeared, [Jean] told friends it was one of her proudest accomplishments.' That makes me proud, too.

At Jean's invitation I visited her in Paris a year or so later. On a cold night in December 1960 we met at an apartment – presumably the one where Jean and Romain were living. Jean answered the door herself. I was thrown. I didn't think film stars did that.

One of her first remarks to me was not 'Have you seen any of my films?' but 'Have you read any of Romain's books?' She pronounced his name in the English way, rather than with the second syllable through the nose in the French way. To a French speaker it would sound like the woman's version of the name.

I should have seen the question coming. Jean had mentioned in a letter that she'd shown Oxford Opinion to Romain. But he wasn't a big name in England, and I hadn't bothered to find out who he was or what he'd written. 'I know him by repute,' I clunkily replied. End of that topic.

The others at the apartment were Romain, Aki Hersay (later Lehman), Jean's housemate at 55 rue de Bellechasse, and a visiting jazz musician from America whose name I remember as Gene Norman. We all of us went on to the seriously top-end restaurant known as 'Chez Moustache'. This famous restaurant was one of the real Paris locations featured a few years later in the film Woman Times Seven, starring Shirley MacLaine.

Jean was warm and utterly charming in an unforced way, not remotely playing the movie star. She wore a simple black dress. As it has emerged in the biographies, numerous witnesses have testified to this aspect of her character. Romain was taciturn. They seemed very comfortable with each other, but their manners were impeccable in avoiding overt displays of sensuality. No doubt Romain's political prominence had something to do with that, too.

My abiding memory of the dinner was that Romain looked bored throughout, disappearing several times to make phone calls. To my 22-year-old self this seemed the height of sophistication. For the next several years, I did my best to look bored at social events.

Strangely, I can't remember a thing that was said at the dinner table. Does this mean that nothing of note was said, or the opposite: that the conversation was so brilliant that my memory crashed from overload? I know I was out of my depth; for me, the occasion was surreal.

The menu might have been written in ancient Egyptian. The only thing I recognised was Chateaubriand steak, which I ordered and then realised to my horror that it was the most expensive item on the menu of this very expensive place. Romain, the host, received my choice my order with aplomb.

At one point I must have said something faintly interesting or amusing because Jean laid her hand on my upper arm – the effect was electric. This was the 'Zuleika Dobson effect' that others have also felt – a devastating, unstudied mix of naturalness and allure that was Jean Seberg.

And then it was all over. We were standing in a cold street. Jean and Romain went off in one direction, I went in another. I never saw or heard from her again. The paths of a young journalist on the treadmill of newspapers and the international film star moving in the company of princes and presidents were miles apart. But I treasure these memories of her, and through Oxford Opinion I'm proud to be a footnote in her fascinating life of triumph and tragedy.

Jean Seberg's Hollywood career never really took off, but she remains a name in France. She appeared in one of the most important films of world cinema, Jean-Luc Godard's *A Bout de Souffle* (in English, *Breathless*), which set a standard for realism and cinematic technique that still applies.

The idyll I imagined for Jean and Romain didn't last. After several good years, they divorced. Always a political activist, Jean became involved with the Black Panthers and was the subject of a determined FBI smear campaign. Her final decade saw the death of her infant daughter, alcoholism, promiscuity, mental breakdowns and suicide attempts, interrupted by periods when she was her old self again. In 1979, she was found dead in a Paris street after her body had lain undiscovered for 10 days. She was 40.

The official verdict was suicide. Certainly the signs pointed to a further and successful suicide attempt. However, circumstantial evidence hinted at something darker: murder. Jean, often unwise in whom she befriended, may have become caught up in the North African underworld. Romain Gary committed suicide a year later, leaving behind a note: 'No connection with Jean Seberg,' it read in part. Not everyone agreed.

In France, interest in Jean has never died, while in America and Britain her story of triumph and tragedy continues to fascinate a small but faithful band of followers. Marshalltown, her Iowa hometown, held a successful festival devoted to Jean and her films in November 2011. I was flattered to be asked to contribute my memories of her. The next year brought an invitation to attend the festival, again to be held in the 'little place in the middle of nowhere' that I'd long been curious to see.

In the meantime, I found myself face to face with Jean's former housemate Aki Hersay Lehman for the first time in 52 years. She took some discovering, but turned out to be living only a few blocks away from her former rue de Bellechasse home.

So here I am sitting comfortably in Aki's rambling old house tucked away behind an apartment block in rue du Bac. She is the longest and strongest link with Jean's Paris life. Aki knew Jean from the earliest days until the last.

I remember Aki very well although I fail to recognise her. She doesn't seem to remember me. Half a century is too long.

Aki receives visitors in a room where almost every square inch is covered with furniture, pictures and memorabilia. Stacks of books and papers on a daybed leave just enough room for the hostess herself to squeeze in. She wears a hat but no shoes. Her clothes appear to be more happy accidents than considered choices. None of this matters.

Somewhere in the pile of stuff is the new book that I've sent her from England, *The Films of Jean Seberg*, but for the moment Aki can't find it.

Aki's father was Japanese and her mother English. She is an original character with some offbeat, not to say off the wall, ideas that probably appealed to Jean. She says Jean had a good sense of humour, and she isn't without it herself. Her star sign is Scorpio – as was Jean's, the women's birthdays being three days apart, with Aki two years older. Her zodiac angel is Ariel so naturally 'I wash my clothes with Ariel powder'.

She didn't expect Jean to take her own life but points out that the 'force of life' had gone out of her in the last years. She blames heavy drinking and some of the people around Jean. Romain – whom Aki highly approves of – and others were powerless to help. And yet, as Garry McGee's 2007 biography *Breathless* makes clear, there were times almost to the last when Jean was her old self again: smart and looking forward to the next picture.

Aki's most interesting depiction is of a Jean needy for love. She says: 'Jean always wanted to be *in* love ... she didn't like to be alone.' That explains a lot; perhaps everything.

I hope to take Aki back to Chez Moustache, although this has now become an upmarket Chinese restaurant, Lily Wang. She seems to like the idea – but next morning she calls off, explaining that she eats very little these days and restaurants are no longer her thing. So I go myself with two local friends. We raise our glasses in Jean's memory.

At Oxford Opinion, my successor Anthony Wade continued to develop the magazine. Then, on the principle of the conveyor belt, it was Geoffrey Cannon's turn. Geoffrey, who was to become a nationally known food writer, was untroubled by humility or caution. He had plans for the magazine. It blossomed forth at more than twice its previous size, on glossy paper, with contents proclaiming that it had broken the bounds of Oxford and was for all the universities.

It was great to look at, but was it affordable? Even more, could a magazine that had Oxford printed all over it appeal to students nationwide, many of whom had chips on their shoulders about not getting to Oxford? Could it appeal to this broader constituency without losing its core Oxford readership. Should it?

David Bell, who had a sharper financial sense than I had, asked me to join him in expressing our concerns to the senior proctor. The proctors were dons with disciplinary powers, including a superintending role over student publications. This official had on his desk, side by side, copies of the new-style, all singing all dancing Oxford Opinion and the previous, more restrained effort. Presumably Geoffrey had sent them in.

When I saw how flimsy our magazine looked by comparison, I sensed that the day would go against us. Sure enough, the proctor made clear that in his view we were merely disgruntled ex-editors indulging in sour grapes. He declined to intervene.

Oxford Opinion soon folded, brought down as many a business before and since by over-expansion. It was a minor tragedy. The university lost a magazine that could have made a contribution for years. Perhaps even now its name would have been as widely known as Cherwell and Isis.

In my penultimate Oxford year, 1959, I offered articles to one of the local papers at home. The Reading Mercury was among the oldest papers in the country, founded in the early 18th century. Its front page had only advertisements and its splendidly antique titlepiece proclaimed that it was read over much of Southern England. In reality its distribution was more modest. To judge from the number of copies on newsagents' counters, it had been outrun by younger and fleeter rivals.

The editor, Mr Hobson, was a distinguished-looking elderly man who was also the owner. He took me out to lunch. His way of eating cheese without buttering the biscuit struck me as the summit of sophistication. Or it might simply have meant that he was avoiding dairy products.

Mr Hobson bought into my idea of a series of feature articles on the theme of 'architecture by Thames-side' – boathouses, chalets, mansions, bridges and so on. It seemed to me that much of the architecture along the river in its middle reaches had a distinctive tone, evoking the Edwardian golden era of regattas and picnics and long, leisurely afternoons.

That Mr Hobson *bought into* the idea is important. He certainly didn't *buy* the idea. No money was offered, and I was too coy to ask for it. I would have major bylines, however, and he would have feature articles – usually in short supply in a local newspaper – so he may have thought it was a fair exchange.

The articles were commissioned against the wishes of the news editor, who protested, 'Everyone wants to write a series when one article will do!'

I borrowed the family car to work the river for buildings that fitted my theme. The results didn't set the Thames on fire, to coin a phrase, but were received by the readers without objection. The following year, in my second series for the Mercury, I put a foot badly wrong. Then we heard from the readers all right!

This series was called Buildings of the Mercury Country. I dealt week by week with different types of mainly historical buildings like churches, mansions, manor houses and market halls. The Mercury's circulation area was a fragment of what it once was, but it was still larger than I could cover in day trips from home. I resorted to writing up some of the buildings from books and describing the scenes as if I was there.

The ruse was painfully exposed when I urged readers to visit Coleshill, a mansion that had burnt to the ground a dozen years previously. There was a correction paragraph, but I was allowed to continue with the series. Chastened, I phoned every building I couldn't reach. I invented trivial reasons for the calls. The real purpose was to check that the buildings were still standing. Not wishing to be thought nuts, I didn't care to say, 'Just checking that you haven't been burnt down.'

TWO
SINKING AND
SWIMMING – 1961-1962

It was devastating to take a third in my finals at Oxford. Devastating but not unjust. Nor was it as bad as it would be now: thirds were more common then. I had a high fever throughout the days of the exam, but it probably didn't make any difference. I simply hadn't done the work. I was sorry to disappoint Sybil Crowe, the politics tutor, who had put me down for an alpha in constitutional history. At least I managed a good beta in that subject.

Today's would-be journalists, more often than not university graduates, commonly take a pre-entry course in journalism. These are valuable in laying down the basics of the trade; they also give a feel for the opportunities out there and where to look for the first break.

When I graduated in 1960, however, formal training in journalism was limited to day-release courses in reporting for those already in the business. It meant that many young journalists, particularly graduates, received only what was euphemistically called on-the-job training, or in other words sink or swim on your own.

Without a pre-entry course for guidance, I spent several months casting around for a job. The opportunities were abundant, but I barely knew where to look. I stupidly turned down Mr Hobson's offer to join the Reading Mercury staff. I saw myself as above being a junior reporter having been a feature writer there and – heaven help me! – the editor of Oxford Opinion. I limited other opportunities by not wanting to leave the London area. There was no good reason for this except that I was too comfortable at my Ascot home with its two acres of grounds.

Inquiries to national newspapers led nowhere. I wasn't aware of the requirement for even the brightest and the best to serve their time in the provinces before going to Fleet Street. This was an agreement between the proprietors and the National Union of Journalists. The Financial Times attracted much anger in union circles by breaking ranks and directly recruiting a few graduates.

Then I became aware of the recruitment firm PA Consulting, to whom I took my needs and talents. They produced what they said was a job in the media, or nearly so. It was in Surbiton, South London, which was commutable by train from Ascot. It was to be a copywriter with the US pharmaceutical group Winthrop, with the understanding that much of the time would be spent with a doctors' newspaper they published called Pulse. It was aimed mainly at general practitioners and was distributed free. It was later sold to a mainstream publisher, but it began with Winthrop as a form of soft public relations.

The company had rights to the famous Bayer aspirin. Its product range of ethical pharmaceuticals (only available on pre-scription) could be described as useful rather than life-saving. It had a drug with a memorably straightforward name amid the myriad tongue-twisters on the market: Lobak for low-back pain.

My few months as a copywriter were grim. I couldn't imagine how anyone could be expected to spend hours, days, weeks even on a single slogan or a tiny chunk of text, especially since the subject matter was so unsuited to flights of fancy. No 'go to work on an egg', the slogan that the author Fay Weldon is proud to have dreamt up, wanted here!

I spent much of the time gazing out of the window in Winthrop's tower building next to Surbiton station, looking down on the steam-hauled expresses to Portsmouth. They were the last days on the last main line to run steam.

Although I failed to make my mark as a copy-writer, I must have given satisfaction with my work on Pulse. It was announced that the newspaper was to be floated into a company called Professional Projects Ltd controlled by Winthrop. It was to be based in Central London, and I was to be the executive editor.

The office was on the top floor of a Victorian building off Drury Lane. It was, and is, an attractive part of old London, all the more welcome after the drabness of outer suburban Sur-biton. I had my own room. I was eager to crown my new status with a red telephone – colours were becoming available to sup-plement the ubiquitous black. I was told there were more urgent issues – and given a black phone.

It was typical set-up for a small trade and professional peri-odical. I was an editor with no staff and with some regular freelance contributors. Over me was an editor-in-chief, the real power in the building. He was Alan Huet Owen, a public relations professional who was probably on a contract to Winthrop.

The unit was equipped with its own business and administrative people, including Jean Shakespeare and John Shepherd. I had a secretary, Sally Smith, without the faintest idea of how to use her. Nor was I given any directions. I sensed that secretaries had to be carefully handled like mettlesome horses, but since I knew nothing about mettlesome horses and not much about women that knowledge didn't take me far. I realised you couldn't just command, 'Go and fetch my dry cleaning.' The secretary had to offer to fetch it, but how to get to that point?

The poor girl must have been bored out of her mind, although she was able to be useful to Alan on his visits to the office.

Alan Huet Owen was a small, rotund Welshman in early middle age, given to pointing out attractive girls in the street and declaring, 'I'd like to roger her!' For all I know, he was unfailingly faithful to his wife.

With Alan it was impossible to know what was absolutely true and what he was bigging up, PR-style. He claimed to have been the first editor of the famous German newspaper Die Welt when it was launched by the British occupation authorities after the Second World War. Certainly he had a fluent command of German and a charming German wife, taller than he, to add colour to his story. He was a very capable journalist who taught me a lot, despite the difficulties that arose between us.

Why Winthrop went to the trouble and expense of running Professional Projects I never knew. Arguably it put some distance between Pulse and the company, making the public relations more effective. Except that the doctor readers continued to see Pulse as a company publication, and liked it just the same.

We were chiefly a lifestyle newspaper. We didn't run clinical reports, unlike the British Medical Journal and the Lancet. In that case there might have been conflicts of interest between the company and journalistic needs. We did cover medical politics, and would have been in difficulty if senior doctors launched an all-out attack on Big Pharma. They were little inclined to do this since many were beholden to the companies for jollies and junkets and fees for field trials.

This quasi-independence helped with an eventual sale. Pulse was later sold to the mainstream periodicals group Morgan Grampian.

Winthrop didn't lean heavily on us, but it was clear who was in control. The newspaper ran pharmaceutical advertisements only from the company. Alan's disingenuous explanation for this was that we offered exclusivity in each product sector. Theoretically, therefore, Rover cars could take out an ad and Ford wouldn't be allowed to do so.

Pulse published weekly so the pace was always hectic. I was given no training in any aspect of the job – journalistic skills like news and feature writing, text editing, headline writing and page layout, or administrative skills like commissioning material, handling contributors and advance planning.

Alan was fond of saying that anyone who worked for him received a good training. This was true in so far as watching him deftly and rapidly at work was instructive. For the rest, I got by as best I could and taught myself in the process. I was a keen reader of the several journalism textbooks then available.

The upside of this process is that in the 1½ years I was with Pulse I became an all-rounder. I was out on the road enough, to medical meetings or interviews for human interest stories and features, to hold down reporting jobs later in my career. The production journalism (sub-editing) was directly responsible for my break into daily journalism.

There is a fly in every ointment. The smaller the company the greater the potential should be for a happy working environment; except that it rarely works out that way. In this case the fly was Alan.

He was one of those compulsive ideas men in journalism who comb every imaginably relevant newspaper and magazine, and spew out ideas, workable and unworkable, for follow-ups. I was too inexperienced to cope with this barrage of cuttings and notes. I didn't know the arts of prioritising or discreetly forgetting the wilder ideas; I didn't have the techniques to develop many of the stories; in any case, I didn't have the staff.

In consequence, the backlog built up and I found myself perennially on the back foot against Alan's complaints. I dreaded his visits to the office, which were greatly relieved when he came with his wife. Then he was a different person, billing and cooing and murmuring endearments in German.

I began to lose confidence in my work, and indeed I wasn't an unqualified success. From what I learnt later about training, I know that when an employee fails the fault normally lies with the management not the staffer. Either he or she was appointed to the wrong job or, more likely, wasn't given the necessary training to do it properly. In today's terms, I was also the victim of bullying by Alan. The concept of workplace bullying was unknown then.

The powers that be must have recognised that too much work was being piled on to me. A deputy editor, Peter Mackenzie, was appointed, after which life in the office improved somewhat.

A pleasant part of the job was dealing with contributors. The longest-serving columnist was Jotter. He was Dr Hertzel Creditor, one of the many doctors drawn to journalism then and since. Jotter wrote waspish comments on medical and political matters. Unsurprisingly, he was very popular with the readers.

Dr Creditor sent his copy by post. I pictured him as a small man, stooped and bespectacled, in late middle age. When I finally met him, I found he was a small man, stooped and bespectacled, in late middle age.

I felt I must watch my words. He had worked with Alan and Winthrop for so long he must be 'one of them'. On the contrary, Dr Creditor was an embittered man. 'I'm just biding my time,' he intoned with relish. 'When the time comes, I'll get even all right!' I didn't pursue the why's and how's of his embitterment. Whether he got even in the end I don't know. When I left he was still jotting.

The editorial staff was gradually built up. Dr John Bradshaw came on board, another doctor turned journalist, valuable for his skills and the 'Dr' bit. The medical press and mainstream newspapers in their medical sections love the credibility of that moniker, and will pay for it.

John was appointed as 'consulting editor' while he demanded to be known as 'consultant editor'. Or was it the other way round? I can see that in the medical world there are nuances with the word 'consultant'. Which way round the argument went, or whether it was resolved, I can no longer remember.

We could have become a happy team with John in sole control. But he wasn't. He suffered Alan's badgering as much as I did, but being older and more experienced he handled it better. 'You're always looking over your shoulder,' he told me. He was right. My self-belief was progressively eroding.

To add to my troubles I was sensitive – too sensitive – about being a lay person with no medical knowledge editing a medical newspaper. I felt it particularly when meeting doctors in person.

I was quick to emphasise that Pulse was non-clinical, but I felt more was expected of me. Yes, the content of Pulse was non-clinical, but the distinction can never be total. Someone writing about life in general practice, for instance, may want to mention the ailments to be seen in the surgery.

The copy of doctor contributors was invariably too long and often a grammatical mess. How to edit this material if you don't know what it means? This is the dilemma that faces lay journalists in the technical and professional press every day. The principle of not putting into print anything we don't understand ourselves couldn't apply on a publication like Pulse; otherwise everything would need to be edited by doctors.

The seasoned lay editor develops an intuition where something is wrong with the copy. At other times, however, the only way to resolve the dilemma is to refer back to the contributor. Writers rarely take kindly to editorial changes, however justified, so the smart editor checks points separately. Exposing the entire edited piece to the contributor can be a good way of producing a row! How many indigestion tablets is it worth for the editor to be in the right?

Pulse was strong on practical features, the most popular subject being money matters. The readership came to life on that one. Doctors, we decided, were very money-oriented – a characteristic they shared with their successors of half a century later. Perhaps doctors are no different from any other group of people; perhaps the difference is that we the public expect them to be different. The British Medical Association (BMA) is famously aggressive in pursuing doctors' interests.

Some of the issues of the times have been with us ever since. Headlines of the 'NHS on the brink of collapse' variety were around even then. In fact, we visited the subject so often that we could have kept the type as a standing head (without the need to reset the line in the days before computers).

Government policy of the day was to concentrate services in district general hospitals at the expense of the smaller, 'cottage' hospitals. Traditionally, GPs had better access to cottage hospitals and might even carry out treatments there. Many strongly opposed the trend to district general hospitals, as did Pulse.

The process was incomplete 50 years later, with many small hospitals surviving and rows continuing over the withdrawal of services – notably Accident and Emergency.

I commissioned an artist friend, Tom Barling, to draw a cartoon that summed it up. He showed a GP standing at the gate of a district general hospital with a porter saying, 'I'll see if you're on the admission list, sir.' Tom continued to draw cartoons for Alan after I left. Later he became a nationally known thriller writer, proving that creativity doesn't have to be limited to one medium.

On the other hand, the hot issue of general practice as a full-time salaried service faded away over the years. This is only because the GPs won the day. Unlike hospital doctors, who are on salaries, general practitioners are self-employed contractors to the National Health Service. This contractor status has empowered the BMA to drive hard financial bargains over the years, including a leap of around one-third in average emoluments to more than £100,000 a year per GP in 2008.

The working environment at Pulse hardly improved and I began to realise that I must leave. I was also aware that journalism comprises distinct streams: newspapers, periodicals and broadcasting. People tended to make their careers wholly in one of these streams. It was particularly hard to switch from periodicals into the other streams. As far as newspapers are concerned, the periodical journalist hadn't 'gone through the mill' of crime, courts, flower shows and funerals – the lot of the junior reporter on a local weekly. There was also a financial motive: a recruit aged 24 or over was classed as an 'adult entrant' and couldn't be got on the cheap.

This time I didn't repeat my mistake of approaching national newspapers. I aimed one rung down, at the regional morning newspapers. These covered most of the country with circulation areas taking in the patches of numerous local weeklies and perhaps two or three evening dailies.

I found the names and addresses from a press directory in the public library, and sent off my speculative letters all over the country. My desire to leave Pulse was so great that staying in the London area was long forgotten. I was delighted when I got a positive response from the most famous of all, the Yorkshire Post. Although aged 24 and an 'adult entrant', they wanted to see me in Leeds for an interview.

After the job had been secured, as described in the prologue, Alan Huet Owen was all kindness while I worked out my short notice at the end of 1962. He seemed to think he was responsible for my big break, which in a way he was. Our personal relations didn't matter anymore as freedom dawned.

THREE
NORTH COUNTRY – 1963-1964

Yorkshire in 1963 seemed like a foreign country. Whether it's changed or I've changed or we've both changed I don't know, but it doesn't seem foreign now. I was self-conscious about my Southern accent. A favourite snack in the canteen was a coostard (custard tart), but I couldn't ask for it correctly. There was the long A and the short A in all-too-common words like bath, class, glass and grass. I couldn't shake the way of saying barthe, clarse, glarse and grarse: in fact, the As stretched themselves the more I thought about them!

The landscape to the north and west of Leeds, including the famous Ilkley Moor, was of a scale quite unlike that of the 'kitchen garden' South East. It was made more dramatic by the snow that lay for weeks that year. Green grass wasn't to be seen until well into the spring.

Before the Clean Air Act that was soon to come, Leeds was a black city, its building begrimed by decades of smoke. Smog frequently hung over the place, laying down yet more pollution on the buildings and, more importantly, into people's lungs.

To this Dickensian scene the offices of the Yorkshire Post made their contribution. They were in Albion Street, right in the city centre, Victorian Gothic in appearance and a rabbit warren of rooms. No nonsense there about open-plan workspace. The news editor was tucked away in a room down the corridor from the sub-editors' room. The editor, Kenneth Young, was on the floor below.

The printing presses were in the building. One of them, the overseer explained, pointing to a handsome installation of well painted metal and gleaming brass, had been doing service since Queen Victoria's day. A plaque revealed that it had been made in Leeds.

Another daily newspaper was produced in the same building, the Yorkshire Evening Post. It was and is unusual for sister titles to have the same name. It led to some difficulties or at least extra work for the switchboard in deciding where to put callers.

I doubt if I would remember the Yorkshire Post building so fondly if it had been a common-or-garden modern office block.

The newspapers moved not long after my time to such a building, in Wellington Street. Some of the distinctive atmosphere of old Leeds was lost when not only the YP building but also much of the Albion Street area was pulled down in the name of development.

Leeds has a poor record in that regard, as a glance at City Square, where buildings are a hodge-potch of heights, styles and periods, will also reveal.

The famous editor of the Yorkshire Post was Sir Linton Andrews, recently retired. Before I joined the paper, I read his *Problems of an Editor*, with its picture of an indefatigable operative with a finger in every journalistic pie, voraciously devouring newsprint almost in his sleep before heading to the office for another cracking day. I looked forward to first-hand accounts of this editorial paragon. I found to my surprise that Sir Linton was held in low esteem by most of the journalists, the objection being that he 'talked a good game'. People thought more fondly of Arthur Mann, who had ceased editing the paper 20 years before and then spent much of his time at the races.

As a news sub-editor I worked under a 'back bench' of, to me, unforgettable characters – Henry Heaton, Arthur Gowers, Sidney Burton, John Edwards and Alan Hague. The first three were Yorkshire, through and through as it seemed. These people between them planned the content and appearance of the newspaper, before the stories were passed down to the subs for editing and headlining.

Henry Heaton was the night editor and therefore the kingpin of the operation. He was a committed Nonconformist Christian. After I'd committed the solecism of referring in a headline to a Methodist minister as a priest, he gave me the useful tip that all Christian ministers/priests can be called pastors. If in doubt say pastor!

Sid Burton was unfailingly cheerful and unflappable in one of the toughest jobs on a newspaper. He was the copytaster, which meant looking through reams of unallocated stories, including news agency copy, and deciding what each is worth (if anything). He then had to give the stories out to individual sub-editors, aiming to keep each person occupied but without swamping them.

Arthur Gowers was also unflappable, but where Sid was outgoing Arthur was inward-looking.

Alan Hague had worked in Africa and John Edwards – later

to be the editor of the Yorkshire Post – had worked on the Daily Express. Both backgrounds seemed terrifically exotic in worka-day Leeds.

The editorial staff was overwhelmingly male. I don't recall any women subs. There were a few women reporters. The women's pages were run by the glamorous Valerie An (she'd heard all the jokes about the missing surname) and her assistant, Ann Simpson, who went around the office like Siamese twins.

The deputy editor was Bill Oliver, who was also, as W.T. Oliver, the respected art critic. Tall, spare and scholarly, he was surely one of the nicest men in journalism. The atmosphere in the office was decidedly lighter when he edited the paper in the editor's absence, although the work still got done. Mr Oliver was to be disappointed when Kenneth Young left. He didn't inherit the chair. The job was handed to the news editor, Ted Crossley.

Mr Crossley often ran his news desk from Yates Wine Bar, adding a twist to the image of the reporters in the pub and the news editor calling them back. He was to surprise everybody, perhaps including himself, by becoming editor of the Yorkshire Post in late middle age. He saw no reason to change his habits. Now he edited the paper from Yates Wine Bar.

The working environment in the subs' room was a revelation to me. For the first time in my journalistic life I was able to con-centrate on a single job, without pressure. Sid fed us one story at a time; then waited until we were clear before giving us the next one. I was to learn that this is the normal way on newspa-pers. It was a liberation after the fraught atmosphere on Pulse. I was able to settle down and learn the craft of editing in depth.

The main work of the 'down table' sub was to edit reporters' and news agency copy and write the headlines. We went through the text particularly for grammatical mistakes and breaches of 'house style', and hoped to develop a sixth sense for factual errors, of which misspelling the name of a local dignitary was the worst. You could more comfortably state that Paris was the capital of Germany than cheat Mrs Small*peice* of her correct spelling.

We might also be required to cut the story to the length avail-able. It was not advised to check with the reporter about what could best be lost. The answer was invariably 'nothing', with perhaps an argument thrown in for free. Best to go ahead and just do it.

The Yorkshire Post had an elaborate style book, said to be based on that of the Daily Telegraph, from where the editor, Kenneth Young, had come. It gave helpful advice about common grammatical and factual pitfalls, and spelt out the paper's preferred presentation style – for instance, whether to abbreviate or spell out military ranks used as titles (Lt-Col Hittem Hard or Lieutenant Colonel Hittem Hard).

The style book was very purist. Catholics were always to be Roman Catholics; ' contact' didn't exist as a verb. There was a contact in the electrical sense, but you didn't *contact* someone: you *got in touch with* them.

A special headache was Conservative MPs who weren't really Conservatives, of whom there were several in the YP area. They were Liberals who were in Parliament during the periods of the National Governments in the Thirties or the wartime Coalition Government, and who now took the Conservative whip. They were Cons-Nat Lib, or sometimes – I never knew why – Nat Lib-Cons. Of course, they were sticky if we got it wrong.

While some of it may sound trivial, this highly developed style was an important lesson. Consistency of presentation is part of printed media's professionalism. It has slipped throughout journalism and beyond with the slimmed-down staffs of later years.

Editors like to run with their style idiosyncrasies, and Mr Young was no exception. He decreed that every name was to have the person's age attached, whether relevant or not (although he didn't put it like that). Reporters spent a huge amount of time trying to find this out as diplomatically as they could, while for national stories we subs made the life of Mr Lord in the library a purgatory. He knew that when the phone rang in the evening it would be, nine times out of 10, a sub saying 'How old is ...?'

Mr Lord appeared to me to be ancient. Perhaps he was only in his late sixties or early seventies. He certainly sounded like a very old man – muttering 'Ages! Ages!' like a mantra while pottering over to his files and reference books.

This idiocy went on until we outed Lady Crathorne, one of the grandest aristocrats around. In those days, most women guarded their age like their virtue, particularly in the sensitive fifties. Perhaps Lady C had been passing for less. She complained, triggering a memo from the editor that while ages were in general important we no longer need use them in each and every case etc etc. The staff didn't need to be told twice. The ages policy collapsed in short order.

In the days before computerised typesetting, sub-editors had to be highly disciplined about headline writing and changes to text. Lines were produced with moulds using hot metal (a lead alloy). If a headline was too long for the specified size and width, it came back to the sub as 'bust'. The adjusted line then had to be set again – no changing it with a computer keystroke or tweaking the size to squeeze it in (incidentally, a dubious design practice).

We had a way of counting headlines that allowed for the different widths of capitals and lower case letters; also taking account of varying widths within a case – lower case *w*, *x* and *i*, for example, are each different in width. On that basis you could usually avoid a bust.

Subs were much less good at estimating the length of copy when put into type. It was common for copy to be cut for space reasons. Before computers were around to provide exact lengths or at least word counts, we had to find the length manually to know how much to cut.

The process involved a known association between words (or lines) in raw copy and words (or lines) in type. If you knew that 40 words of type in the standard body size averaged one inch in the standard column setting, you had only to estimate how many words in the raw copy to know how many inches it would make in type or how much needed to be cut. Simple in theory, but in practice most people's 'casting off' was often wildly wrong. All over the country overseers would point to lengths of metal type on galleys and moan about the waste of time and money. Every line on these galleys had been set to no purpose by a highly paid Linotype operator.

When the typeset story was too long, it often meant that changes were needed to the portion that would be used. This meant yet more lines being set. Even a small change at the beginning of a paragraph usually meant all the remaining lines in that par being reset. No wonder that making avoidable changes to typeset copy was a great sin! Now it matters much less because everything is adjusted on screen ahead of any physical output. Some writers in consequence have become very casual about changing content at the proof stage. It still takes time, however, and time costs in one way or another. I remain frugal in changing type once it's been signed off for setting.

I was well used to seeing my headlines in print because of my time at Pulse, but still I was thrilled to see my first headline in the Yorkshire Post. Perhaps I recognised the difference between scoring a goal in the Conference and the Premiership (or the Championship, to be strict about the metaphor). The headline was as I wrote it. Arthur Gowers, the chief sub, hadn't found a need to change it.

My sense of thrill was absurd in one sense – it was a small item on an inconsequential matter – but in another sense not absurd at all. When we stop being thrilled at firsts in our professional lives, that's the time to change our work.

My greatest friend from the subs room was Francis Ashborn, whom Mr Gowers had chosen to induct me into the Yorkshire Post way of doing things. He was almost 20 years older than me, a Sri Lankan who had held a senior journalistic post in his home country. He was chief assistant editor on the Times of Ceylon, a Methodist who reluctantly turned Roman Catholic to marry his wife, Renee. The marriage, as it turned out, was childless. Francis was stick thin; Renee was big. They were a strange couple in the proportions ½: 1 ½.

Although I was to know him for many years, I didn't get to the bottom of why Francis had come to Britain. Was it politics or a desire to swim in a bigger pond? Either way, he seemed to work contentedly in Leeds. In his knowledge of English language and literature, he was more English than the English. He gave much practical help to his younger colleagues as well as a slightly odd take on some English expressions.

'You can't *have your cake and eat it,*' he insisted. 'You must *eat your cake and have it.* The *lion's share* doesn't mean most of it, as you seem to think; it means all of it.'

Francis was one of the many journalists perennially working on a book that remains ever unfinished, or at least unpublished. He was a superb grammarian and a capable editor, but so far as I know his novel was never published. The skills of editor and writer aren't necessarily transferable.

I must have been seen as a likely lad because I was asked to fill in as a holiday relief in the leader writers' department. Extraordinarily for a provincial newspaper even then, the YP had three full-time leader writers (who doubled up by writing features from time to time). Two young men and a middle-aged chief made up the department. Plummy-voiced Hugo Young had an unassailable academic pedigree of Oxford and Harvard.

Andrew Alexander's narrow face and lean build gave him an air of solemnity ahead of his years.

Both went on to become national 'names': Hugo Young, an Ampleforth-educated Roman Catholic, as chairman of the Scott Trust, owners of the Guardian newspaper with its Nonconformist provenance, as well as a columnist for the paper; Andrew Alexander as an acclaimed writer on economics and politics for the Daily Mail. When I encountered Hugo Young years later on his visits to the Guardian newsroom, I found it easy to forget he was a working journalist. He was tall and imposing, with an air that would not have disgraced a grand duke.

Tom Greenwell, the chief leader writer, was a divorced ex-diplomat who composed his pieces on a bottle of whisky a day. He never seemed affected by it unless the extreme conservatism of his leaders owed as much to the bottle as to his intellect. Either way it suited the paper, which was owned by the unambiguously named Yorkshire Conservative Newspaper Company Ltd. (Much later it was taken over by United Newspapers and then Johnston Press.)

Tom lived in a shared house in a rundown part of Leeds. It seemed bohemian to me, but was probably simply squalid. He would not have been a good candidate for life insurance. What happened next demonstrated the redeeming power of love. He fell for a girl in an ordinary occupation who was many years younger than himself. She was a clerk in the Inland Revenue. Ten years later, when I returned to Leeds and met the now remarried Tom, he was free of the bottle. The years had fallen off him, and he looked exceptionally happy.

My short time as a leader writer showed me that it wasn't for me. I found it boring to spend the whole day mugging up on a subject, all in order to write 300 or 400 words. That's the sort of length that most journalists can manage in an hour. And some leaders didn't need all day to research. What do you do with the rest of the time? I wanted more action, so it was with relief that I returned to the subs' room.

My time at Pulse had given me the taste for being an all-rounder. I was happy subbing, but I also wanted to write. I had the time, before I went to work. The hours of the news sub are deeply anti-social. The typical shift begins mid-afternoon and continues until late evening. He or she is free when most of the world is at work, and at work when most of the world is at play.

Add to that Sunday shifts in rotation, and you can say goodbye to amateur dramatics or being in a sports team, not to mention crippling your chances on the social scene.

So I had the spare time. I wrote some 'news features' for the newspaper. These are articles on topical subjects in which the issue is worked out through the opinions of several sources, rather than the writer presenting his or her opinion. It was a genre that suited me. Two of my subjects were clean air and spa treatments. Both were on the cusp of prominence, one coming in and the other going out.

Clean air in those days had nothing to do with carbon dioxide or diesel particulates. The problem was more down to earth and highly visible – coal belching soot and noxious chemicals from thousands of factories, offices and homes. The legislation that was to transform the air of Leeds and other industrial towns and cities was coming in as I wrote.

Ironically, it was also this time, the early Sixties, that the motor car began its ascent to universality – from just three million on British roads then to 30 million in 2010 – creating another type of unclean air that has yet to be fully addressed.

Harrogate, just down the road from Leeds, is nowadays a spa in name only. The era of taking the waters for a cure has gone. It was a surprise to find that, despite the Victorian and Edwardian image of spas, the era hadn't gone in 1963. It remained possible to take a cure on the National Health Service. (The facility was later withdrawn.)

As a result of writing these features, I was invited to join Bernard Dineen in the features department as a sub-editor. Bernard, the features editor, in his early thirties, was an accomplished journalist who became an inspiration to me. He had the enviable ability to appear absolutely unflappable on deadline whatever the complications. A reader might phone in precisely at the moment when the composing room overseer was screaming for copy; somehow Bernard managed to satisfy both without seeming to rush.

He could do this, I suppose, by being totally in control of what he was doing. It was not achieved without effort. Sometimes the tension was written on his face. He admitted to having had an ulcer.

Bernard was rumoured to have been politically very left-wing as a younger man. By the time I worked with him he was expressing admiration for the United States: 'Considering their power it's surprising how little they throw their weight around' was one of his observations that wouldn't have passed without challenge in left-wing and other circles. He later became business editor and a long-running and well loved columnist, expressing vigorous free market views.

Features were in a separate room in the rabbit warren that was the Albion Street building. I soon gave offence to my former colleagues by walking through the subs' room and ignoring them. It seemed I was getting above myself with this modest promotion. In reality, I was simply preoccupied. Bernard gently put me right, and from then on I 'did a Bernard' – made a point of not being preoccupied, however pressing the matter.

One of my jobs was to edit readers' letters for publication. There were surprisingly few for a newspaper of such standing and reach. This was a reminder that because people don't write you can't assume they don't read. Even so, every feature writer prays that the article will stir some reaction.

Letters occupied a fixed space on the main comment page. Sometimes we struggled to fill. I would pen something myself, always locating my fictitious correspondent in Darlington or Sheffield with the hope of rattling the competition. These places were the heartlands of our adjacent dailies, the Northern Echo and the Sheffield Telegraph.

The Yorkshire Post had a sensible policy of contacting correspondents, usually by phone, ahead of publication as a safeguard against hoaxes or indeed the writer dying before the letter could appear! Of course, you couldn't ask 'Did you really write this letter?' or state 'I was just checking that you're still alive'. You invented some inconsequential reason. The letter writers probably found it a bit odd, but I doubt that any realised the real purpose.

One of the highlights of the features coverage was a daily column called People. This was a gossip column about authors and artists but especially Top Society. In Yorkshire this meant, or was taken by the Yorkshire Post to mean, the aristocracy and gentry. There were plenty to choose from although, as is the way with gossip columns everywhere, the same names came up again and again.

The column was ambitiously relaunched when the editor hired the well connected Angus Wolfe-Murray to run it. The column became 'Angus Wolfe-Murray's People', with the writer's picture. His tenure was relatively brief, and Mr Young didn't repeat the experiment of like calling to like. The column would again be simply People, put together by the subs. The choice fell on me to do it. This was retrenchment. No name, no picture, minimal expectations. However, to everybody's surprise, including my own, I was able to maintain the momentum of the column and develop it further.

The format of the column was very much to my taste. Short items encouraged tight writing and neat turns of phrase if one could think of them. Anything to avoid the journalistic sin of being 'flat'. I lived vicariously – daydreamed really – with the aristocrats on their acres or the writers comfortably tapping away in their cottages. I encountered many of them although this was mainly on the phone.

I learnt a lasting lesson about the law of libel when I wrote an item about a prominent landowner. Henry Varley owned the Studley Royal estate (which contained the historic ruins of Fountains Abbey). He ran a bookshop in London and was about to open a second. Hardly hold the front page material, but a typical People piece. After talking to the agent I wrote, 'Mr Varley lives mainly in London and only rarely visits Studley.'

Soon afterwards I was called downstairs to see the editor, who told me that Varley's solicitors were proposing to sue for libel. They alleged that the sentence contained the innuendo of his being an absentee landlord. That was when I learnt that innuendoes (hidden or extended meanings) lurk everywhere for those who look for them. They can bite you as much as plain statements.

'I can't see the problem either,' Mr Young told me, 'and I don't blame you. But our insurers are going to settle.'

It was a classic libel case in point. The statement could almost certainly have been successfully defended as true. However, because of the difficulties of proof and uncertainty over damages, provincial newspapers or their insurers almost invariably preferred to pay to get rid of the complaint.

In any case, was the statement libellous? In other words, is a landlord blameworthy if he lives elsewhere and delegates his duties to a capable agent? If the statement wasn't libellous, no defence would have been needed.

The editor was less easy with me after I was asked to write an 80th birthday tribute to a prominent Leeds businessman, Sir George Martin. It was impossible to get on to a wavelength with Sir George. With the intolerance of youth, I found him an old bore. His idea of demonstrating that he was a plain man was 'I don't own a racehorse'.

The resulting article failed to rise to the occasion. I began with a tired quote from Shakespeare: 'One man in his time plays many parts.'

'Never begin an article with a quote that is a cliché!' the editor stormed. He was right. And since then I never have. Such intros continue to be seen even in newspapers that should know better. The world of journalism needs more Kenneth Youngs to tell writers not to do it.

I warmed more to a man the editor described as Leeds's leading gourmet (name forgotten). Nor was this damning with faint praise; the man knew his food. A top hotel was selected, and we went to lunch. The gourmet's point was that even at the highest level food was corrupted by processing and lack of freshness. He quizzed the staff about the vegetables, forcing them to admit that many were out of frozen packets.

I hope he lived long enough to survive the horrors of the microwave era and enjoy the renewed emphasis on fresh, unprocessed ingredients.

A highlight for the People column was the Yorkshire Post Literary Lunches, which Mr Young had started. These occasions were as much social as literary. I got to recognise the fixtures among the guests who would be good for a quote or who might be prodded into a quip.

The organisers mixed established writers with promising newcomers – three authors at each lunch, as I recall. I was interested in Edna O'Brien for the wrong reason: she was smoulderingly sexy – at lunchtime! – without trying. Annabel Dilke, barely more than a girl, had written a fun book called *Rule Three: Pretend to be Nice*. Actually, Annabel didn't need to pretend; she was nice, as I confirmed when I lunched with her in London. She returned to the headlines years later as the widow of Georgi Markov, the Bulgarian dissident who was murdered in London with a poisoned umbrella tip.

Randolph Churchill, Sir Winston's son, lived up to his reputation as an alcoholic by delivering his remarks to the luncheon when clearly drunk. Turning to Kenneth Young, who was in the chair, Churchill referred to Sir Linton Andrews as 'your unworthy predecessor'. In Yorkshire this was like saying 'F*** God'. A collective gasp ran round the room – and Mr Young failed to distance himself from the remark.

Lawyers say that *after* the incident (post hoc) doesn't necessarily mean *because of* the incident (propter hoc). Whatever the reasons, soon afterwards the editor's contract was renewed for only a year rather than the three that would be expected. It was an invitation to depart, which he soon did into a career of writing books.

After several months of editing the People column, I began to question the value of the work I was doing. Why were we writing about the Zetlands, the Crathornes, the Worsleys (whose daughter Katharine became the Duchess of Kent) purely because of their social position? What had they done to deserve this publicity except to be born into their ancestral acres?

In those days the concept of celebrity hardly existed, but I suppose this sort of *angst* afflicts at least from time to time those who make their living from writing about or photographing celebrities. The paparazzo with the soul of a scholar, perhaps. It was, however, somewhat precious of me to indulge these feelings. I was months, not years, into the job, and I was learning valuable journalistic lessons. This is with the hindsight of many years. At the time the thought never occurred. No sooner had I fallen out of love with the work than I resolved to move on. That meant leaving the Yorkshire Post.

In mid-1964 my friend Francis Ashborn had landed a job with the Guardian in London. It was soon after the start of London printing, and the newspaper was gradually building up an editorial operation there as well as in Manchester. He urged me to follow if I could. So I applied and for good measure also approached the Daily Telegraph. I didn't see any conflict in seeking to ride horses of such different colours as the Guardian and the Telegraph. I wasn't engaged enough politically for it to affect my job choices. Many journalists find themselves reluctantly working for a news organisation of opposite views to their own; I was willingly putting myself into that position.

I saw myself in the progressive centre. Never a Labour supporter because of the party's commitments to big government and state ownership. I believed in localism, civil liberties, small businesses and rural life. That pointed to the Liberals, which I supported for years, while later the agenda better fitted the progressive wing of the Conservatives and also the Greens. The Liberals and their successor, the Liberal Democrats, destroyed their credentials for small government through their continuing infatuation with Europe even as it turned before our eyes into a monster of big government and democratic deficiency.

The reputation of the Yorkshire Post was such that I had interviews with both the Guardian and the Telegraph – and each offered a job as a home news sub-editor. I chose the Guardian. My political stance tilted my choice after all.

Kenneth Young tried to get me to stay at the Yorkshire Post. He offered a pay rise and my name and picture on the People column – elevating me to star columnist status. I was savvy enough to recognise this as an eventual entree into personality journalism nationally, but I knew it wasn't what I wanted or was ever likely to want. Nor has it been. So after just under two years in Yorkshire, it was off to London.

FOUR
FLEET STREET – 1964-1968

If my two years at the Yorkshire Post were among my happiest in journalism, the next four years in Fleet Street were the most miserable. This was nothing to do with the 'Street of Adventure' or the demands of the work; my mental state was the problem. The difficulties must have built up gradually, but emerged with explosive force and cast a shadow over the later part of my time there.

None was apparent as I reported for work at the Guardian in October 1964, days before the general election that saw Labour into power for the first time in 13 years. The offices were in Fleet Street only metaphorically. They were in Gray's Inn Road well on the way to King's Cross. We were on the third floor of a building (since demolished) owned by Lord Thomson of Fleet, whose Sunday Times was produced there. The two newspapers shared a composing room where advance pages of the weekly were to be seen lying around. I managed to resist sneaking a look at these formes (completed pages in metal type), particularly since this was the heyday of investigative exposures under editor Harold Evans.

Not for Lord Thomson the pretentiousness of a private lift. One day I entered the building just ahead of him. Staff held back as he made for the lift with an attendant. But I thought, he's not my proprietor, and got aboard. The attendant said nothing. We three rode together, the lift delaying his lordship at the third floor while I got out.

Like a Cinque Port from which the sea has receded, the Guardian's original London office – which was in Fleet Street – lost its role with the transfer of editorial operations from Manchester to London. The London editor, Gerard Fay, remained, with nothing much to do except lose himself in the pleasures of the bottle.

The Guardian's long journey from provincial newspaper with a national following to a true national had been going on for many years. Distribution was as much an issue as editorial content. In the mid-Fifties, for example, I took the paper daily at our home in Ascot, west of London. But it was frequently a day late because it had to be sent around the country from Manchester. The other nationals in those days typically had two production centres, London and Manchester, which allowed same day availability in all but the remotest parts of the country.

A symbolic change was made in the late Fifties when 'Manchester' was dropped from the title. More importantly, London printing and the transfer of editorial operations began soon afterwards. Another symbolic moment came when the editor, Alistair Hetherington, transferred his chair to the capital. The editorial move was carried out in stages, and when I joined in 1964 the process was far from complete. Foreign news, for example, remained in Manchester.

Stories were exchanged in type between the two centres – hence did not need to be set twice over – by a process called teletypesetting. Innovatory in its day, it involved a Linotype operator working his own machine and a slave machine at the other end. In theory, the output of both machines was identical. The process, unfortunately, was prone to failure, leading to late setting and rushed corrections at the remote centre. Rushed corrections meant further mistakes – the main source of the reputation for mistakes that beset the Guardian (or Grauniad, as Private Eye called it) for many years.

The night editor was John Putz. Not only was he king of the newsroom but also he had been the central figure in the successful switch of editorial to London. Whether out of recognition of his age, which must have been in the fifties, or his status, he was 'Mr Putz' to me; his deputy, Michael Hides, later editor of the Sheffield Telegraph, was 'Michael', and of course it was first names to all below him. The back bench was completed with Peter Large and Arnold Kemp.

Arnold was the copytaster, a young man who was marked out for great things. A Scottish nationalist at a time when they were a small minority, he abandoned his national career and he and his wife Maggie went to Edinburgh. Later, he became editor of the Glasgow Herald, married Ann Simpson (from the Yorkshire Post) as his second wife and died prematurely.

He was replaced as copytaster by Donald Wintersgill, a cultivated man who lived on his nerves – among the last qualities needed in a copytaster. Donald, whom I would team up again with two decades later, found his metier as a prominent arts correspondent as well as the Guardian's syndication editor.

The newspaper attracted 'lifers'. Many of those I knew in

those days were still on board towards the end of my second association with the Guardian almost 40 years later: Peter Preston, David McKie, Victor Keegan, Ian Wright, Campbell Page, Philip Osborne, Bernard Jolly and others.

Among the memorable figures from the early days was the Kremlinologist Victor Zorza. He sat in a tiny cubicle piled to the roof with files and papers. Authoritative is probably too weak a word for his articles, but I wondered how many readers were that interested in the highways and byways of Soviet policy. It's unwise in a general newspaper to publish material of minority interest only.

Another extreme specialist – although possibly with more general appeal – was Patrick Keatley, the Commonwealth correspondent and a pleasant character in the Bill Oliver mould. His cubicle was also piled high with papers, although it was chaotic where Victor's was neat and tidy. Patrick specialised, without meaning to, in late copy. It had to be delivered to the typesetters 'take at a time' (meaning that the story could be composed in bits by several operators rather than one operator having the whole story before him). One of my jobs was to stand over Patrick while he frantically wrote the next two or three pars, then dash back to my desk to fix up the English as another sub took my place breathing down the writer's neck.

This method of production meant it was virtually impossible for anyone to know how long the story was. The result was to be seen in the overmatter galleys the next day. These were time and money wasted.

Ian Aitken's copy, on the other hand, was both accessible and neatly written. It was a revelation after the discursiveness of typical Guardian material. He joined from the Daily Express and brought with him that paper's ideas of readability. Ian showed us that it's possible to be profound without also being obscure.

Clare Hollingworth had been a war correspondent at a time when women were a rarity in the role. By now she was defence editor. The content was good, but her copy was a jumble. She never minded it being fixed up by the sub-editors. When she won the prestigious Hannen Swaffer award for her journalism, she was reported to have said 'I owe it to the subs' – a gracious recognition that few writers manage.

The routine of news subbing was much as I'd known it at the Yorkshire Post. My friend from Leeds days, Francis Ashborn, was there. We sat around a block of desks, which allowed for badinage unimaginable now that everyone is lost behind a computer terminal. We traded tricky points of house style and grammar; double-checked our concern about some factual inaccuracy in copy. This team effort was one reason that standards in those matters were higher then. Another is the presence of proof readers, now one of the lost jobs of newspapering.

The proof readers' job as they checked galley proofs was, officially speaking, to 'follow copy out of the window'. Invariably they did more than that. They were the unofficial custodians of house style. Reporters, and the subs who passed the copy on, were often saved from grammatical and factual mistakes.

I enjoyed stone subbing as a welcome change of routine. This meant working in the composing room putting together the pages. It was a crucial part of the production process to keep the paper on time. Rather than over-length stories going back to editorial for cutting, a stone sub made cuts on the spot and handed them to the compositor. The same applied to headlines, which could be quickly rewritten 'in situ' to make them fit.

A further job was to select fillers, which were sitting on a galley with a 'pick me' expression like dogs in a rescue centre. Pages weren't made up of the rectangular story blocks that became universal later. On a broadsheet newspaper like the Guardian, they were presented as vertical strips. This sometimes produced 'legs' of uneven length, requiring a filler to be dropped in at the end to even things up. To select a filler you had to be able to read the lead type in mirror-image form. (When poring over a page with the compositor, the sub saw it upside down too.) You had no way of knowing how many fillers would be needed over the evening so the tendency was to pick the best first to ensure they got in. This produced the paradoxical result that a filler on the front page could be one of the weakest.

Thanks to the problems with teletypesetting, and perhaps other factors, the newspaper seemed always on the brink of going to bed late. The overseer, Don Borritt, would run around frantically exclaiming, 'We're in the shit tonight, Mr Cedric!' As a form of address it was an echo from another age. He was the only one in the composing room who addressed me like that, everyone else naturally using my first name.

The printers had a powerful, nationwide taboo against editorial people touching the type. You could never, ever speed the makeup by picking up a filler and bringing it to the page. You could point to an item with the pen hovering a quarter-inch (6 mm) above the surface, but never, ever let your hand slip or shake! I became friendly with several of the printers, but this was a line never crossed. The first time I handled type was years later when someone gave me a slug of headline type. By then it was as much of a museum piece as a shard of Roman pottery.

It was always a thrill when, mid-evening, the first edition of the newspaper arrived from the printing presses in the same building. You saw neatly fixed in print on crisp newsprint not yet spoilt by handling the stories that you had worked on perhaps as little as an hour ago, when they were a mess of typewriting and hand-written subbing changes, additions and instructions. In London, there were three more editions to go (others in Manchester), the farthest destinations receiving the earlier editions. Pages were often 'tidied up' with editorial and proof-reading changes after the first edition. This procedure – to some extent inevitable in the rush of daily production – was fine for London; not so good in Plymouth, which received the first edition! Better to get it right first time ...

With not much going on in my private life – not hard when your play time is your friends' work time – I looked for work as a Saturday sub on a Sunday newspaper. These relied on 'regular casuals' on their main production day because their permanent, week-round staffs were small. The Guardian (before it bought the Observer) didn't have a Sunday counterpart, but there was no restriction on trying my luck elsewhere.

After a few not-too-successful shifts at the Observer, I found a regular berth at the Sunday Telegraph. This was soon after it had launched as a compact newspaper aiming to 'fill the gap' between the heavy broadsheets (Sunday Times and Observer), which even then were felt to be getting too big, and the lightweight tabloids. Whether this gap was more than a marketing slogan is open to doubt. The Sunday Telegraph circulation struggled for years. Although it eventually overhauled the Observer's, it has never matched that of its weekday stablemate – a reverse of the typical situation.

The newspaper had only two full-time staff among the news subs – Bill Aitken, the night editor, and Matthew Rock, the chief sub. The rest of us were casuals gathered from all over Fleet Street. I found the work environment very congenial. There were long periods with nothing to do except read the New Statesman and the Spectator – it was the heyday of those magazines – punctuated by challenging bursts of activity. I suppose the newspaper was over-staffed, but this at least allowed plenty of time for thorough editing.

I discovered a knack for the running story. In subbing terms, this is a breaking story near the deadline. It has to be put together – perhaps from several sources, say two or three agency reports plus staff copy – not only hurriedly but also perhaps take at a time, with a page sent to the compositors while one is working on the next one. Therefore it needs a clear head, an overall 'feel' for the story and writing ability to make links between the various sources. I was often chosen for front page running stories and when I left, Bill Aitken and Matthew Rock, in a joint reference, picked out this aspect of my work.

The editor-in-chief of the Sunday Telegraph (who was also the proprietor), Lord Hartwell, had one of those editorial idiosyncrasies so beloved of editorial main men. Every ship mentioned by name, from the smallest tug to the grandest liner, had to include its tonnage. Happily, the answers were usually readily found from the Jane's reference books in the library.

Lord Hartwell, although a rich man who might have lived comfortably on his dividends, commanded respect among the staff as a working newspaperman. I never heard him bad-mouthed. On Saturday evening he ploughed through galley proofs, making frequent suggestions in pencil in a small, distinctive hand. They were invariably apt. It seemed to me an effective form of quality control. Kenneth Young used it at the Yorkshire Post, presumably having picked it up from his time at the Telegraph, but I never knew it used elsewhere in a systematic way.

It was, however, an expensive practice because it meant resetting type, sometimes whole paragraphs. It was another example of the heroic but unwise emphasis on editorial quality with little regard for costs. This unworldliness led eventually to the Telegraph's forced sale to the Canadian robber baron Conrad Black.

I continued to work at the Sunday Telegraph until I left for America in 1968, leaving the newspaper with feelings of great affection.

Meanwhile, the Guardian suffered a crisis that threatened its closure or merger. It hadn't covered its costs for years. This hardly mattered because the owner, the Scott Trust – uniquely in British newspapers – had as its overriding purpose to publish the Guardian using whatever resources were available to it. At the time, this mainly meant the piggy-bank of its regional sister paper, the Manchester Evening News.

I discovered the bitterness that this caused among MEN staff when I was entrusted with taking flongs (papier mache moulds) of the 1966 election results to Manchester so they could be used in the northern editions (such complicated material not being trusted to the error-prone teletypesetting system!). The Evening News staff couldn't see the justice in subsidising a paper whose journalists were paid more than they were and which was in process of deserting its native city.

The time arrived, however, when the resources of the MEN and the few Lancashire weeklies that the company also owned were no longer enough. Voluntary redundancies were invited at the Guardian. Closure was contemplated. So was the fate worse than death of merging with the Times.

The editor Alistair Hetherington, dismayed at the threat to the paper's identity, led opposition to the move. The trustees were eventually persuaded to call off the merger.

Survival came when an outside hire, Peter Gibbings, devised a way of dramatically breaking out of the box. He invested in more local weeklies, which were highly profitable, and local radio stations. He bought the car buyer's bible, Auto Trader. This was to be a cash cow for the Guardian for many years, leading to the irony that this most right-on of newspapers was supported by that most unright-on of activities, motoring.

In the internet age, the Guardian's financial base again looked precarious. The perennial loss-maker was testing its assets to the limit. The rise of online advertising meant a steady loss of income from classifieds (the small ads) for its weekly subsidiaries, while the newspaper itself was throwing many millions at its website. The weeklies and the radio stations were sold, as was a half-share in Auto Trader. These moves produced welcome capital but they meant selling the seed corn. The Observer, which the company had bought, was also a perennial loss maker. It looked vulnerable (although was ultimately spared). It was clear that the Scott Trust's requirement to maintain the Guardian to its last pound didn't extend to the sister paper.

Thanks to Gibbings, the 1960s crisis passed. At ground level at least it was business as usual. I started to find work at the Guardian monotonous and oppressive. This was compounded by personal difficulties. I'd left home years before and, returning from Leeds, made the mistake of moving back in. Evening shifts meant it was hard and often impossible to catch a train to Ascot. I drove to the office and back each day – a return trip of more than 50 miles mostly through suburbs. One route took me past Heathrow Airport, where in those more peaceable days airliners were parked next to the main road, a thin chain-link fence the only barrier.

In other words, I was exhausted. Matters weren't helped by the habit I had for a time of dropping in after work at the Press Club in its splendid Victorian premises in Salisbury Court, off Fleet Street, sinking two or three pints before driving home.

Late at night, the Press Club was a place for serious boozers. This was before it became a lunch club for PR executives and, later still, an occasional social club meeting in a pub having lost its own premises. An executive on the Daily Express was famous for holding court to the stage where he had to be carried horizontally back to his office. I found I couldn't keep up because alcohol made me tongue-tied – not helpful in a gabby place like that.

At other times I stopped at a late-night cafe in Bayswater where I lost my heart to no effect to the singer. The most sensible thing I did to 'wind down' was to give a lift home to a colleague, Martin Revis, and drop in at his place for a coffee. These were all attempts to get a bit of normality into an abnormal work pattern. My free time was in the morning before work, when I had no use for it. I started to make aimless drives through the Berkshire and South Oxfordshire countryside as a way of passing the time.

Eventually this lifestyle caught up with me. One day I experienced a shudder of revulsion as I picked up a piece of copy. I told myself I didn't want to read sentence after sentence after sentence day after day after day. A nightmarish future of nothing but words on paper stretched before me. In fact, I didn't want to read at all. I stared at the paper willing the letters to turn themselves into meaningless patterns as they would appear to an illiterate. There must be comfort in that. This they refused to do. They wouldn't even dance around although they managed an abnormal glare off the page.

Then I was troubled by the opposite thought, that I was losing my ability to read, to extract meaning from those patterns. I would be helpless, an imbecile. Then again, if the patterns meant nothing perhaps it would be a worthwhile challenge to learn what they meant. A lethal idea popped into my head that having learnt to read there was nothing left for me to achieve.

I see now that this was an undiagnosed nervous collapse, brought on by exhaustion and an unsatisfactory lifestyle. These feelings lasted intensely for months. They continued in diminishing form long afterwards, only shifting when I moved to the United States in 1968. I suppose this was enough of a challenge to shake me out of my anxiety state.

Through it all I presented as normal. Friends and family had no idea what was going around in my head. At work it was another story. I was still able to do the work, but I became withdrawn, not taking part in the jokes around the subs' table. On one occasion a fellow sub complained that I sat there all evening saying nothing, then emitted a manic laugh at something that amused me in copy, then relapsed into silence. If he had only known!

Nervous attacks have continued to plague me intermittently through the years. After finally recognising them for what they are, I learnt ways of keeping them in the 'worry box'.

There was a finely graded hierarchy at the Guardian among the home news subs. This declared itself in the weekly roster. The late shifts were an important step up from down table subbing, like being made a corporal. They brought authority to change contents when Mr Putz and the rest of the top table had gone home. The last shift of all, lasting into the middle of the night, left the sub and a few printers in sole command of the Guardian's destiny. If there was a major story at that stage, the sub would have to remake the front page.

I was never selected for these late shifts. I was overtaken by sub-editors who were younger and junior to me on the paper – in one case, by someone to whom I'd shown the ropes when he joined. No doubt I deserved it, but my competitive instincts were engaged. I don't stand for being overtaken! It was time to look around.

Always an admirer of popular journalism, I decided to try my luck in that sector. I felt it would add further variety to my CV. I did a write-around, as I had before joining the Yorkshire Post and was to do again. I landed a job at the Sun as a news sub at a substantial increase on my Guardian pay. This was the newspaper that Rupert Murdoch was soon to buy and turn into a slam-bang tabloid – in fact, a new paper with the same name. At that time, however, the Sun was a worthy but failing broadsheet that had been born out of the old Daily Herald. This had

been the organ of the trade union movement. The formal connection was cut when it was bought by Odhams Press, but its
readership remained ageing and left-wing. Even though failing
and, as it turned out, in its death throes, the Sun still had a circulation four times that of the Guardian.

I speedily discovered how different popular journalism was
from so-called quality (or 'unpopular') journalism. The sub-editors truly were king. A sub would rewrite a story from top to
bottom, and then add the reporter's byline. The writers probably
thought murder, but knew better than to complain.

Whatever one thinks about that degree of editing, it was
skilled work by the subs. I soon discovered that it was harder to
hold the job down than it was on the Guardian. I was impressed
by the emphasis that the chief sub, Ken Rowe, put on almost
every word, especially in first paragraphs.

He sat at the head of a long table. Every so often he would
call up a sub for a query. The method of summoning was to call
out the man's name, rather loud, whereupon he would leave his
seat to see what the problem was. Ken would say things like,
'This word "nearby" ... do you think it should be "close by"?
Go away and think about it, will you?' I dreaded the 'Cedric,
please!' more than once a night because you felt like a miscreant
summoned to see the headmaster. My seat was at the bottom of
the table, which made for a long walk.

This approach meant high standards and was typical of the
mass circulation press. At the Daily Mirror it was said, doubtless
apocryphally, that if you subbed a two-par filler in less than an
hour they thought you were rushing it.

At the Sun I encountered page designers for the first time. (At
the Guardian the editorial back bench laid out their own pages.)
The designers would rough out pages for a journalist to
approve, after which stories had to be cut (or expanded) into the
spaces required.

The style was very neat and tidy, the clean look of Helvetica
– then a new and adventurous typeface – for headlines matching
the ethos of the pages. It was a designer's paper although perhaps not a reader's one, lacking the urgency and impact of the
tabloid Daily Mirror or the then-broadsheet Daily Express.

The Sun's innovative design approach extended to a front
page novelty that deserved to be copied by other publications.
I encountered it again among the exuberant news media of the
Philippines. The titlepiece (or masthead) changed shape and

position from issue to issue. It might be a box at top left or a strip right across the top – both classic positions. At other times it would be at top right, or in the middle of the page surrounded by editorial content. It even made an appearance as a strip across the bottom of the page. The last was deeply impracticable because it meant that when the newspaper was folded in a news rack the title wasn't seen. Otherwise, though, the variable positions were unusual and they were fun.

I was no hit as a Sun sub-editor because I lacked the 'popular' touch. Staples like sport, television and crime weren't my scene. I fitted better with the Sunday Telegraph, whom I continued to work for on Saturdays after leaving the Guardian. So it suited everybody, me included, when I was transferred to the Sun's business section. This was enjoyable work, a one-person job involving selection of contents as well as sub-editing. Nor was it too taxing: the business coverage was typically one page.

The section was made up most days by the same compositor, Nelson. He had no other pages, and was expert in stretching out the work so that any passing management wouldn't notice that he had too little to do. This was a courtesy on his part. Even if management had noticed, they couldn't have done anything such was the grip of the union, the National Graphical Association.

With the circulation constantly in decline, the Sun was clearly heading for sale or closure. However, there was no sense of gloom among the staff. Rather the opposite as people thought about their redundancy payoffs. No-one worried about the next job. We simply assumed, and we were right, that we would easily find something.

For me, however, it was pointless to drag out the months waiting for redundancy. I'd been there so short a time that the payoff would be small. Nor was redundancy guaranteed. I might have been taken on by the new owner – not a prospect I relished. I continued to be troubled by the anxiety state that had struck in the latter part of my time at the Guardian, and knew I must do something about it. Once again, I did what I was becoming good at – and went somewhere else.

The Sun was sold to Rupert Murdoch for a nominal amount a year after I left. He had bought the title and access to the editorial staff, many of whom were kept on. Nothing else was recognisable from the Odhams newspaper. Format (size), content and demographic (target readership) were all transformed.

Page three replaced politics ...

I had turned 30 and was still living at home, which by then was a large flat in Kensington. Tolerably affluent after a working life of 50 years, my father was able to afford this as well as the Ascot house (later the house in the country was at Sway in the New Forest). My anxiety was fuelled by what I felt was my mother's clinginess, although I may have ascribed inadequacies to her in order to avoid addressing my own.

Professional counselling would have revealed that sub-editing itself was a source of misery. I was unaware of this at the time but, looking back, it seems crystal clear. No-one comes into journalism to be a sub-editor. Vital as the function is, it's best as a job for those who've had their fill of 'the road'. I had unfulfilled road ambitions. My experiences at Pulse and the Yorkshire Post – news reporting, feature writing, diary items – had shown that I was strong in writing. But I had allowed it to drift during the Guardian and Sun years.

My response to the suffocating atmosphere at home was to seek work abroad. Incongruously, I looked simultaneously to Africa and the United States. My school friend Roderick Thomson had an enviable National Service posting in Uganda. Another schoolfriend, Tony Noel, had been a district commissioner in Northern Rhodesia (now Zambia). My Guardian colleague Martin Revis had worked on the East African Standard in Nairobi. I envied them these experiences. Africa seemed an exotic place in a 'Sanders of the River' sort of way.

At the same time, I had my own brief experience of the United States, and wanted more. Like many people coming to consciousness when Britain was prostrate and the United States the ruler of the world – one of my earliest memories is of asking GIs for gum ('Got any gum, chum?'), which underlined our dependency – I was in awe of Americans. Despite my Fleet Street experience, I wondered whether I could hack it over there.

I saw an advertisement for sub-editors in Tanzania, and applied. I also did my by-now customary write-around. I contacted the 20 or so largest dailies in the US, having found their names and addresses from Ayer's press directory. Be careful about casting your net too wide ... Soon, I found myself looking at job offers in Dar es Salaam and Cleveland, Ohio. How to choose between such different locations?

Most of Britain's African colonies had recently become independent, but it was still common to recruit expatriates for white-collar jobs. I expected this situation to continue, as it did for a long time, and reasoned that the American experience would be stronger on my CV. So I accepted the offer from the delightfully and uniquely name Plain Dealer newspaper in Cleveland. I could always do an African contract later. But it didn't work out quite like that.

FIVE
AMERICA – 1968-1971

When much of the world was protesting about America's war in Vietnam, I prepared to go to the United States as an immigrant. I presented myself for a medical at the embassy in London when the dust had hardly settled from the famous 'battle of Grosvenor Square', where protesters fought with police in March 1968. I was barely aware of the protest. My level of political awareness was such that I worried only about being drafted into the US army. I quickly learnt that for somebody of 30 that would not happen.

When I think now about that day, I think about Henry V's speech before Agincourt – 'gentlemen in England now a-bed shall ... hold their manhoods cheap whiles any speaks that fought with us upon St Crispin's Day' – and know it fitted me. In 2003, among a million marchers in the streets of London protesting at the war in Iraq, I was conscious of doing what I should have done 35 years before. That radicalisation – if joining a mass of respectable citizens who barely smashed a window between them can be called radical – had its origin in the United States when the country was tearing itself apart over Vietnam and the air was alive with the lovely ideas of the counter-culture, when everything seemed renewable and everything seemed possible.

I knew nobody in North America when I arrived in September 1968, but I was warmly welcomed in New York by Eric Frankland, a Briton, and his American wife, Sue. Eric worked on the Wall Street Journal, and he was a contributor to the National Union of Journalists' newspaper in Britain. I had written to him out of the blue for advice. With characteristic generosity, he invited me to stay at their home on Staten Island. That made my landfall very easy.

I was among the final few to travel by train from New York City to Cleveland, Ohio. By then, traffic had already deserted to planes at one end of the social spectrum and the Greyhound bus at the other. My fellow passengers – apart no doubt from one or two people afraid of flying and too proud to take the bus – mainly used the train for short hops, getting on and off at the various stops along the 500-mile route.

Not long afterwards, train services were withdrawn entirely from Cleveland's Union Terminal. The US government set up Amtrak to maintain a skeletal passenger presence on the railways. This turned out to mean, apart from some East Coast commuter runs, tourist trains on the old romantic routes.

It was not 'end of an era' sentiment that put me on the train, just accident. In Britain (although motorways were starting to make a difference) that was how you made long distance journeys. I just assumed that America was the same.

The Cleveland Plain Dealer, where I was to work as a copy editor – in Britain, read 'sub-editor' – was a strangely named newspaper in a country with plenty of strange newspaper names (the Sacramento Bee being another oddity). It was work I'd been doing on daily papers back home for six years. But I was bored by the sub-editor's upside-down routine of free days and working evenings. Never mind that the same routine would apply on the PD, as it was universally known in Cleveland. There's much to be said for being bored in another place. Several of the American newspapers I approached had offered a tryout, but only the Plain Dealer proposed to file the work permit application. The treasured 'green card' conferring permanent resident alien status was mine with minimal effort.

Such a process would probably be impossible now short of being a brain surgeon, but those were still the days of nationality quotas. Immigrants were admitted in the same proportions as the original population. That put the British, as the first colonists, in a favourable position with the quota constantly undersubscribed.

In Cleveland, I booked into the YMCA (having arranged this before leaving London; it was the only place I could think of). On my first Sunday, having nothing better to do, I asked for the nearest Anglican church and was directed to the cathedral. Here was another surprise: this was no Canterbury or Winchester, or even a Southwark. It was the size of a parish church, jammed in among commercial buildings. The clergy staff consisted of the dean, Perry Williams, and one other man, whose main role was as minister to Cleveland State University nearby. The reason for this is that the Episcopal Church of the USA is a small church although with more than its share of the rich and powerful and 'old families'.

After the service the dean shook my hand and I joined the

congregation for coffee. Both these practices later became common in British church communities, but for me then they were strikingly novel. The welcome worked because I went to the church throughout my three years in the city, and was confirmed there.

Cleveland, population about two million, was and is part of the American 'Rustbelt'. It was then at its nadir because of the decline of heavy industry, particularly steel. The Cuyahoga River, running through the city, was so polluted that a few years before it had caught fire. Accustomed to the well maintained parks of London, I was shocked at the overgrown and run-down state of the several parks. In any case, I was told, it wasn't safe to walk in them anymore. Little wonder the city was nationally known as 'the mistake on the lake', the butt of many jokes!

To me, one of the city's most obvious features was its seemingly endless suburbs, although in this it was the same as other American cities, reflecting the abundance of land. In downstate Ohio, I was to see fields left uncultivated because there was more land than anybody wanted to farm. Suburban sprawl is one of the most unpleasant aspects of US land use. It is far away from the smalltown America of national myth. Even in those days, thoughtful commentators were calling attention to the formless developments that disfigure both east and west coasts. On the east, the infill from Boston to Washington was called Boswash – an inspirationally ugly name for an ugly phenomenon. The name for the west coast counterpart, from San Francisco to San Diego, was almost as telling: the prison-like San-san.

Settled from the early 19th century, Cleveland was classically Midwestern in appearance. There were few terraced houses of the sort to be found in earlier American cities. The typical home was a detached, wooden house with verandah running across the front. More prosperous, newer homes on large plots lined the main roads farther from downtown.

The East Side, that is the eastern side of the Cuyahoga River, was solidly black out to about 100th Street, where the prosperous white suburbs began. The most affluent was Shaker Heights. The West Side was equally solidly white but without the differences of wealth that marked the East Side. Thus the city's most affluent citizens had to run the gamut of some of the most troubled areas to get downtown.

The Hough riots were a recent memory. They were part of the series of race riots that racked American cities in the Sixties. The best known are the Watts (Los Angeles) riots of 1965, when 34 died and more than 1,000 were injured over six days. We were told to lock our car doors as we headed downtown along the main road, Euclid Avenue, through the black area. I suspect this was exaggerated fearfulness, but I never put the alternative to the test.

One time the whites braved it and got out of their cars was to go to the Cleveland Theatre, which was a company with a national reputation. As the ghetto expanded the theatre stayed put while the landscape about it changed. The other famous cultural facilities – Severance Hall, home of the Cleveland Orchestra; the art museum, and the former Case Institute of Technology (by then part of an amalgamated university) – were on the farthest edge of the ghetto and formed a natural barrier to the affluent areas beyond.

The city had turned its back on Lake Erie. There was no promenade where citizens could enjoy this vast inland sea with Canada on the farther shore. Beside the lake was a fine fish restaurant called Captain Frank's. A favourite place for drinks after work on Saturday was Di Poo's Tool and Die Works in the Flats, a mouldering industrial area where the river runs into the lake. Nearby was the resort town of Sandusky, with a good and popular beach. Small insects came off the lake at a certain time of the year in their hundreds of thousands and dashed themselves to death. They were known as 'Canadian soldiers'. (Reciprocally, it was said, the same insects on the opposite shore were known as 'American soldiers'.)

Downtown Cleveland was not a mini-Manhattan. There was only one real high rise – the tower of the railway station, Union Terminal. There were plenty of substantial buildings, however, which crowded in on the main street, giving it a gloomy appearance. This feeling was eased by so many stars and stripes on display – more flags on an ordinary working day than on a national holiday in Britain.

I heard about 'the death of downtown' as shops followed customers out to the suburbs. The two main department stores, Higbees and the May Company, were still in the city centre, although – a new idea for me – they also had stores in the suburban shopping malls. Undeterred, I wrote a starry-eyed feature article about shopping malls for my former newspaper, the Yorkshire Post. It expresses the exact opposite of what I believe now.

'In the malls, thankfully, one can forget about motor vehicles and the noise, pollution and danger that they bring. One can walk and window-shop at leisure,' I wrote. (Present position: malls are hideous temples of consumerism.)

Then: 'Suburban shopping centres and malls are part of the automobile-orientated society, which has also produced free-ways streaking to the hearts of cities, drive-in restaurants, cinemas and banks, multi-storey car parks …' (Present position: 'the automobile-orientated society' has done much to degrade that society)

Then: 'Establishment of American-style shopping centres in the suburbs of British towns and cities would make our "downtown" areas better places to be in.' (Present position: it means the opposite.)

I was stunned by the range and display of goods, although I was merely observing for the first time trends that were soon to become common in Britain too. In the American hardware supermarket, home-owners could find everything from plywood to stereo sound systems. The girls at the check-out counters were unfailingly helpful, with little of the 'take it or leave it' or 'I'm too busy to talk to you' that one found in Britain at that time. British shop staff have subsequently become more polite – perhaps another trend imported from America.

Ready mixes, from cakes to sauces, were prominent, with enormous displays of low calorie foods. Every solid and liquid food item, from fruit pie to cola, seemingly had its diet equivalent. Meat was usually strictly flesh, with 'innards' like kidney, liver and heart (let alone brain and eyes!) less common. The national sweet tooth accounted for the many items high in sugar and starch.

Many of the goods seemed to me to be over-packaged, being smothered in paper and polythene-wrap. Branded items tended to be even more elaborately packaged. To reach the toothbrush or the ballpoint pen or the tranquilliser tablets amid all the wrapping was like finding the diamond in its bed of satin or the pearl in the oyster …

Looking over these paragraphs now, I could be describing 21st century Britain. These US shopping practices were a revelation to me in 1968; it was to be many years before they struck the UK with full force.

The ultimate emblem of American consumerism and the determination of manufacturers to gratify it was the sandwich filling that combined cheese and luncheon meat without the need to bring these ingredients together. The stores made it easy for people who liked this lunchtime treat by providing a pre-sliced loaf that was meat one side, cheese the other.

Similarly, there was no longer the need to laboriously mix peanut butter and jelly from their separate jars. Producers pre-mixed the two – a feat that equalled putting the stripe in the toothpaste – and the resulting mixture looked like the coloured sands from Alum Bay in the Isle of Wight.

Another in the occasional series of articles for the Yorkshire Post found me interviewing half a dozen or so British doctors working in Cleveland hospitals. We all huddled around a tape-recorder. When I played the tape back later, I'd lost track of who was saying what. This meant the article was light on sourced quotes, at least accurate ones, which are the essence of a good feature. The doctors insisted they were there for the superior research facilities. Of course, no-one mentioned the money.

An article on American women, written out of a slender knowledge base, found they were more pushy than their European sisters. This is a theme, if I'd known it, that has been going since the beginning. They were, I reported, still appreciative of the small compliments like holding doors open and praising a dress. It was a gross generalisation. No doubt some were; others would have punched you to the ground for saying so.

I learnt a valuable journalistic lesson later on a visit to Washington. I wanted to interview a senator who was speaking out against the Vietnam war, but he was said to be too busy. Instead, his aide would be happy to meet me. I found myself asking the aide 'What does the senator say about … ?', 'What are the senator's plans for … ?' and so on. This duly appeared as 'Senator X said', ' Senator X plans to' etc. For him this was publicity on the cheap. Probably the Yorkshire Post, as a leading British regional newspaper, was considered worth meeting but not in person. Nowadays I simply don't do secondhand quotes. At the least it would be 'Senator X's spokesman said'. More likely I'd decline the story if I couldn't reach the main man. Peversely, the tough approach usually means you get to meet your source after all.

In my memory of Cleveland it is either extremely hot or exceptionally cold. Of course, it wasn't that way, but we remember the extremes. I could tell when it reached zero Fahrenheit (-18C) because my beard froze at just that temperature. The snow was continuously on the ground from January to April (no doubt a trick of memory). Then the car had to be laboriously cleared of ice at least twice a day – to go to work and to get home. The summer heat was relieved by air conditioners, which were commonplace in private homes. My friends the Brecklings, with a substantial house in Cleveland Heights, one of the better suburbs, were seen as eccentrics for not having air con. Jane believed that constant switching from cool indoors to heat outdoors made people more vulnerable to colds. (She was almost certainly right that sharp temperature contrasts encourage viruses.)

It was striking how slowly the huge cars travelled in town, and how strictly lane discipline was observed. The same behaviour applied with pedestrians crossing the street. Everybody waited at traffic lights for the green WALK sign even if there were no cars in sight. I found out why. In what seemed to be a totally deserted street, I wandered across with the DON'T WALK sign showing. The street was indeed empty apart from me and, as it turned out, a motorcycle policeman who appeared out of nowhere as in a cartoon. Only my British accent and what he assumed was my lack of understanding of the rules saved me from a ticket.

Americans follow the rules more than Britons do. They are less chippy. I saw this again at the newspaper, where there was a strong sense of hierarchy, and people tended to do what they were told. One wonders where this compliance comes from. Perhaps it is to do with the German influence in the country. Or perhaps Americans naturally see authority as legitimate, and not to be resisted, because in a republic born of revolution all authority is ultimately the people's authority.

The Plain Dealer belonged to the elite group of 'major metropolitan newspapers'. It was the biggest in Ohio, one of the most populous US states. However, it had never won a Pulitzer Prize. This had become a preoccupation of the editor, Thomas Vail (whom I rarely saw in the newsroom). He was a member of the family that formerly owned the paper, although by then it had been sold to the Newhouse brothers.

Another family member was W. Holden White, who wrote for the paper from London. He was known in the office as a 'remittance man', a term then unknown to me having led a sheltered life where I never met remittance people. Some of his copy was charming and interesting in an idiosyncratic way, but he didn't operate as a foreign correspondent providing mainstream coverage. That, as he might have said, is what news agencies are for.

American journalism, I discovered, operated with the same practices and conventions that I was used to. Both traditions had the same understanding about what news was – and wasn't. Both maintained the distinction between news and comment, the American even more than the British. One striking difference was in legal coverage. It had become impossible to libel someone in US journalism unless malice was involved; in Britain it was, and is, easy to libel someone by accident. Pre-trial coverage was tightly restricted in Britain for fear of prejudicing a fair trial; in America it was common to read lines like 'Police said Smith stabbed his wife to death in an argument over money and tried to incinerate her body' – the argument being that jurors know very well that these are merely police claims.

Work as a copy editor was largely the same as in London, so adaptation to the new environment was not a great issue. It was the same hot metal production process. We worked with pen (or pencil) and paper, with the copy re-typed by compositors. Computerised type-setting was on the horizon. The paper adopted it soon after my time; London followed much later, in the late Eighties. I had to adjust to a few different spellings, some American forms of English including widespread use of the subjunctive mood ('The mayor asked that it be done' rather than 'The mayor asked for it to be done') and a very different style of newspaper publishing. The papers, which we got before we went home in the evening, were commonly 64 or 72 pages, and much more on Sunday. To me this was enormous, but I quickly learnt to exclaim 'Small paper tonight!' (meaning 64 pages) with the best.

The greatest difference between the work of a copy editor on the Plain Dealer and what I had been used to in Britain was that less was required of me Stateside. I checked writers' copy, wrote headlines and cut content to fit available space but (even though the PD was among the more actively edited US newspapers) there was less of a tradition of positive intervention with the copy – improving sentences, deleting or altering adjectives and even changing the all-important first paragraph in a news story known as the 'intro' or 'lead' . Writers call this process 'mucking the copy about', but usually it makes it better. None of us is the best judge of our own material. The alternative US term for the job, 'copy reader', seemed more accurate: we were reading the copy for accuracy rather than asking ourselves how it could be improved. The job was somewhere between that of a proof-reader, who looks at typeset copy for outright mistakes, and a sub-editor in the British sense.

The work of the rank-and-file copy editor therefore was limiting. The staff of the copy desk fell mainly into two groups: recent journalism graduates, who hoped to move on quickly, and old hands whose best years were behind them. (Back in Britain, I heard of a former Cleveland colleague who delayed his retirement 'so he could get his teeth fixed'. Since Britain's dentists took to charging private fees, I can easily understand it.)

One man, who sat opposite me at the horseshoe shaped desk, liked to loosen his false teeth and play with them in his mouth. I was frightened of him. His neighbour Art Milner used to encourage his antics, but despite these early high jinks later became an effective and pleasant slot man (ie chief sub-editor). Another was an alcoholic who frequently left the room for a reviving tot and had to be helped with his work by his neighbours. At the end of the night he got in his car and drove home. Once, I was told, he had been 'a real sharp guy'.

A recovering alcoholic, Gerry Lee, a taciturn Southerner, became my greatest friend on the copy desk. He never touched a drop. He lived with his wife Nicky in an apartment block within walking distance of the office. The Chesterfield was about the only decent housing in the central area, and was seen as a harbinger of the renewal of downtown. Gerry and Nicky had spent a year living in London, which he was always keen to talk about. Gerry insisted on referring to the War Between the States, not the Civil War (which implies a single entity of the United States). He frequently found a way to drop into the conversation references to the fictitious 'John Wilkes Booth Memorial High School'. He wasn't entirely joking with this reference to Abraham Lincoln's assassin.

The greatest character on the desk was Charlie Mulcahy, whom we called 'Sarge'. He had been a sergeant in the US Army, and the persona suited him. He had a wide repertoire of jokes and quips. Inevitably we soon knew them all, but he brought them out at a time and in a way that they were still funny. He told us about the Catholic boy and the Protestant girl (or vice versa), both five years old, who went skinny-dipping. They got an eyeful of each other. The girl said she never knew there was 'such a difference between Catholics and Protestants'.

Of headlines that made a good typographical shape at the expense of content, Sarge would say, with intentional lack of grammar: 'It don't say nothing but it fits like a sonofabitch!' Some towns in the United States, he pointed out, were so small that 'folks read the paper to see if the editor got it right'. When I published a journalism manual, *JournoLISTS*, in 2001, I used this joke to illustrate the point that information is not news – however important it may be – if people already know it. Sadly, Charlie had died before I could get a copy of the book to him to let him know he was still fondly remembered.

There were several Britons at the Plain Dealer; evidently I was part of a recruitment stream that had been found worthwhile. They included a top executive, Thomas Guthrie, who had been with the paper a long time, a couple of old hands and some recent recruits. We never formed a group although I was close to a couple of people. It was perhaps an example of the commonality of culture, starting with language, between the United States and Britain that we didn't feel the need.

When the National Union of Journalists back in Britain heard about so many Britons buried in the American Midwest, they asked for a picture for their newspaper. I arranged for the group pic to be taken in the newsroom. I was told afterwards that some American colleagues took exception to this very visible reminder of a foreign presence. It never occurred to me at the time, but I don't blame them. A bunch of Americans on a British newspaper would stir stronger feelings.

As copy editors our main creative activity was to write headlines. Sometimes these presented considerable difficulty. Headlines had to include a main verb, in contrast to the practice in Britain, which saw this as desirable but not always essential. In fact, the insistence in all cases on verbs means weak headlines in some cases. We could not write *New Hope for Cancer Sufferers*, for example. It would have to be *Cancer Sufferers Gain New Hope*, which is clumsier. Nor could we say *City's Bonanza from Speed Tickets*. It would have to be *City Has Bonanza from Speed Tickets*, which wouldn't fit, and a weaker idea would then be substituted. We weren't allowed to win space with verbal heads as used on some US papers, eg *Sees Hope for Lakefront Rebirth* (read the story to find who is seeing the hope). Nor could we abbreviate 'government', although 'prescription' could be 'rx' (after the traditional notation on doctors' pads), as in *Stokes Has Rx for City Woes*.

The Stokes we were always writing about, and whose name was so handily short, was Carl Stokes, the first black mayor of a major American city.

For some reason, there always seemed to be a lot of stories around featuring Japanese. The Irish were much to be preferred because the word was shorter. We weren't allowed to abbreviate 'Japanese' in headlines, which meant the heads often bust (exceeded the available space). In copy, too, 'Japs' was strictly banned while 'Nips' was even worse.

It was common for the newspaper to sell advertisements to occupy a whole page except for one column or, alternatively, two or three inches (5 to 7.5 cm) across the top, the remaining space being occupied by editorial material. The rationale was that readers were more likely to look at a page that included editorial. When the editorial space was horizontal, this meant extremely long heads of 60 letters or so. A full line was insisted on. Even a couple of characters short meant the headline had to be re-done. It was surprising how easy it was to tweak the wording to get an exact fit.

This process of fitting heads by calculation and adjustment has been wholly superseded by computers, where the copy editor trials the wording on screen and can see instantly whether it works or not. It remains a useful back-up skill for when we're separated from our computers or the system is down!

With advertising-led newspapers the 'news hole' is enormous. A lot of copy is needed to fill it. This, I suspect, is a key factor behind the well known prolixity of American journalism. The Plain Dealer's newsroom was organised around four desks – city, suburban (known as 'metro', for metropolitan), state and foreign/national. Shortage of copy was never an issue with the state and foreign/national desks. An almost infinite amount of news agency material was available. Nor was it an issue for the city desk resourced with a large reporting staff. It was certainly an issue with the metro desk, which often seemed at risk of running short. It was obvious that brevity isn't always a virtue in journalism.

In general, American newspapers have a much larger news hole than is usual with their European counterparts. This derives from the practice of selling advertising cheaply but in volume, which leaves a lot a space between the ads. While much

US journalism looks prolix to outside eyes, it is serving a very practical purpose.

The need to fill space was behind the abundance of 'turns', or 'jumps', of stories from the front page to their continuation inside. It was a practice I disliked, feeling that many readers are deterred from continuing when they have to turn a page. I particularly disliked it when the turn proved to be only an inch or two (2.5 to 5 cm). That's where cutting copy comes in! Once upon a time, there was an idea in London to have only one story turning from the front page. Sadly, the practice has been lost sight of even there in recent years.

In Ohio, I found myself on top of two of the main events that decided the course of the Vietnam war. In the case of the My Lai massacre pictures, I was as close as the next desk in the Plain Dealer newsroom. Seymour Hersh had broken this story of atrocities by American troops, but PD readers were the first to see pictures.

My Lai is a village where in March 1968 US troops murdered 347 unarmed civilians including old men, women and children. The troops were fired up to fight the guerrillas they didn't find, and angered by the loss of a well liked sergeant. So they cut loose. Hersh broke the story in November 1969, and the PD ran the pictures four days later.

They came to the paper's notice because the combat photographer who had taken them lived in the Cleveland area. He showed them to local groups without anyone apparently realising their true significance. This went on for months. Eventually, two reporters, Joseph Eszterhas and Alan Wiggins, heard about them.

After the paper published, national interest erupted. I watched in wonder as Eszterhas and Wiggins, my 'next door neighbours' in the office, spent hours on the phone to rival buyers. They were very much the office heavies, a pair of Jack the lads, so I'm sure they did a good job pushing up the price. It was this exposure to the national media that started Eszterhas on the road to a career with Rolling Stone and then to Hollywood where he became the million-dollar-man and scripted *Basic Instinct* (1992), with Michael Douglas and Sharon Stone.

Eszterhas recalled the episode in an interview with Ellen E. Heltzel (Poynter Online, February 2004): 'One day this guy called me and said his name was Ron Haeberle, and he was a photographer, and he'd been in this village where the American

GIs had massacred everybody, including women and children. A few weeks before *(sic)*, Seymour Hersh had broken the story of My Lai, and some newspapers ran the story, but most didn't. Now here comes Ron Haeberle, saying he had these photographs, part of a slide show he'd been taking to Kiwanis [business and social] groups around Cleveland. I said, "Get down here".

'To my utter shock, he had colour and black-and-white photographs of the most startling kind possible. I broke the story of the photographs, of Haeberle's account, in the Plain Dealer. The photographs immediately caused an internal firestorm, but more importantly, they proved everything that the Hersh stories alleged. The combination was a body blow to the American psyche and really helped end the war.

'After that, I wrote an article for the Evergreen Review called "The Selling of the My Lai Massacre", in which I was critical of the way the photographs were published. I was summarily fired for biting the hand that fed me.'

The second pivotal Vietnam event was the killing of four student protesters at Kent State University by the Ohio National Guard. These were shots that echoed around the world. KSU was only about 30 miles from Cleveland and therefore very much our home territory. Most memorable were the hapless excuses of the commander, but the tragedy on May 4 1970 had its roots in US history. The national guardsmen were not regular soldiers or even police. They were militia – the people who made the American Revolution – part-time troops who found themselves in a situation they were not equipped to deal with.

An article I wrote for the Yorkshire Post soon afterwards captures the divisions of those times. 'Students have achieved the near-impossible [I reported]: middle America as it retires for the night now is more apt to see long-haired anti-war protesters under the bed than Reds.'

Later, about a poll: '(T)he great majority of respondents rejected the proposition that those who pulled the triggers were primarily responsible for the slayings at Kent State. Only 11% blamed the Ohio National Guard; 58% blamed the demonstrating students, and 31% had no opinion. The soldiers certainly were under provocation, perhaps under menace – but there is something terrifying about a public that can shrug off a volley of bullets on a summer's day that easily.'

Soon after the Kent State killings, two black students were

shot dead at Jackson State College in Mississippi, and six more blacks were killed in Augusta, Georgia – all by law-enforcement officers. The American public seemed stunned by the turn of events. The reaction was: 'We thought it couldn't happen here.' Many people did not trouble to conceal their belief that the country was coming apart at the seams. Or they used high flown language, like: 'What happened to the American dream?'

The man in the street – the great mass of people who live 'west of the Hudson River' – blamed college students, their professors and East Coast liberals for all the nation's troubles. The students for their part blamed the military-industrial complex when President Richard Nixon ordered the invasion of adjacent Cambodia in April 1970 as an extension of the Vietnam War.

The peace movement got 75,000 people to a rally in Washington on very short order. Nixon, who had spent a sleepless night, courageously made an appearance before dawn among the amazed demonstrators. But a girl commented that, as he spoke to them, the president's mind seemed to be somewhere else.

The Kent State deaths triggered a nationwide series of campus riots, boycotts, strikes and shutdowns. Often professors openly allied themselves with the students' cause; many put their names to published petitions condemning the war, the slayings or the action of Ohio's governor, James A. Rhodes, in ordering the National Guard to the Kent campus.

The incendiary situation produced some imaginative responses by university administrators. Many Ohio colleges closed in the wake of the shootings, but in Cleveland both Cleveland State University and Case Western Reserve University were able to stay open.

At CWRU, a private school with many students from comfortable family backgrounds, the factor that probably headed off trouble was the administration's quick offer to students of alternatives – to continue with their courses as usual or to take final grades (marks) as of before the Kent tragedy, which would free people to engage in protest activities. In the event, the student union was transformed into a great hub for the areawide anti-war movement.

At Cleveland State, with students drawn generally from a lower socio-economic background, the students voted to continue with their studies. But 'alternative education' courses in 'relevant' topics like the war, racism and the environment were started by faculty volunteers, and these could be taken for academic credit.

The furore on the campuses and the accommodations it produced seemed appalling, if not completely subversive, to many ordinary people. Communists were entitled to despair of America once again when construction workers paraded in Wall Street in support of Nixon's Indochina policy. A pro-war student tried to join the parade with the flag of his college fraternity. This was mistaken for a Viet Cong flag, so he got the same fisticuff treatment that was meted out to his hirsute brethren.

On the eve of Nixon's announcement of troop action in Cambodia, identical majorities of 59 per cent of the American public specifically rejected the sending of United States combat troops, advisers or bombing missions into either Laos or Cambodia. Just weeks later, the public was voicing approval of Nixon's decision to send United States troops into Cambodia by 50 per cent to 30 per cent. Much of this switch-around represented reaction to the anti-war outcry raised by the young and the liberal.

With hindsight, the apocalyptic stances of both sides are seen as typical American over-reactions. Once the trauma of Vietnam was removed, the fissure that seemed to threaten the very nation closed up again into the normal politics of intergenerational and ideological differences.

My time in the United States coincided with the height of the Vietnam war. It was remarkable how the newspaper's coverage changed over those three years in step with the American public's growing alienation from the war. In the beginning, the smallest battles were reported in detail; at the end, only the biggest actions rated space.

Rarely were 'US forces' in action. It was 'Allied forces' or 'the Allies', even if these were nothing more than the ramshackle army of South Vietnam. The nomenclature has provenance: Americans don't like to act alone (while wanting to keep control). 'The Allies', with its heroic echoes of the Second World War, suggests added legitimacy. Fast-forward to Iraq 2003 and 'the Coalition': Britain's greatest help to the United States was not soldiers on the ground but the C-word.

The first manned landing on the moon took place during my time at the Plain Dealer. The grammarians and strict constructionists were quick to note that Neil Armstrong's first words included a slip of the tongue and therefore didn't make sense. He said: 'That's one small step for man, one giant leap for mankind.' He meant to say: 'That's one small step for *a* man, one giant leap for mankind.' Curiously, this was not widely commented upon. Years later, Armstrong was to acknowledge the slip.

I remember talking with some black people and getting excited about the achievement. I was totally unprepared for their dismissive comments that the money would have been better spent on health, schools and urban renewal. No national pride there, but why should there have been? The Cleveland black ghetto on the east side of the Cuyahoga River ran to almost 100 city blocks. Drivers from the suburbs beyond kept their windows shut and their doors locked as they drove through it ... arguably their minds shut and locked too.

It was natural that I should be chosen to sub-edit a big story from Britain in February 1971: the introduction of decimal currency and the end of pounds, shillings and pence. The newspaper led the front page with this story – a counter-example of the supposed parochialism of the US press. To give the headline a bit of oomph, I referred jokingly to Britons coping with 'funny money'. This was deemed insulting to Britain and its new currency, and wasn't used. I was certain, however, that readers in the UK would have liked the joke.

My time on the copy desk was interrupted by a brief, and unsuccessful, spell as a reporter. A young woman copy editor was always bad-mouthing the job, and this affected me. When she transferred to reporting, I thought I must too. My request was granted, but at that time I didn't have enough experience of news gathering to hold the job down. On one field assignment I had to be prompted by the accompanying photographer to ask the most obvious question. The couple had a tame fox. For some reason it didn't occur to me to inquire how they came by the animal.

I was quickly transferred to the obituaries desk, a low status job that involved working up obituaries from some of the paid-for death notices supplemented by phone calls. I followed in the footsteps of a veteran reporter. He was never known to use an adjective except on one occasion when he described someone as 'handsome, affable and debonair'. This turned out to be a friend of his. I asked Sarge about this extraordinary character who was handsome, affable and debonair. 'Well,' said Sarge, 'he sure was affable.'

I almost became an obituary candidate myself when I was driving in rural Ohio. At an ungated level crossing the flashing light warned me not to cross. In due course a freight train passed by – one of those interminable trains which have since become common in Britain. After the train had passed the light continued to flash for what seemed an eternity. This is absurd, I thought. I persuaded myself that the light was faulty and impatiently, without even checking the tracks, drove over the crossing. I was missed by a whisker by a train coming from the other direction. It would have been the stupidest way to go.

Before long I asked to return to the copy desk. I was not seen as a prodigal son, but nor was I treated as a returning defector. This time I was part-time because I'd taken up an activity that was far more absorbing than journalism.

A copy editor on a morning daily works, say, from 3pm to 11pm – deeply unsocial hours. Varying shift times provide no remedy because only minor alterations of an hour or two are possible depending on what job is being done. The question of what to do with my days arose as it had in London. There I went for fairly pointless walks, but Cleveland had fewer walking opportunities. There were fewer parks – none at all downtown – and those were rundown and uninviting.

Production of the Sunday paper was integrated with the weekday paper. A plus side of working five shifts over a seven-day cycle was that days off could be bunched. In that way during my first full year, 1969, I made trips to Montreal, Toronto, Chicago, New York and New Orleans. The pay helped. The difference even with national papers in Britain was striking (these were the days before Fleet Street pay rose by a quantum leap). For the first time ever I had money to spare.

By the summer of 1969, nine months into the job, I was bored. I was also homesick, at least in the sense that I responded avidly to places that reminded me of home. One such place was the campus of Case Western Reserve University, which was part of the 'cultural complex' forming a wedge between the ghetto and the affluent suburbs. Its Victorian gothic buildings and grassy setting reminded me of Oxbridge.

They were offering summer school courses, and I was admitted to one on the history of US labour relations. It was not the most riveting subject, particularly since the lecturer just regurgitated his own textbook, but it still beat boredom. The course earned credits towards an MA in political science. In the autumn I signed up for more courses and set about the programme in earnest.

Now the copy editor's hours became a positive advantage. I spent most of the day on campus, then drove downtown for my shift. Finding the energy for both wasn't a problem in those days. The degree course was absorbing, with the facility to make up your own pattern of courses. I stretched this to the full, even bringing social anthropology into the political science package.

The only time in my life I've been headhunted was when one of the senior editors at the PD, Jack Foster, was appointed to a bigger job down-state, and wanted to take me with him in an important role. I thanked him but refused, explaining that I couldn't break off from my studies. It was true, although another reason (not mentioned) was snobbery. After London and national papers, the Cleveland Plain Dealer was small beer. I couldn't see myself going alcohol-free in Nowheresville.

For the rest of my time in Cleveland I led a double life. The newspaper became increasingly peripheral to the university, which took up most of my effort and where I made several friends. I was loving both the work and being a student again, feeling that I was making a much better fist of both than I had the first time around at Oxford. By the end of 1970, I had amassed enough credits to take the final exam to earn the degree.

By now I was so into it that I decided to continue in the doctoral programme. Hence I went part-time at the Plain Dealer and full-time at the university. I was allocated a little office in the political science building – Hayden Hall, happily one of the most Oxbridge-like buildings on the campus – which I shared with another mature student, John Breckling. I was a quasi-academic doing a little newspapering on the side. Breck became one of my closest friends. We had a running joke about our plan to form 'the Institute of Creative Studies'. This meaningless title was inspired by some fatuous name we had encountered in real life. It prefigured the equally meaningless Department of Administrative Affairs in the TV show *Yes, Minister*.

At this time I produced my one and only academic paper. It was a content analysis of the East African business community. As part of my CWRU coursework, I spent hours trawling through a who's who-type directory, pulled out the business people and recorded a variety of characteristics like age, education, position and career path. I wouldn't have been pretentious enough to call these 'variables'. I then made a few general observations, and thought that was it.

My tutor, a committed Africanist, Kenneth Grundy, had other ideas. I had produced, unknowingly, raw data, that valuable resource for behavioural social scientists. Grundy enlisted another faculty member, Barry Hughes, a quantitative research specialist. My material blossomed in the approved language of hypotheses and chi-square correlations.

These were the early days of using computers for correlations (eg a strong positive correlation between business success and elite education). The work involved laboriously transferring the information to punched cards and feeding these into the computer. I remember the process stalling several times because of a mistake on a card, and then the magic moment when the computer spewed out reams of paper with the result. My messy data were tidily turned into neat hypotheses with chi-square numbers attached!

All this effort was directed towards the forthcoming conference of the African Studies Association. The paper, by Grundy, Hughes and Pulford, was presented there by Grundy and Hughes. Breck, my friend and fellow student, said I should have gone too. I didn't mind. I suppose I'd been used as indentured labour in the time-honoured tradition of American graduate students, but I had my mention. Like plastic bags, academic papers take a long time to disappear. This one was reprinted in a book. Forty years later it was readily traceable on the internet.

The project produced a payoff in other ways. It reawakened my interest in Africa, and prompted me to find ways of working there. Almost three decades later, the experience gave me the confidence to research and write my first book, *Eating Uganda* (about the colonisation of the country in the 19th century). In that, the idea of hypotheses remained helpful but they were unstated. There wasn't a chi-square correlation in sight.

Sometimes I wondered if my academic activity was fair to the PD, which had brought me to America to work for them not to be a student. Hopefully, though, all debts were fully discharged. It was, however, entirely through the newspaper that I could work out my student aspirations: the pay was good enough that I could afford the fees at the private university (although I needed help for my year in the doctoral programme, when the department made a small grant). I was, in fact, living out the American legend of 'working my way through school'. I became aware that in our department I was a rarity: everyone else seemed to be on grants, loans or family support.

In autumn 1971 I had been at the paper three years. The excitements of university life – it was the heyday of the counter-culture – combined with the boredom of copy editing to leave me desperately unhappy when I had to tear myself away from the campus and go to work. I felt nauseous as I entered the office. I was never actually sick; plainly, it was psychosomatic. Nor did I feel ready for the next stage of academia. The political science doctoral programme at CWRU consisted of course credits, a qualifying exam and a thesis. I had assembled enough course credits, but I simply wasn't reading enough to pass the exam.

Whether it was my part-time job or simply an inability to get into the deep detail needed for academic research, who knows? I decided not to take the exam because I was certain I would plough it. I preferred to leave my up-to-then sparkling record intact. It was against the urgings of my friends – but they didn't know how little I'd read. Looking back, I wonder if my friends (who had grown up with the system) knew something I didn't. Perhaps the exam was a formality and everything hung on the thesis. Perhaps the authorities would have passed me however abysmal my exam paper. No matter. I'm usually not one to refuse a fence, but this is a decision I've never regretted. I'd had an enjoyable year of post-MA study, and had no need of a PhD. I didn't want to become an academic. I was also thinking about leaving America.

As I got to know the place better, America seemed more, not less foreign. The dominant WASP ethos at the top – the white Anglo-Saxon Protestantism derived from the original settlers – makes it very easy for Britons to get along; but ultimately it is not what America is about: it is about populism and prodigality, 'regular guys' and 'the American way of life', in a way that no European can fully understand.

I didn't particularly seek out Britons for my social life, but the Americans I had as my friends were Anglophiles. When it dawned on me that I was relating to people according to their 'Europeanness', the conclusion was obvious: go back to Europe.

There was nothing in my private life to keep me in Ohio. S was a fellow political science graduate student. Her apartment was in the same building as mine. She was jokey and laid back, and I spent many hours with her chatting and drinking sangria. Together with her friend T, a student in another department, we were keen film-goers. T was apparently a much flintier person but, in what may have a window on their true characters, at the end of *Love Story* T was crying and S was dry-eyed.

The inevitable happened, and I was head over heels for S. But how to declare it? Grabbing her out of the blue would have seemed simply weird. So helped by an extra glass or two of sangria, I nerved myself to make a declaration. S's reaction was mainly shock. My feelings certainly weren't returned. It's so unusual to find a man who wants nothing more than friendship, she said. Now I too had fallen from grace. While all this was going on I was unforgivably ignoring the far more suitable J, who worked at the paper. I caught up again with J in San Francisco, but the tide had gone out.

In December 1971 I returned to Britain after approaching the Thomson Foundation, based in Cardiff. It's a measure of the assumption we all made in those days that jobs were there for the taking, as well as my own tendency to leap before I looked, that I gave up a secure, permanent job for a one-year contract. The foundation, an offshoot of the newspaper empire then owned by the Canadian Lord (Roy) Thomson trained journalists from the Majority World. The attraction was the guarantee of a field trip to Africa. It turned out to be the first of many. Meanwhile, the heat of Africa was a long way off. Ohio was cold but Wales was damper. Huddled in a Cardiff bedsit, I yearned for the apartment I'd left.

SIX
TURNING TEACHER
– 1972-1975

The Thomson Foundation editorial study centre was based in a utilitarian office block with sweeping views of Cardiff bus station. The city itself was saved from Victorian industrial meanness by the handsome public buildings befitting its role as Wales's capital and by the castle, a Gothic fantasy with Roman origins. The owner of the castle, the 2nd Marquess of Bute, turned Cardiff into the world's greatest coal exporting port with 'black gold' from the nearby Welsh valleys. His son John, the 3rd marquess, was reputed in the 1860s to be the world's richest man. As the Butes prospered so did the city until in 1955 it was designated as the national capital.

Our study centre was for print journalists; television journalists were more fortunate, with a handsome building in its own grounds at Newton Mearns, on the outskirts of Glasgow. There was no radio training, this being the preserve of the BBC.

Kirkhill – the Glasgow college – was residential, but our students (a word not to be used to their face) stayed at International House in Penarth, down the coast from Cardiff. This was a student hostel – of a superior type but a hostel nonetheless, and looking back I wonder at the grossness of putting them there. Many were senior editorial figures in their own countries, perhaps with secretaries, staff and chauffeured cars. They took it in good part. The experience built an esprit de corps in adversity when, for example, those who wanted it had to smuggle alcohol into the bedrooms. International House was a Methodist institution.

The Thomson Foundation had been created a few years before by Roy Thomson, famously characterised by his fellow Canadian, Lord Beaverbrook, as 'a little guy – owns a lot of little newspapers'. That was not how he ended, however, becoming owner of The Times and the Sunday Times, the Scotsman, STV (Scottish Television) and a string of regional papers including the Western Mail next door to where we worked in Cardiff. His company evolved into the first among equals of the financial information giant, Thomson Reuters.

The foundation developed unique expertise in the news media of the emerging countries. The BBC's radio training unit based in Bush House, London, might dispute the claim, but it was embedded in the BBC itself. The Thomson Foundation was a free-standing operation. I never found anything to suggest that it was under the control of the Thomson commercial interests.

Back then, the term 'Third World' described a meaningful reality. The West was the first world and the Communist bloc was the second world. The remaining countries became the third world and were far more nearly united in their underdevelopment than they later became, when some countries were nudging the development levels of the industrialised West while others stagnated.

The foundation knew a lot about the special issues of Third World media, from widespread state control (although hardly ever as crude as a censor poring over copy with a blue pencil) to the poverty of journalists leaving them open to inducements or (hopefully rarely) outright bribes. It knew about the flagrant partisanship of newspapers owned by political parties, and the difficulties of reporting corruption in government or tribalism in the country. This was a collective body of knowledge that incoming staff members like myself absorbed over time. There was no induction programme. Perhaps there should have been.

Cynics said that the foundation had been set up to help Mr Roy Thomson to his peerage, and even that the then-enormous £5 million launch fund was an accounting transaction rather than real money. Whatever the truth, the foundation was still running long after the donor had been ennobled or was even alive. It also continued to do much good on the ground.

Its success, in its courses at home and assignments abroad, was to provide down-to-earth, practical training at a time when the emergent world was awash with media sociologists and mass communication specialists. The men and women who came to the foundation weren't mainly interested in such lofty aims as nation building and what was later called civil society, but they did want to know how to put out a better newspaper or TV programme. Political independence, recent for many countries, had barely affected the skills gap in news media between north and south.

The Thomson Foundation could never be accused of the 'talking shop' approach to courses that is regrettably common. The style was to keep courses active, with plenty of assignments and exercises to test and improve the various skills of journalism. Ever afterwards, I've followed this talk-do-discuss format, usually insisting on something practical every half-day. And after lunch not too much talking before getting into the doing if one wants attendees to stay awake!

While the foundation gloried in its 'shirt-sleeves' approach, this tipped over into anti-intellectualism. The Cardiff lecturers were rarely seen with a textbook, much less an academic volume. They – we, for I plead guilty – relied on mimeographed handouts generated in-house (albeit with the partial justification that these were tailored to the special needs of our Majority World participants). This attitude of mind was still on display 20 years later when a new set of lecturers clashed with media academics at an open meeting I organised for the British government's Overseas Development Administration (later the Department for International Development).

The head of the Editorial Study Centre was Don Rowlands, who had been briefly editor of the daily Western Mail based next door. Don was good at expounding, but no longer spent much time preparing his sessions. With five minutes to go, he would rush into the lecturers' room and dive into a filing cabinet in search of cuttings he wanted for his talk. We considered it good sport to hide the papers and leave him to flannel his way out of trouble.

Don's first-hand knowledge of the Third World derived from deepest Cyprus and Malta. The rest he learnt from his students at Cardiff. This situation continued until 1981, when James Coltart, the Thomson Foundation chairman, ordered him to go to China to head an important, 2½-month project with the China Daily newspaper. Even then, he found a reason to return early, leaving myself and fellow consultant Barry Harding to carry on for the final month.

The cause both of the lack of preparation for classes and of the lack of interest in overseas work was Don's uxoriousness. Touching in its way, he simply didn't care to be separated from his wife, Mary, either for lunch or for weeks.

Six of us made up the full-time staff at Cardiff. Until I joined, the only university graduate was Jennifer Palit, the secretary. Don's deputy was John Cardownie, who had the habit of pacing up and down the room when delivering his remarks in class. His clipped style of speaking in a clear Scottish accent added to the suggestion of a sergeant major on parade; yet this authoritarian delivery masked deep concern for the emerging world and the condition of journalism there. He knew what he was talking about, having completed numerous projects on the ground.

The director of the Thomson Foundation, Tom Neil, presided over Cardiff and Kirkhill (the television college) from a base in neither. He occupied a small and lonely office in London. Mr Neil was a tallish man with physical presence. He had been in the colonial service in Kenya. His duties at the foundation didn't appear to be onerous, allowing him to depart in good time to cultivate his roses at his home in Bourne End.

From time to time, he visited us in Cardiff. On an occasion when he took the staff out for a lunchtime beer, the talk turned to the subject of sex. Mr Neil, who was in his early sixties, remarked: 'I'd rather have a pint of beer!' He proceeded to have his beer – and somehow I thought he wasn't joking.

I told the class about the director's visit (in expurgated form) and observed that Mr Neil was aged 62. There was an audible intake of breath. To me it was no great age, but it was an introduction to the fact that in the Third World life was usually shorter than in the privileged north.

Teaching was not my motivation in joining the foundation – that was the promised assignment in Africa – but I found the job suited me. I was able to combine my journalism skills with an element of reflection on the role of the news media in society. Having recently completed a master's degree in political science, I was happy to dress up some of my lectures in the language of behavioural sociology. However, I was forced to draw the line somewhere: subjects like cropping and scaling (measuring) pictures or cutting out waffle in copy didn't lend themselves to my academic enthusiasms.

Inevitably, some sessions were more successful than others, but nobody said so because of the foundation's 'good session' culture. No one ever had a bad session! The lecture theatre was one floor below our offices. When we returned from being on deck, as the expression went, the question would invariably be asked 'Good sesh?' Just as invariably, the answer was, 'Absolutely!' This gung-ho culture meant that inexperienced lecturers like me had to develop our skills in isolation because we couldn't admit any shortcomings.

One of my subjects was Transatlantic Similarities and Differences, based on my working experiences in the United States and Britain. Two Indians were in the particular group where I first gave this lecture. I made what I thought was a good point, to find them shaking their heads. I sent down another winner. Still they shook their heads. Galled now, I progressively threw in ever stronger points – and they shook their heads ever more vigorously. No one else seemed to have a problem. I left the room with a dejection I couldn't hide despite the 'good session' culture. Then one of my colleagues explained that when Indians shake their heads it means they agree – an early example for me of the cultural minefield through which I was picking my way.

An African student told me that the dinner I'd hosted was 'quite nice'. This was depressing until I realised that in Africa and many other places 'quite' has the single meaning of *very* – in this case *very* nice. Result: a happy host. 'Quite' is an absurdity in the English of many countries, including Britain. It has two, opposite meanings. When we say a meal was *quite nice*, we mean only moderately nice; yet when we are *quite well* we mean we are very well.

The three-month Cardiff course combined talks about press structures and practices with ground-level journalism training. This reflected the fact that, although they were senior people, the students hadn't had the training opportunities, on the job or at colleges, that we in Britain took for granted. Even where they had done journalism at a college, they usually needed retraining in the practicalities of putting out newspapers and magazines, making us wonder what went on in the colleges. (This criticism is not unknown about journalism courses in Britain and the United States!)

A long-running issue was the standard of English – not written English, which for those from English-language publications was often better than our local journalists', but the ability to understand what was said in class. South Korea was particularly inclined to send senior journalists with poor English. Applicants were able to self-certify their language ability, with the predictable result. I argued that we should screen applicants with the British Council's language aptitude tests, which were available in the countries of origin. It was to no avail, so we continued to have groups where one or two people could hardly understand what was going on.

Even the fluent speakers of English might have difficulties with speakers if they had strong accents or talked too quickly. I developed a way of speaking that was slower than normal but not so slow that it seemed to be talking down to people. I was often praised for my clarity. No-one as far as I know complained about hearing baby-talk from me; therefore I concluded that the approach was working.

The standard number on a course at Cardiff was 12, usually one per country. Men heavily outnumbered women, but this was decided in the countries of origin, not by the Thomson Foundation. They came from countries far apart in geography and in journalistic styles – from the Philippines, for example, whose exuberant and unhindered press made the News of the World look restrained, and Malawi, where no picture on the front page could appear higher than one of the aged dictator, Kamuzu Banda. We staged a role play exercise featuring a burning building in which the students had to carry out interviews and then write up the story. The participant from Malawi decided not to bother talking to eye-witnesses, but instead to get a statement from the fire brigade.

Life in the lecturers' room was enlivened by the affair of Neville's suspension. Neville Kros was a chippy South African (who became a close friend at the foundation). He fell out over some small matter with Don, who suspended him. Neville announced, 'I'm not prepared to be suspended!' Don failed to have him removed from the building, allowing Neville to stay at his desk but not giving him any work. The rest of the lecturers weren't supposed to talk to him, but of course we did. The stalemate went on for several days until the issue petered out and Neville was back in the team.

He wasn't the only non-conformist on the staff. Fellow lecturer Tony Thompson drove Don wild by wearing an ear stud. He refused to remove it, claiming he had gipsy ancestry. With his swarthy complexion that was credible, but it may or may not have been true.

For a short while, an Indian journalist joined us as a staff member. Our collective mindset struggled with this idea. 'Is he an officer?' someone asked. 'More of a warrant officer,' Don replied. We weren't being racist, supremacist or even paternalist. The foundation's training was justified by the expertise gap that existed between the journalism of the West and the rest. To close that gap was what the people came for, so it was curious to appoint someone from the wrong side of the gap – particularly from India, famous as the land of old-fashioned English and conservative page layouts. These were among the main issues we were struggling to overcome.

Towards the end of the year, 1972, I was offered a permanent job with the foundation. And my African assignment came through. Lasting 14 weeks, it scooped up most of Anglophone West Africa: Sierra Leone, Nigeria, Ghana and the Gambia. This was being thrown in at the deep end. Nowhere illustrates better than Nigeria the affectionate saying 'In Africa anything can happen – and usually does'. Zambia and Lesotho took up 10 weeks at the end of 1973, while 1974 and 1975 saw month-long visits to Bangladesh and Zambia respectively.

The main purpose of these extended trips – described later in the book – was to run training workshops in journalism. Sometimes the foundation took advantage of a lecturer's presence in the region to show the flag and develop contacts, as with my visit to apartheid-era South Africa.

It sounds glamorous, and in a sense it was; but there were a lot of lonely evenings in hotel rooms. Sometimes I travelled with a fellow lecturer; at other times I was alone. In the end, I preferred to work solo. To be locked into the company of someone else for a month, morning, noon and evening (at least we slept in separate rooms!), to suffer the mannerisms and the repeated remarks, is tough enough for close friends; with mere colleagues it was like the drawbacks of marriage with none of the benefits!

The days of free trade, with customs barriers torn down at the behest of Western paymasters, were far in the future. Imported products were prized either for their status or to cope with shortages. I always took in a few items as gifts, ranging from razor blades to whisky (and on one occasion, salt).

One bottle of whisky was always for myself. I applied the 'hotel alcoholism' test: can you bring in a bottle of whisky, keep it in your room and a month later have some of the contents left? If the answer is yes, you're not on the way to alcoholism. I passed that test – although I admit to frequenting the hotel bar.

Thus I began my career as a member of the Development Set:

Excuse me, friends, I must catch my jet
I'm off to join the Development Set:
My bags are packed, and I've had all my shots
I have traveller's checks and pills for the trots!

The Development Set is bright and noble,
Our thoughts are deep and our vision global;
Although we move with the better classes,
Our thoughts are always with the masses.

In Sheraton hotels in scattered nations
We damn multi-national corporations;
Injustice seems easy to protest
In such seething hotbeds of social rest.

We discuss malnutrition over steaks
And plan hunger talks during coffee breaks.
Whether Asian floods or African drought,
We face each issue with an open mouth.

We bring in consultants whose circumlocution
Raises difficulties for every solution
Thus guaranteeing continued good eating
By showing the need for another meeting.

The language of the Development Set
Stretches the English alphabet.
We use swell words like 'epigenetic',
'Micro' , 'macro' and 'logarithmetic'.

It pleasures us to be esoteric
It's so intellectually atmospheric!
And though establishments may be unmoved,
Our vocabularies are much improved.

When the talk gets deep and you're feeling dumb
You can keep your shame to a minimum:
To show that you too are intelligent
Smugly ask, 'Is it really development?'

Or say, 'That's fine in practice, but don't you see:
It doesn't work out in theory!'
A few may find this incomprehensible,
But most will admire you as deep and sensible.

Development Set homes are extremely chic,
Full of carvings, curios, and draped with batik.

Eye-level photographs subtly assure
That your host is at home with the great and the poor.

Enough of these verses, on with mission!
Our task is as broad as the human condition!
Just pray God the biblical promise is true:
The poor ye shall always have with you.
　　　(Ross Coggins, Adult Education and Development,
　　　　　　　　　　　　　　　　　　September 1976)

The metre may be sub-Tennysonian in places but the sentiments were oh so true! Sadly, they remain true more than three decades later.

SEVEN
AFRICAN DAWN

The African dawn was my own. The destination was Nigeria, where I was to be attached to a fledgling journalism training school for three months. Lagos was extreme Africa, the place that every expatriate had a story about. Pandemonium at the airport was an early sign. Officials rummaged through every bag while passengers, many of them loaded down with enough items to equip a small house (very likely their purpose), jostled and shouted for attention.

To me it seemed like a madhouse, but in Nigerian terms it was probably situation normal. Mercifully, I didn't have to negotiate airport arrivals alone. I was met by the school's Australian director, Keith Harris, who proved well able to shout for attention. He had to do it again at the hotel, where my booked room had fallen off the list. Eventually a place was found for me. No money appeared to change hands in either episode – just lots of sound and fury.

This hotel, booked from London by a travel agency, proved to be entirely impracticable as a location with Lagos's perennial traffic jams. Given the chronic shortage of hotel rooms, I was threatened with homelessness for a while. Then the British High Commission came to the rescue. The acting chief information officer, David Skinner, kindly let me use the comfortable guest bungalow of an empty embassy house.

I found myself the master of a staff of two, a gardener and a cook/houseboy (who was a middle-aged man!). The gardener seemed to spend all day raking leaves with the rest of the garden looking after itself. The cook required me as the acting memsahib to say what I wanted him to buy in the market each day – an impossible task for me because I couldn't name a tropical fruit or vegetable to save my life.

Nevertheless, it was pleasant to relax in post-colonial splendour. This went on for three weeks until a room became vacant at the Ikoyi Hotel, where I remained for the rest of my stay.

Practically nothing about life in Lagos was easy at that time. It was an unusual day when all the main utilities – water, electricity and telephone – were working at the same time. The hardest was a lack of water. The others were merely inconvenient, but it was deeply discouraging to be unable to wash or shower in the humid climate.

The Nigerian electricity authority was called NEPA. My colleague John Cardownie tells how children thought they had learnt a new swear word. When the power went out, parents would yell 'NEPA'! So when a child bumped his toe or broke a toy, instead of saying 'damn!' he'd yell 'NEPA!'

Travelling around Lagos was a luxury. Road congestion was so bad that it was usually easier to stay put.

The main street, once Broad Street and now Yakubu Gowon Street after the current military ruler, was almost derelict in places. After Gowon's overthrow it became Broad Street again …

Lagos showed the classic effects of an overgrown city, the natural and mainly unregulated growth being compounded by the effects of the recently concluded Biafran War. Many thousands of refugees had flocked into the city after the Ibos of Nigeria's Eastern Region declared independence as Biafra.

The dislocation of Biafra's secession was profound. The Ibos were known as 'the Jews of Africa' for their education, industriousness and commercial nous. They filled a disproportionate number of posts in the federal government service, many of which now fell vacant. General Yakubu Gowon was praised for the relatively clement way in which he put down the rebellion. In many respects, however, he and the Western powers were on the wrong side of the intellectual argument.

Biafra enjoyed wide support in the West by people who couldn't see why if a people were united in wanting independence (as the Ibos were) they shouldn't have it. How naïve, say the practitioners of realpolitik! Britain's Foreign Office for one has an aversion to dismantling borders, as the examples of Kurdistan, Somaliland and Sarawak also show. And above all it was the oil, stupid: Biafra had the bulk of Nigeria's oil.

For all the difficulties of life in Lagos, I had to tell myself that this was what I wanted, what I'd planned for in icy Cleveland and damp Wales. Through the open windows of the classroom at the journalism school – the Nigerian Institute of Journalism – poured the sounds and smells of the inner city. Traffic competed to make itself heard with non-stop and loud High Life music. Delicious fried food added its aromas to the characteristic tropical smells of vegetation in a humid climate.

Directly outside the institute sat a beautiful girl selling oranges. Shades of Nell Gwynne, except I'm sure that the girl was more virtuous! I was a regular buyer of her oranges, rather more than I needed. Keith pointed out that through the mother I could buy the girl as a wife. I expect he was joking, but there may have been an element of truth in this.

Nigerian newspapers were numerous and exuberant, a mixture of the official, or government-controlled, and the privately owned. It was the first time I met 'sex' as a verb (apart from 'sexing chickens'), as 'And then he sexed me'. The papers ranged from the Daily Times, a tabloid with the same look and style as Britain's Daily Mirror – no coincidence because it was part-owned by the Mirror group – to the starving amateurism of the West African Pilot, a famous nationalist paper started by one of the fathers of Nigerian independence, Dr Nnamdi Azikiwe, which was living on its past glories.

Total daily newspaper circulation in Nigeria was around 350,000. The figure for the United Kingdom, with a somewhat smaller population, was more than 20 million at that time. This was a measure of the development and literacy gaps needing to be closed.

The media, I concluded at the time, had a relatively large amount of freedom, but censors weren't needed on political issues when self-censorship often did the job for them. A columnist complained that editors and writers had taken to 'boot-licking'. The sting was a 1964 press law that held journalists responsible for the truth of what they wrote.

It was to meet the needs of this extensive media network that Lateef Jakande, politician, newspaper owner and the then-chairman of the International Press Institute, set up his Nigerian Institute of Journalism. The Thomson Foundation gave its support.

For three months, jointly with Keith Harris, I ran the NIJ's current course, News Reporting, for 43 mainly young journalists. The difficulties of Lagos life reached into the classroom. Two hundred copies of the IPI's *African Newsroom* arrived at the docks in July, but four months later had disappeared from there. Not to be outdone, the airport lost 30 copies of an important textbook, *Practical Newspaper Reporting*. Three reels of Thomson Foundation educational films created by John Cardownie reached us in the end, although it took five trips to extract them from the airport.

It was a relief to spend a couple of days outside Lagos on a visit to Benin City, capital of the former Midwest province. (Gowon abolished the old provinces after the Biafran War and cut them up into smaller states.) The Midwest had briefly seceded along with the Eastern Province, but the oba or king of Benin had managed to keep his throne. This was the man whom the regional information officer, a former 'Thomfound' student, Johnson Abaide, had arranged for me to meet.

We went to the oba's palace. I wish I had been more aware at that time of how Africa's traditional kingdoms continued to exist while having been absorbed into the colonial framework. Few have a more traditional provenance than Benin, with its glorious, world famous bronzes.

Johnson advised me to shake the ruler's hand and utter a few pleasantries. I wasn't at all prepared for Johnson throwing himself prostrate on the floor but, mindful of his advice, I stayed upright. An official photographer recorded the occasion, where I can be seen executing a stylish bow that happened of its own accord.

The elderly oba seemed to have only limited English, or at least that's what I assumed. This was surprising for an important person in a former British colony. I found myself speaking in a slow and simple way as for an uncomprehending foreigner. Afterwards, it worried me that he was being polite and he could have replied in rapid and fluent English if he'd chosen to.

Christmas 1972 came and went. It was my first experience of sun-bathing on Christmas Day. Keith and his charming wife, Jude, invited me to join them for an outdoor meal.

The Thomson Foundation had arranged visits to three other West African countries, partly for me to do an on-the-ground assessment of journalism training facilities.

On the way out, I had touched in for five days at Sierra Leone (where the humid climate of Freetown hit me like a brick wall). I gave two teaching sessions. And the rest of the time was filled with a busy round of visits and discussions with media figures. Six out of the 11 former foundation course members met me at a pleasant reunion.

On the way home, my stop in Ghana was even briefer – just 48 hours. I was there to make contact with Bill Hachten, an American friend of Don Rowlands, and to take a quick look at the journalism teaching facilities he was organising in Accra.

After the cheerful chaos and the crowds of Lagos, Accra – Ghana's capital – seemed very orderly and quiet. I had a feeling of whiteness. It was full of buildings looking fresh and white. I heard that Ghanaians were known as 'Nigerians with mufflers'. I started to understand that not all of Africa was like Nigeria. As in Sierra Leone, Thomson Foundationers turned out to greet me. Some came to the airport the next day to see me off, which was a touching gesture.

The tiny, English-speaking country of the Gambia is surrounded on three sides by Francophone Senegal, the fourth side being the coast. This was my final stop, for a three-day visit. In the company of M'Backe N'Jie, a recent Thomfound graduate, I carried out a programme of visits and teaching sessions. One of the sessions drew 60 people. Most were school pupils – a good omen for journalism, yet in a country that small there would never be enough jobs for them.

The Gambia later became a huge magnet for package tourism because of its relative closeness to Europe, but in 1973 the tourism boom was only beginning. The economy was undeveloped, and this showed in the news media. There was no television and limited radio. Two newspapers and the government news bulletin were printed; the rest were cyclostyled.

If the news media in Nigeria and Ghana were more developed than those in Sierra Leone and the Gambia, that was nothing to do with how sophisticated or cultured the nation was. It was and is down to economics, to having a big enough commercial sector to support advertising revenue and a big enough population to buy the papers.

West Africa had been an absorbing experience, but the climate and the chaos in Lagos made for a difficult time. Seven months later, I was to see another Africa. In fact, I could hardly believe how different it was. The jacaranda trees were in full bloom when I arrived in Lusaka, the capital of Zambia, for a month-long course – street upon street of glorious purple blossoms. The streets themselves were wide and, away from the Cairo Road shopping district, almost empty. The place seemed to operate in an ordered way.

Lusaka has one of the world's most pleasant climates. At more than three-quarters of a mile above sea level (4,265 ft or 1,300 m), it is hot but without the enervating humidity of the coastal areas. The seasons were varied enough to keep things interesting.

The tutor team for the course was my fellow Thomson Foundation staffer, Norman Cattanach, and myself. Norman, who had been chief sub-editor of the South Wales Echo, went on to a distinguished career in training. He ran the in-house journalism scheme for the Straits Times in Singapore, where he recanted his previous life running short courses of the type we were engaged in. He described them dismissively as 'flying workshops'. In due time, he found himself the director of the foundation – when presumably he recanted his recantation.

We stayed at the Ridgeway Hotel, where the terrace was built around a pond. I was enchanted by the weaver birds busy with their nest building. The Ridgeway was owned by Anglo-American, the dominant force in the copper mining that made Zambia wealthy. The editors' committee organising the course gave us a car for our exclusive use for the month. This was unthinkable on my many later visits to the country, as the economy deteriorated.

Zambia was on the way to becoming a one-party state under Kenneth Kaunda's United National Independence Party. Of the two daily newspapers, the Zambia Daily Mail was owned by the government. The other, older newspaper was the Times of Zambia. It had a bigger circulation and was owned by Lonrho, a conglomerate with businesses throughout Africa. It too had links with government: the editor was Vernon Mwanga, a former minister. When Kaunda instituted the one-party state, the Times was nationalised.

Radio and television were also state-owned. There was no satellite TV in those days and short-wave radio could be erratic. The internet was more than two decades in the future. Thus the Zambian public had few opportunities to hear other views than the government's. The newspapers were freer than the broadcast media. They did an adequate job in providing 'bread and butter' domestic news, and were quite adept in presenting foreign news from the agencies. They were weakest with the dug out material that is to be found 'off diary' – stories that don't come from press releases, press conferences or official announcements.

The importance of active news in this sense was one of the issues we took up on the course. This was a seminar-workshop held in ideal circumstances. Around a dozen journalists took part from all parts of the media. It was held in stylish Mulungushi Hall, which had been recently built for an international meeting of African officials.

Despite Norman's later doubts about 'flying workshops', I

felt confident that some of the course insights would prove lasting. Nor need we expect too much of ourselves. The poet
Edmund Blunden said that one poem could justify a lifetime.
The same can be said of a month-long training course if participants come away with a single, game-changing insight.

Some of the 1973 course participants were at the top of Zambian media when I worked in the country 20 years later. Sadly,
one of the brightest, Emmanuel Chayi, died after he had become
the director-general of Zambia Broadcasting Corporation, a
casualty of the Aids epidemic.

A general post ensued. While Norman and I were working in
Zambia, another Thomfound team – John Cardownie and Tony
Thompson – was working in Tanzania. I now met up with Tony
in Johannesburg, bound for the exotic mountain kingdom of
Lesotho (the former Basutoland), where a six-week course had
been arranged.

While in Joburg, we met journalists and managers of the main
newspaper groups, Argus and South African Associated Newspapers, publishers of the liberal Rand Daily Mail. An incident
at a SAAN training seminar illustrated the indignities of petty
apartheid. The event was integrated in a modest way. Two of
the 16 participants were black – probably a radical step at that
time.

The seminar took place in a fine, large house called Mountain
View. Participants worked, ate and slept there except for the
blacks, who had to go away at night to a hotel – not through any
wish of the company but because it was the law. This shocked
me because I hadn't realised how far and wide South Africa's
racial policies reached.

Lesotho was entirely surrounded by South Africa, a black-
ruled island in an apartheid sea. It had been a British protec-
torate after having been briefly annexed to Cape Colony. Its
mountain fastnesses meant it had never been conquered by
Britain. It resisted all efforts to bundle it in with its dominant
neighbour. Britain can claim credit for respecting the wishes of
the Basotho.

A group of South African journalists roundly and rightly criticised Tony and me for having no idea who 'Mokhehle' was.
How can you run a course in Lesotho without knowing that,
they asked. They were referring to Ntsu Mokhehle, the rightful
but displaced prime minister of the country. His Basutoland
Congress Party won the 1970 election, but the prime minister,

Leabua Jonathan, declared a state of emergency and stayed put. Chief Jonathan, it was claimed on the street, was ready to hand over but was persuaded to stay by South Africa and Britain, who feared the left-wing BCP leader. (Mokhehle finally became prime minister as an old man, between 1993 and 1998.)

In our indifference to the politics of a country we were about to work in, Tony and I were succumbing to the Thomson Foundation culture. There was no pressure or expectation to brief ourselves. The foundation proudly declared itself non-political, but on an occasion like this it was more like institutional negligence.

Lesotho seemed like an enchanted country. The landscape was bathed in late afternoon sunshine as we headed for the border, looking down on the River Caledon and the Sotho capital Maseru – merely a small town hugging that border. It had a single, wide main street, which gave an effect not a million miles from that of a Wild West town. I rejoiced in its intimate scale.

This part of Africa is home to the curious click sound of the Sotho and Xhosa peoples. The Xhosa themselves are pronounced KLosa. The sound is like clicking your tongue and making a sound at the same time.

Tony Thompson and I stayed at the Holiday Inn, whose grounds went to the Caledon with South Africa beyond. Most evenings a beautiful black singer called Abigail provided cabaret entertainment. I committed a bêtise by remarking to Abigail that I'd seen an interesting play in Johannesburg – her hometown – and had she seen it? 'We're not allowed to go to theatres,' she replied. She resolutely refused to dance with the guests, except that I persuaded her. I gloried in the honour of the only man who danced with Abigail. Ever since, Help Me Make It Through the Night has been among my favourite tunes.

Our course, at six weeks, was longer than usual for the Thomson Foundation. It was also unusual in having participants from three nations in substantial numbers. Ten of the 22 attendees were from Botswana and Swaziland. These countries were black-ruled former British protectorates in South Africa's orbit. They thus had much in common with Lesotho. It seemed to me to highlight the value of regional rather than national training workshops, although this idea was not developed during my time with the foundation.

The media scene in Lesotho was much like Zambia's on a smaller scale. The Ministry of Information was the dominant supplier of news to broadcasting and newspapers, with all the limitations that this meant. In the background was the election of three years before, when the victorious Basutoland Congress Party was kept out of office.

The two main newspapers were small affairs, both owned by Christian denominations. Moeletsi oa Basotho was run by the Catholics and was more elaborate. The Protestant paper, Leselinyana la Lesotho, printed most of its pages in Sesotho. Lesotho had and has the advantage denied to most African countries of a single indigenous language.

We were told that relations between the newspapers were poor. I thought nothing of it at the time, but many years later when I researched a history of Uganda in the 19th century * I realised that Catholic-Protestant hostility to each other has disfigured the African continent as it has Europe. It was one thing to read about how things were in the 1890s; another to encounter it in 1973.

Jessica – not her real name – was tall and slim and beautiful, and a member of the class. She was a Mosotho and she was married with a young daughter. It was the only time I fell for one of my students, or at least did anything about it. Soon we were carrying on a discreet affair at the Holiday Inn, with my colleague Tony in on the secret, constantly dreading discovery in a small place like Maseru. An added problem was that Jessica's husband was a senior government figure. I looked out of my window at the Caledon and South Africa beyond, wondering whether one day I would have to swim for it.

The course ran to the brink of Christmas, but I felt no festive cheer as I flew home. I was bereft at leaving Jessica behind, because I was falling in love. It was not to be the end of the story, however.

Back in Cardiff, life resumed its usual pattern of three-month courses. Jessica and I exchanged letters and had the occasional phone call, which she took clandestinely at a friend's house. In those days an international phone call was a big deal: it had to be placed through the operator, and the quality of the connection was variable. I was 36 but like a teenager hanging on the post – joyful when an air-mail letter with its red and blue edges fell on to the mat; in deep depression when one didn't arrive as expected.

The Thomson Foundation occasionally supported individual students to come to Britain. I persuaded Tom Neil, the director,

---

Eating Uganda (1999)

that Jessica was a bright candidate who would benefit from a
BBC radio course in London (this being an area of media not
covered by the foundation). It was true, but no truer than it was
for half a dozen others on the Lesotho course. I didn't tell him
about my personal motives.

Jessica in London was a different person from the poised individual so at home in Maseru. She seemed not to cope with the
big city, spending much of her time sleeping. The course director, in a comment that got back to me, complained that the only
time he could be sure she would attend was when the weekly
spending money was issued.

Somehow it came out that Jessica and I were having an affair.
I could only agree with Mr Neil that I had seriously misled him.
He could hardly have taken it more seriously than I took it
myself once the scales had fallen from my eyes. I've always been
grateful for his forbearance in refusing my offered resignation.
He probably felt I was in a scrape of the sort he'd seen before in
his days as an administrator in Africa. Although I deeply regretted tricking Mr Neil, I saw no reason to end the affair when Jessica returned home. We continued to write and phone.

Nineteen seventy-five found me back in Zambia, this time in
the idyllic setting of the Mindolo Ecumenical Centre at Kitwe
on the Copperbelt. Tropical flowers blazed forth their colours in
winter temperatures of around 30C. Tea was taken on the lawn,
mornings and afternoons. I was allocated a bungalow and a
vehicle for my month-long stay as a guest lecturer and consultant with the centre's offshoot, the Africa Literature Centre
(ALC).

All was not as comfortable as it seemed, however. This was a
time of severe food shortages in Zambia. As part of the boycott
of apartheid South Africa, President Kaunda had closed the
Zimbabwe (then Rhodesia) border through which most imports
had arrived. Much of the day was taken up with looking for
food staples. A message would arrive on the bush telegraph,
'There's bread at ...' or ' ... has sugar' and off we'd go. I suppose
Mindolo engaged in collective buying because students didn't
go short of food, but other campus residents like me fended for
ourselves.

Mindolo was where I encountered sliced avocado being
ladled from a large bowl in the canteen, in the manner of cab-
bage at my English school. Truly, other places, other customs
(and other costs)!

The ALC director was E.C. (Zeke) Makunike, a Zimbabwean and former magazine editor and director of Methodist Publications in Rhodesia. The head of journalism was Michael Traber, a Swiss Roman Catholic priest, also a former magazine editor and director of Mambo Press, Rhodesia. Although the centre had a chronic lack of lecturers, the agreeable Zeke didn't do any teaching. One of my main recommendations in due course was that he should put aside any considerations of status, and pitch in. Unfortunately, this sense of hierarchy was too common in Africa.

Mike Traber had the best command of English I've ever met in a non-native speaker. His vocabulary and grasp of idioms were astonishing. He wore his clericalism lightly, and his priestly dress not at all. Only once did his Catholicism burst out. I'd made some remark about Anglicans, and he spat: 'That heretic church!'

The Africa Literature Centre's programmes had been strongly criticised the year before (1974) separately by three visiting consultants: my Thomson Foundation colleague, John Cardownie; a training warhorse and International Press Institute stalwart, Frank Barton; and John Musukuma, the ablest Zambian journalist of his generation.

Part of the issue was that Zeke and Mike's backgrounds weren't sufficiently hard-edged for newspapers and broadcasting as well as magazines; secular media as well as religious media. In consequence, the courses weren't rigorous enough. A comment from one of the visiting examiners sums it up: 'Less than five students [out of 19] showed evidence in their examination papers that they had learnt anything from the course - if there was anything to learn from it.'

Zeke and Mike to their credit wished to raise standards. Mike had visited the Thomson Foundation centre in Cardiff to observe the training techniques in use there; now I was assigned to the ALC for a month to inject 'the Thomson touch'.

As always, I stressed the need for practicality: mass communication theory to be retained but given in the latter part of the course; African ideologies to be spread throughout the course rather than delivered in indigestible lumps. The course timetable was to be based on the talk-do-discuss sequence. The general standard of English on the present course was poor. I urged compulsory English lessons for two hours a day at first, phasing out over the six-month programme. A student from

Portuguese West Africa (Angola) had practically no English – a situation we were not unfamiliar with in Cardiff. It was impossible to help him, but the others were from Anglophone countries – Uganda, Tanzania, Malawi, South Africa and Zambia itself – and would benefit from the forcing-house approach.

Zeke Makunike and Mike Traber in a letter of appreciation were kind enough to describe my ideas as 'most valuable innovations', citing the areas of course programming, lecture preparation and presentation, content of exercises and tutorial administration. The Africa Literature Centre month had been a learning experience for me, too, in my dual role of guest lecturer and consultant adviser. In Nigeria, I had been a guest lecturer but made little impact as an adviser. Now, with three years' experience and a hard journalism background I had the confidence to bring about improvements.

Tom Neil hadn't forgotten about Jessica any more than I had. He was well aware that Lesotho was a short hop from Zambia, and had wondered whether to send me. No doubt he wanted to avoid the foundation being drawn into a messy situation involving a senior Sotho figure. Tony Thompson, my colleague in Maseru, gamely assured him that the affair was over. Except it wasn't.

We met in Gaberone, Botswana, for an idyllic few days. And then it really was over. There was no happy way out of Jessica's dilemma. Her daughter was in one continent, with the husband refusing to let her leave the country, and the man Jessica wanted to be with was in another continent. We sputtered on for a few more months until the engine of our love affair died.

The hereditary chief of Botswana's main ethnic group had morphed into the president of the independent country. This was Sir Seretse Khama, who years earlier had caused a sensation in those colour-conscious days by marrying a white British woman, Ruth Williams. Lady Khama's sister lived in Zambia. When she heard I was going to Botswana she asked me if I would deliver a package.

Presenting myself at State House, I was mildly surprised that my package was scanned by a security official. How innocent we were in those days! The room where I was received was comfortable but unostentatious – typical British upper-class style. Sir Seretse and his wife were charming. A small incident typified the graciousness of the man. When I went to light a cigarette, the president – also a smoker – got out of his chair and set me going with his lighter. I suspect that few heads of state would be capable of such a gesture to a visitor of no consequence.

Back in Cardiff yet again, I was well into my fourth year. My friend Neville Kros, a heavy smoker who was soon to die of lung cancer, was a talented and conscientious lecturer and tutor. He felt his promotion prospects were damaged by never having risen, as it were, above the rank of corporal in the journalism trade. He had been the deputy news editor of a provincial evening daily. Don Rowlands, the head of the Cardiff team, by contrast had been the editor of a significant morning daily. These things matter, Neville felt, at least as much as and probably more than ability in the job.

The point spoke strongly to me. I was aware that I had accumulated worthwhile experience with a variety of good publications, but my moves had all been lateral ones. I was a lance-corporal, nothing more. I started looking around for a ladder to climb. I was attracted by an advertisement for the manager of Mirror Group Newspapers' editorial training scheme, which the company ran in Devon through local newspapers it had bought for the purpose.

After a trip to Plymouth for interview, the job was mine. I was sad to exchange my Development Set hotels for a utilitarian office building on a Plymouth main road, soon to be a Portakabin on an industrial estate, and hoped to return to overseas work some day. But meanwhile I had become a member of the officers' mess.

EIGHT
OUTSTATION PLYMOUTH –
1975-1978

The city of Plymouth, my home for the next seven years, was a workaday place set in a stunning physical environment. Dartmoor was close at hand on one side; the rugged and beautiful coastline of the South Hams on another. Seen from the Hoe and Sir Francis Drake's statue, the bay known as Plymouth Sound is surely one of England's finest seascapes.

Historically, Plymouth's raison d'etre was the Royal Navy dockyard, from where ships commanded the western approaches to the English Channel. Drake chose his spot well to play his game of bowls! The centre was badly blitzed in the Second World War. It was quickly rebuilt. The cheap and plain architecture added nothing worthwhile.

The city's position, well down in England's south-west peninsula and a long way from supposed civilisation, was both a blessing and a curse. It attracted comments from disenchanted incomers like 'Is there intelligent life west of Exeter?' while companies were perennially unwilling to relocate because it was so remote.

On the other hand, I cherished the sense of separateness that the peninsula gave, with almost an island feeling. People spoke of 'going up the country' as if the rest of England was somewhere else.

Devon and Cornwall are holiday land so anyone working there was at risk of a hayseed reputation. Nor did we spend most of our time on the beach although, prudently, when the boss phoned from London it was always raining in Plymouth. The locals had mixed feelings about the invading hordes without whom the economy of the two counties would collapse. In Devon the visitors were known as 'grockles', in Cornwall 'emmets'. The latter means woodlice, so the intention was clear.

The Mirror Group training scheme had been established in Plymouth for about 10 years when I joined in 1975. It was the only programme for journalists run by a national newspaper group at a time when direct entry to Fleet Street, without going through the legendary provincial mill, was effectively blocked. A local company, West of England Newspapers, had been bought specifically to provide journalism training.

The flagship was the Sunday Independent, which was one of only three regional Sunday newspapers in England (the others being in Birmingham and Newcastle upon Tyne). The accompanying flotilla comprised weekly papers in Plymouth, Torbay and Totnes, later joined by Newton Abbot and later still Kingsbridge.

When the Mirror bought West of England Newspapers, their district reporter Reg Scott found himself catapulted into the managing directorship – a transfiguration rivalling that of William Boot in *Scoop*. The MD in my time was Frank Slater, an accountant by background who had worked for the Mirror in West Africa and who was said to be able to 'talk his way out of a paper bag'. His director colleagues were a mixed bag: two holdovers from the previous ownership, a mystery man who eventually disappeared no-one knew where and, as editor of the Independent, John Theobald, a Mirror veteran with a substantial journalism background.

The board's day revolved around lunch at a restaurant down in the city centre, from which they would return mid-afternoon for a little work. Before long, they would migrate to a local pub to unwind at the end of the day. It was a dreadful example to set the staff, even with the different conventions of those days.

The chief accountant, David Meyer, and I occupied the next tier down from the board. Throughout my time in Plymouth, it rankled with me that the manager of the training scheme – the very raison d'etre for the company – was not on the board. I did not envy them their lunches or their company cars. However, I felt affronted that we were all there because of training and training hadn't been given its due. This was especially the case since the board acted so unprofessionally and unsuccessfully. There were other reasons behind the company's perennial losses, but the board's lack of commitment was part of it.

WEN's chairman was Duncan Campbell, who was based in London and was also a main board director. From a London point of view, I suppose the losses were too insignificant to bother with. They went through the motions of attacking the losses, but these were the palmy days when the Daily Mirror was the biggest-selling newspaper in the country. It had a daily sale of more than three million. Now it ranks third behind the Sun and the Daily Mail, with little more than one million.

From the Plymouth journalism factory many big names of tomorrow emerged. They included David Montgomery, News of the World editor and later a famous hatchet man as chief executive of Mirror Group plc; Alastair Campbell, Mirror political editor and then prime minister Tony Blair's henchman; Patrick Bishop, Daily Telegraph defence editor; Nick Davies, investigative reporter for the Guardian; Tom Utley, a star columnist for the Daily Mail, and Lindsay Nicholson, editor of Good Housekeeping. Authors included Andrew Morton, author of *Diana: Her True Story*, which first lifted the lid on the princess's troubled marriage, and two acclaimed thriller writers, Val McDermid and Stephen Leather.

I found on arrival that the graduate-entry training scheme had lost much of its impetus. Applications had dwindled, reaching a low in 1973 of 151, of whom only 83 were graduates – far fewer than a national scheme of its stature ought to attract. The current group of trainees, I was alerted, were disaffected because they felt they weren't getting proper training. One of their training managers had left and the other, himself on the way out, was based in another office.

It was necessary to act quickly. Among the innovations was a practice that I'd decided upon before starting the job. This was a copy clinic. Trainees made an additional copy of everything they wrote (a carbon copy in those days), and passed this to me. In due course I returned these articles with my comments, good and bad, not failing to include the traditional 'ugh!' (which nowadays would probably be construed as harassment).

With 20 or more individuals to be critiqued each week, I'd made a rod for my own back but I was convinced it was worth it. It provided writers with guidance they weren't getting in the working situation. The editors might change a story, but rarely explained why. Equally, a good story was likely to get into print little changed – but without any words of congratulation. That's where training could make a difference.

Increasing the number of applications for the training scheme, and therefore improving the potential quality of the intake, was a long-term project. Eric gave me assiduous support in publicising the scheme to the universities. In just two years we increased graduate applications fivefold. The number eventually reached around a thousand a year. This gave plenty of choice for the dozen places we had to offer.

The selection process was simple but effective. From a plain two-page form – much of it occupied by an 'essay-type' answer – I had to produce a shortlist of around three dozen candidates. These then went to London to be interviewed one-to-one by Mirror executives and senior journalists (plus Eric and myself). The selectors met in a conference led by the group chairman to make the final choice.

The national training manager, Bill Mills (possibly sore that he wasn't part of the process), said of the initial shortlisting: 'You could throw all the forms out of the window, pick some up at random and get the same result!' I felt sure that such cynicism was misplaced. I spent hours winnowing the applications into the final list. The author-to-be Val McDermid wrote her way onto the shortlist with the quality of her essay. Val was raw from a romantic break-up just days before, and the agony shone through. She then impressed the selectors at interview in the same way.

Nick Davies, later an important investigative reporter for the Guardian, applied to the training scheme a year after having left university. His application caught my eye because he had done a variety of jobs of the 'cattle ranching in the Argentine' variety in this 'second gap year' in the traditional manner of aspiring authors. Once on the shortlist, he came through the interviews with ease. He told me later that the other training schemes had turned him down because he didn't fit the mould. And yet Nick has abundantly proved his value in the world of journalism.

A killer question on the application form was 'what other training programmes have you applied to?' An applicant might fear that listing other training schemes would prejudice the application, showing lack of single-mindedness. 'None' might seem to be the best answer. Here, however, was proof that honesty is the best policy. I was looking for several other names to be mentioned because it showed drive and serious intent to get a start in journalism. I eliminated anyone who wrote 'none' on the grounds that either the answer was untrue or the applicant was insufficiently motivated.

By now, I felt the need of some training myself – in training. Plymouth Polytechnic ran a one-year evening programme for the City and Guilds further education teacher's certificate. I was grateful to Frank Slater, the managing director, for supporting me on the course, financially and with time off.

The course was worthwhile and thorough going. As well as class sessions, there were essays to be written, two lessons monitored and marked, and a three-hour examination (no multiple choices here). In one of my sample lessons I eccentrically chose to use an epidiascope, an obsolescent piece of equipment that nevertheless had the advantage of allowing writing on paper to be instantly projected. This was a benefit for a lesson on headline writing, for example. Trainees' work could be collected in, round by round, and shown immediately to all

To use the epidiascope the room had to be dark. This meant either that you addressed the group in the pitch black or that you constantly switched the room lights on and off. The examiner commented on this problem and, with unbecoming lack of humility, I argued the point. I was lucky not to be marked down.

The three-hour exam consisted of four essay-type answers. I fell into the most basic of traps. One of the questions was about audio-visual aids, something of a speciality for me. Instead of quartering the available time and answering each question accordingly, I wrote at massive length on AVA. This meant I had too little time for the other questions, affecting the marks overall. As a veteran of this type of exam, I should have known better. I was awarded the certificate but with a lowish grade.

For the course to stress the presentation aspects of teaching was entirely right. Ever since, I've been conscious of how many trainers get carried away with their own eloquence and don't leave enough time for questions. A simple tip like leaving your watch on the table not on your hand should be more widely known. It means you keep track of the time without reminding the audience of the clock (and how long it is to the break). In later years, PowerPoint has been abused as much as used. Among the presentation faults is talking by reading off the slide. Even worse – and a common practice at press conferences – is to issue a printout before the talk has started. This makes it pointless to attend to the speaker.

It was a new training team in Plymouth so nothing stood in the way of making a new start. Frank Slater, while showing a helpful interest, left us to our own devices. Eric Grimes, who was to be my deputy for three years, had joined the company just a month before me. He made his own new start before I arrived by throwing away almost every piece of paper accumulated over 10 years. I would have preferred to keep some items for archival interest, but I had to admit that operations weren't harmed in any way.

Eric and I had very different personalities. He was a bouncy extrovert who had been chief public relations officer for Somerset, a big band enthusiast who kept his hand in journalistically with Saturday subbing shifts on the Independent. Whatever his private feelings about me – for example, he disliked my puritanical insistence that trainees claim only for what they spent: he felt that making a little extra was a time-honoured way of supplementing low wages – he supported me loyally throughout our time together.

I was also fortunate in my secretaries, successively June Baskwill (later known as Jude Brent-Khan) and Jane Larsen. Later, I worked with Fiona, my successor's secretary. There was nothing to choose between the three in pleasantness and efficiency – crucial qualities in a small unit like ours. Thirty-five years later, with West of England Newspapers a distant memory for both of us, Jude and I continued to work together.

The calibre of these women was such that we received an accolade from the editor of one of the weekly newspapers. He said Training was the only efficient department in the company.

Because West of England Newspapers was built around the training scheme, a special and very potent method of training had evolved. In other companies, trainees would usually attend an initial course and then disappear to their newspapers. That was more or less it apart from brush-up courses to prepare for examinations like shorthand and press law. With the Mirror scheme, trainees attended an initial block-release course, then throughout their two years with the scheme returned to the training department weekly for day-release training. They were posted to two, sometimes three newspapers – a weekly and then the Sunday Independent. At the end of the programme, they had an attachment to one of the national titles in London, Manchester and Glasgow.

This was the Rolls-Royce approach to journalism training.

I quickly realised that the 20-week initial training, held in the autumn, was too long when trainees were itching to get on with the 'real work'. This was a feeling I knew very well from my student days. Furthermore, the trainees weren't getting enough training time in the spring when they had exams, including shorthand. I proposed a simple change to higher management – split the block into two of 12 weeks in the autumn and eight weeks in the spring. This was agreed. It was a great success, greatly improving the mood of the course.

A further unique advantage of the Mirror training scheme was that we could call on national-level stars and executives from the parent group to talk to the trainees. Usually, they didn't need to be persuaded. We evolved an attractive package in which we brought speakers down the day before, gave them an excellent dinner and put them up in the leading hotel, and let them loose on the trainees the next morning. At lunchtime the speaker met the trainees over 'a pie and a pint' before returning to London by an afternoon train. From the speaker's point of view, what was there not to like?

One of the most engaging speakers was Keith Waterhouse, successful author and playwright – his *Billy Liar* was a book, a play and a film – and at that time a Daily Mirror columnist (he later decamped to the Daily Mail). Keith was an astonishing man who somehow disproved the rule that heavy drinking gets the Fleet Street warhorses in the end. He never seemed to let his writing get in the way of his drinking, and as a writer died in harness in 2009 aged 80.

He came to Plymouth several times, on one occasion as a double act with the editor of the Daily Mirror, Mike Molloy. Not for them a sedate dinner with the training staff and early bed. Late at night they were to be found leading a trail of trainees, Pied Piper style, into a club.

Dan Ferrari, the Mirror news editor, offered us a valuable insight into investigative reporting. When the heat is getting too close to the main man, he said, a senior figure will be offered up for sacrifice. This person invariably will not be the one ultimately to blame for the scandal. It's been useful to attach this thought to the many scandals that have followed.

Sir Edward Pickering and Tony Miles, both chairmen of the Mirror Group at different times, on their visits to Plymouth were well liked by the trainees. I overheard one of the trainees address the then-chairman as 'Tony'. I told him later that this wasn't the way to speak to the big boss, to which the young man replied: 'He told us to.'

Sir Edward had a remarkable rapport with the trainees, to whom he could give about 60 years. They responded, as we all did, to this fascinating man who seemed to have worked everywhere and done everything. But jazz-loving 'Pick' had not come to talk about himself. The secret of his success with the young was simple: he was truly interested in what they had to say.

The guest speakers signed their bills at the Holiday Inn, and these were sent to me for settlement. Sir David English, editor in chief of the Daily Mail and unusually for us a guest speaker from the outside, was the only one to overdo it. Perhaps he felt the opposition was fair game. His bill contained items from the hotel shop that were plainly intended as presents. This seemed to me to be way outside the spirit of the deal, and I was minded to refuse. Given Sir David's stature I was smart enough to refer the matter to London. I was told to settle the bill as it stood.

As well as a day-to-day induction into 'doing journalism', the Mirror training scheme followed the examination syllabus of the National Council for the Training of Journalists. This non-governmental, industry-based body ran a test of reporting competence called in those days the proficiency certificate. It was a thoroughgoing exam that I was happy to support. Subjects included: a simulated interview and write-up, usually involving some hideous catastrophe in the fictional town of Oxdown; producing a story from a 10-minute speech; producing another story from handout material, and a paper on 'newspaper practice'. The test could be taken only after passing preliminary examinations in law and government (central and local) and law, plus a shorthand requirement of 100 words a minute for four minutes.

The NCTJ deserved credit for making the proficiency certificate a meaningful test. It was common for upwards of a third of candidates to drop one or more of the subjects. Candidates certainly weren't nodded through, and nor could they pass on the basis of an editor's recommendation – a system that would have guaranteed an exaggerated pass rate.

The proficiency certificate contained no test of typing skill, although at the Mirror we taught that too. Arguably, it would have been more useful for the test to include typing rather than shorthand. Such a statement is a heresy for the British newspaper industry, although over most of the rest of the world it is a truism. Elsewhere journalists manage perfectly well without shorthand.

Elderly editors, remembering or mythologising the time when newspapers ran long, verbatim reports of speeches and court cases, insist to this day that shorthand is a vital tool; yet it is many years since journalism worked that way. Not to mention the existence of audio recorders or the recording facility on mobile phones.

I'm a heretic about shorthand through personal experience. Having come into mainstream journalism through sub-editing, I never had to learn it. I've held down many jobs as a reporter and feature writer over the years. The lack of shorthand has not handicapped me in any way, nor has my accuracy been challenged.

A moment's thought will show the impracticality of compulsory shorthand. The NCTJ requirement of four minutes' transcription at 100 words per minute, modest as it was, proved impossible to maintain. The test was changed to two two-minute blocks with a pause between. However, in the real world speakers don't deliver in convenient two-minute bursts, and then sit down for a breather. Nor do they speak at 100 wpm. Even the slowest speakers speak faster than that. If we try it, we see how slow that is.

In other words, the 100 wpm note-taker will be left behind after a sentence or so. He or she might as well jot down key names, facts and phrases, and reconstruct the direct quote from that – as most of the rest of the world does.

At the Mirror we taught shorthand to a higher standard – 120 wpm – but even that was not fast enough for any except the shortest passages.

We used the Teeline shorthand system in common with most other centres. Teeline has kept its popularity to the present day in journalism training. It is an ingenious system that combines word abbreviation with symbolic notation (based on sounds). It is faster than an abbreviation system using, but nothing like as fast as a full-out symbolic system like Pitman.

Teeline's advantage is that it is more readily learnt than Pitman – just the thing for journalism trainees who have to be whipped like recalcitrant horses to get up to speed! Our experience at Plymouth was that Teeline starts to fall apart above 120 wpm (unlike Pitman, which has hardly started at that speed). We had several trainees who volunteered to try for 130 wpm, but no-one succeeded.

The Mirror training intake was more or less equally divided between boys and girls. Some of the young women, with the vibrancy of youth, were attractive, but I wasn't aware of any of the permanent West of England Newspapers staff forming relationships with them, or even trying to. Nor did the trainees seem to pair off much among themselves. Some had relationships 'up the country'; others no doubt were concentrating single-mind-edly on succeeding at journalism.

An exception was Alastair Campbell, later to become notorious as Tony Blair's fixer and bully boy. Alastair in those days had Grecian handsomeness. He was easily over six feet tall, and came with the added attraction of a bad boy reputation, having written for an erotic magazine. In short, he was a proposition for any girl. His choice among the trainees was Fiona Millar, who had cute, girl-next-door looks.

Almost from day one they were together. I caught a moment when it was clear what was happening. At the top of the Civic Centre, during an induction tour of Plymouth, a bolt of electricity seemed to pass between them, making clear how they felt. More than 30 years later, they were still together, twin powerhouses in the Labour Party.

Alastair's looks coarsened over the years, mirroring perhaps the dark arts he practised. I never saw him again after the Plymouth years, but the arrogant bully of popular repute was not the Alastair Campbell I knew. He was a thoroughly pleasant chap, neither aggressive nor domineering. For me, he is a conundrum. Do people change so much, or is his media image simply wrong?

The Plymouth years were among my happiest. For a while I considered spending the rest of my days in Devon with its physical beauty and relaxed lifestyle. But it wasn't enough. I had told Frank Slater at my job interview that I planned to do three years, and as my third anniversary in the job approached I became restive. Always conscious of age, I was aware that I was about to turn 40. The fact that I was not on the local board continued to rankle. Eric Grimes, who had joined the company one month before me, resigned to return to public relations with a job in Bristol. Above all, agreeable as life in Plymouth was, my heart was in overseas work.

All these factors came together and led me to request a meeting on my fortieth birthday (March 7, 1978) with Frank and Duncan Campbell, who was visiting from London. Having chosen the day for its symbolism, I dramatically announced that I was resigning to become a consultant. I had made no sounding about employment prospects in that role; I simply trusted to luck. If the chairman was surprised, he didn't show it. He responded almost immediately: 'Well, would you like to be a consultant for us?' Full marks for quick thinking because he couldn't have seen my announcement coming. But nor had I seen his offer coming. It simply hadn't occurred to me.

His plan was for me to work full time with the training scheme for 20 weeks a year – corresponding with the two periods of block training – while the rest of the time I would pursue my other work. Of course, I said yes. It got the freelance venture off to a very easy start. Those 20 weeks guaranteed bread, butter and mortgage. The chairman must quickly have spied the advantage for him too – saving half a year's salary. Two training officers had run the scheme. Now there would be one, who was Jim Dalrymple, moving across from feature writing for the Independent (he was later to make his name as a feature writer for the national newspaper of the same name), plus myself as part-time consultant.

Jim's heart wasn't in training, and he left most of it to me. This suited both of us. Things changed when he was succeeded by Colin Harrow, who had a news agency background and who was brought in from the outside. Colin understandably wanted to put his own stamp on the department. Still the arrangement worked. It can be hard when you've run the department to be working under someone else in the same department. In those days it didn't bother me. Perhaps later, with the inflexibility of age, it would have done. The crucial factor, though, was that I had stepped down from choice.

The consultancy arrangement lasted for four years until the Mirror Group, by then owned by Reed International, started to run down the training scheme in preparation for closure. Colin stayed on while the last batch of trainees worked through the system, then transferred to a senior post with the parent company in London.

I felt that the accumulated expertise of years in Plymouth and the unique and effective pattern of training were too valuable to lose. I put forward a proposal to transfer the scheme to the Berrow's newspaper group in Worcester, also owned by Reed. It was no use. Perhaps the powers-that-be concluded that the parent group was too small to absorb the output of the training scheme and that therefore it was providing training free for the rest of Fleet Street. It was an accurate perception.

I had a house in Plymouth for several more years although I rarely visited it. I had accepted that once again my future lay elsewhere.

NINE
GLOBAL HEYDAY 1 – 1979-1987
(AFRICA)

The following decade, to 1987, was my busiest internationally, not only in Africa but also in Asia and the Caribbean. From my London base, I spent up to half the time on the road some years. These were mainly training workshops lasting from one month to four months. That was a lot of hotel rooms, but I didn't mind. The sights and sounds of worlds so different from the comfortable, cosseted West more than compensated. Friends would ask, 'Where are you off to next?' They were projecting their travel fantasies on to me. I was happy to play up to this image of the globe-trotting man of the world.

My clients included the Thomson Foundation, the Commonwealth Press Union and the British Government's Overseas Development Administration (later the Department for International Development), In between times, I worked within Britain, particularly for the NCTJ (National Council for the Training of Journalists). And for the first four years I had that valuable consultancy with the Mirror training scheme.

There was plenty of what factories call 'down time' – when I wasn't working. But the jobs when they came were well paid, and I had no financial worries beyond never knowing when the phone would ring next. Somehow it always did – a lesson learnt.

I had got to know Colonel Terence Pierce-Goulding, the secretary (later styled director) of the Commonwealth Press Union, when I was at the Thomson Foundation. The CPU was an association of newspaper proprietors from around the Commonwealth, run from a tiny office under the eaves of a Dickensian building in Fleet Street. In summer this was known as the 'CPU sauna'.

Its flagship scheme was the annual Harry Brittain Fellowships, when a dozen or so journalists from various countries spent three months in Britain. Their package of activities included a residential training workshop. Terry became dissatisfied with the previous providers so I hosted it in Plymouth for him. The Mirror trainees enjoyed meeting their international counterparts while the visitors got a different perspective on British journalism.

Now Terry returned the compliment by sending me on my first international assignment as a consultant. It was back to Zambia in 1979. I felt at home on this my third visit. Again, I marvelled at the spaciousness of the capital, Lusaka. It was no wonder that it had room to spread: the city was established on the open savannah because it was the midway point on the railway between the Victoria Falls and the Copperbelt. It took its name from the nearby kraal of a local chief.

The Ridgeway Hotel was in the 'government area', about a mile from the business district of Cairo Road. This reflected the social divide in colonial times between the officials and the traders. Beyond Cairo Road was the third element in the demographic makeup, a shantytown for the urban poor. It wasn't extensive in those days, but I was to see it grow hugely over the years. These shantytowns are often forgotten when we speak of life in Africa and the Majority World generally. They are neither urban nor rural: they are in the city but not fully of it.

If my work for the next six weeks was familiar, there was a new element to this training workshop. I was alone. It was hard work with no-one to share the teaching or the course organisation. It gave added piquancy to the sundowner, the welcome first drink at the end of the day in that brief, magical time before the African sun disappeared.

I remember especially the magical evening when on a visit to the Victoria Falls I had the falls to myself. It was sundown and no one was about in the garden of the tourist lodge. It was a few hundred yards above the falls. I took a table at the edge of the Zambezi, lingered over a beer and marvelled at the spray rising above the lip of the cataract after dashing on the rocks 355 ft (100 m) below. In fact, the wall of spray can reach 1,000 ft (300 m).

The falls are twice as deep as Niagara, and at 5,500 ft (1,675 m) far wider. They are known to the local Lozi tribe as Mosi-oa-Tunya ('The Smoke That Thunders'), a name sensibly adopted for the nearby hotel on the Zambian side. Visitors to Vic Falls stand at the edge and look down at the rainbow. Nor is it a fugitive band of dissipated light. It is substantial enough to snap and show the people back home.

I've been fortunate to visit the Victoria Falls several times. I found the undeveloped Zambian side peaceful and relaxing. It was so unlike the crowds and the hustling on the Zimbabwe side (where I saw a package tourist with his feet on the table in the formerly select Victoria Falls Hotel).

My overseas work mainly lay in capital cities, but wherever possible I got out to see something of the country. Often I extended my stay privately. I never understood many of my colleagues, who, finding themselves at no expense to themselves in some of the world's most interesting places, could think only of getting home again. Sometimes I had to discourage colleagues from leaving on the same evening that the course ended, which was a discourtesy to our hosts.

Taking photographs in public places was risky in Zambia at that time. The authorities were edgy about security because of Kaunda's confrontation with South Africa and Rhodesia. They feared that spies were everywhere. Not only was the border sealed for South African goods but also Zambia hosted the guerrilla training camps of Joshua Nkomo's ZAPU. (Robert Mugabe's ZANU was based in Mozambique.) Not being a war correspondent, I've heard shots fired in anger only once. This was when aircraft of the Rhodesian air force shot up the camps near Lusaka.

I hated to be thwarted of what I foolishly saw as my divine right to take pictures where I pleased. I was snapping away in the street in Kitwe on the Copperbelt when an expatriate pulled his car over and gave me a friendly warning. Didn't I know that people were arrested for doing that? Stupidly, I gave him a graceless reply and carried on. On that occasion nothing happened.

I was taking a photograph of Lusaka's new Pamodzi Hotel when I was stopped by a man who said he was a plain-clothes policeman. His manner suggested that it wasn't a good idea to argue, or even to demand his ID. He was all too believable. He demanded my camera, ripped out the entire roll of film thus destroying the images, handed the camera back and walked on. In the circumstances I got off lightly.

The government launched newspapers in four or five vernacular languages to expand literacy in the rural areas. This worthy objective ran into the central difficulty of a lack of books and other reading matter in the indigenous languages. An adviser told me that without fresh material to tackle, reading skills erode. I learnt that reading isn't like riding a bicycle: once you can do it, you can do it forever. If you don't keep reading, you will eventually forget how.

My next African assignment the following year, 1980, was far removed from the usual run. This was a clandestine workshop for black journalists in apartheid South Africa, arranged by the World Association for Christian Communication. It illustrates how set in concrete the South African political situation had become that a reputable international organisation like WACC would contemplate a covert meeting. At that time, few saw any outcome for the country but bloody revolution.

The moving spirit was Michael Traber, the Roman Catholic priest with whom I worked in Zambia in 1973. Mike, as an anti-apartheid activist, was afraid that he would be refused a visa for South Africa, in which case he would try to enter the country secretly. In the event, the visa came through with no problems. He was perhaps a touch disappointed that he wasn't considered worth banning!

We were joined as lecturers on the course by the prominent Zambian journalist, John Musukuma. John reported a chance conversation he had had with a white South African. 'If we had people like you,' the man told him, 'we wouldn't need apartheid.' The tragedy of South Africa was that it had its own John Musukumas, but they weren't allowed to come forward.

Mike was in his element on the course, with his eyes alight and his voice trembling with passion as he descanted upon the media's role in securing social justice. It wasn't my sort of journalism. Clearly the media have a role, indeed a responsibility, in social justice, yet even considering the provocation (and in South Africa this was at the top of the scale) overt advocacy journalism is self-defeating. Information is the most valuable commodity, not interpretation or opinion.

I wondered whether the authorities were aware of the course and preferred to let it continue rather than make a cause celebre by banning it. The possibility of a mole in the group could not be excluded. Whether or not they knew, Mike, John and I came, talked and left without molestation.

In 1982, the Thomson Foundation sent me to Ethiopia with two others to design a media development programme for the government. I had an argument at Heathrow Airport with the team leader, Jim McIntyre, and things went downhill from there. He was an overbearing Scot who was probably covering up insecurity. What a cliché! Matters weren't helped by the fact that he and the third member of the party, industry veteran Bill Ward, were TV men to my print background, leaving them with plenty to talk about but me with little to say.

Addis Ababa, the capital, where I was to spend a month, stays in the memory as one of those special places. Ethiopia was never colonised, apart from a few, late years of Italian occupation, so the Western flavour was less. Most African cities have a modern quarter built by the Europeans and a traditional sector. In Addis the two were mixed together. Cows wandered unherded past the gleaming new building where I was choosing a seat on a Paris to London flight. The computer technology seemed like magic at the time.

At 7,726 ft or 2,350 m, Addis is one of the world's highest cities. We struggled when we had to climb several storeys to reach an office. I spent the whole month feeling I had a band of iron clamped around my chest. I was told this wasn't unusual, and that some people couldn't cope at all with the elevation. They felt better a mere 1,000 ft (300 m) lower down. It seemed that was some sort of threshold. I made a mental note never to work in La Paz (11,942 ft or 3,650 m).

Despite the strains in our consultancy team, we managed to get out an impressively bulky set of recommendations. But should we have done it? 'Media development' in a dictatorship is far removed from Western ideas of a linchpin of civil society: it means more effective propaganda and tools of oppression. Colonel Mengistu, the military ruler, was later acknowledged as an especially brutal leader. Perhaps this wasn't fully apparent at the time.

Maybe a harbinger was that Ethiopia remains the only country in the Majority World where I've been frisked while going about my business. The senior civil servant I was with, who was also rubbed down, was embarrassed that I had been subjected to the indignity, although I thought nothing of it.

The morality of the project was troubling. The Thomson Foundation, which sent us, did not pass judgement on the regimes it was assisting. This was justified on the grounds that it was better to help progressive forces within a dictatorship than to abandon them. It is a familiar dilemma, not limited to news media. The justification comes more easily in some cases than others. As for individual consultants, does our hunger for work – or our fear of saying no to a client – blind us to the rights and wrongs of what we do? Or do we too say that it's better to help progressive forces ...

I had passed through Zimbabwe in that brief period of semi-

independence, or sham independence if we prefer, under Bishop
Abel Muzorewa when the country was known as Zimbabwe-
Rhodesia; in 1982, two years after full independence, I was back
for a six-week training workshop.

Harare – the former Salisbury – was physically much like
Lusaka but on a bigger scale. There were the same wide streets,
the same jacaranda trees, the same spacious homes. The similarities were not surprising since both countries had similar histories as settler societies.

The main newspaper, the Herald, previously the voice of the
settlers, had made a comfortable accommodation with the
incoming regime of President Robert Mugabe – too comfortable,
I felt. I met the (European) senior managers. They appeared to
be happy to fill the paper with propaganda on a scale that made
the Zambian state-owned papers look like models of objectivity
and balance. Maybe they really didn't mind. Maybe the owners,
South Africa's Argus Group, knew which way the wind blew.
Either way, the result for the readers was the same.

This was long before Robert Mugabe's government became
a byword for brutality and corruption, but it was a bad omen.
Mugabe at least deserves credit for the clemency he showed the
former leader Ian Smith, the man who had imprisoned him.
Smith didn't suffer a day's detention until he died. But independence slightly altered his situation. He still walked openly
around Harare and Africans still greeted him. Smith himself
explained: 'The only difference independence has made is that
before they said "Good morning, Mr Smith" ... now they say
"Good morning, Ian".'

If Mugabe's clemency deserves credit, so does Smith's
courage. A student on one of my Zambian courses told how he
set out to interview the former Rhodesian leader. The man had
been depicted in the Zambian media as an ogre, a giant of evil,
scarcely human at all. As the student approached Smith's house,
he wondered whether he would get to see the great man and if
he did how many layers of menacing security he would have to
go through. He knocked at the door, which was answered – by
Smith himself, who affably invited the journalist in for a chat.
The astonished student was lost for words.

My bedrock consultancy with the Mirror training scheme
ended amicably in 1982 when plans were put in hand to run the
scheme down. For me, this raised the issue of where to earn
money instead. Happily, it had been my busiest, and most prof-

itable, year for overseas work – Ethiopia and Zimbabwe were joined by Sri Lanka and the West Indies to make five months spent on the ground. But I couldn't expect that level of work each year, and a couple of overseas assignments would not be enough.

Thanks to connections made in my Plymouth days, I worked in domestic training for the National Council for the Training of Journalists. I also worked extensively for the Thomson Foundation in its UK-based programmes. The editorial study centre had left its Cardiff home to embark on a period of wandering. Don Rowlands, the head of the centre, was short of lecturers. He relied on external consultants, including Ken Meadows, Barrie Harding and myself. I was the only one who had been on the staff, so was correspondingly more useful to him.

We found ourselves working in a charming country house at Fleet, Hampshire. Always keen to arrange comfortable quarters, I quickly bagged an unused attic room as my private office. It was summer. The pub was a short walk away along a lane.

I also worked abroad with Ken and Barrie, in Zambia and China respectively. Ken had worked on the East African Standard in Kenya before moving into government public relations in London. Now retired, he welcomed the opportunity to 'get the sun on my back again', as he put it. Unusually for my travelling companions, Ken was never to be seen with a book. He read newspapers, and for the rest of the time just sat and thought (or perhaps just sat).

Ken was something of a radical. He irritated me once too often with his anti-royalist remarks. I burst out: 'If you feel that way, Ken, why did you accept the MBE from the Queen?' 'I felt I was doing it for journalism,' he replied. It was one step better than saying he had accepted it for his wife.

Barrie was a more sophisticated character than Ken. He had been a Fleet Street news editor. He made a successful late-life switch to training and became popular in China, carrying out several assignments there.

Don Rowlands sent me to Tanzania in 1983 for a six-week assignment with a Foundation staffer, John David, and a BBC man, David Crawley, who was to deal with the broadcasting side of the multi-media course. This three-hander didn't present the problems I'd experienced in Ethiopia, but still I was reminded that two's company, three's a crowd.

The rundown condition of the capital, Dar es Salaam, contrasted starkly with the new buildings and glittering shops of Nairobi, Kenya's capital. President Julius Nyerere's noble attempt to build African socialism had not delivered the economic benefits or the free-spending tourists. Both were to be found in adjacent Kenya.

At the same time, tourists were advised not to walk about Nairobi after dark. The risk of being mugged was considerable. Nobody found it necessary to give that warning in Dar. My greatest feeling of insecurity was in the decrepit hotel lift, never sure whether I could get out of it as easily as I got in it.

Books were a scarce and prized item in Tanzania at that time because of a lack of foreign exchange. The hotel shop had a simple but effective way of pricing secondhand books – the bigger the book the more expensive it was. This was without regard to author or subject. I felt there was rough justice in this approach. Customers deserve something for their money, especially when they may not be able to afford the next book.

The Tanzania assignment was to be my last one for the Thomson Foundation and the end of my 12-year association with them. Silence descended. No more overseas or domestic work was offered. Simply not offering work is the standard way of dropping freelances, but in some circumstances it is disrespectful. I had worked intensively and conscientiously for Don in the last couple of years, helping him out when he needed it most. Now, it seemed, he no longer had that need.

After a year, I felt I must close the issue. I went to see Don and asked him if I could expect further work. Struggling to keep a look of relish from his face, he told me that he didn't expect to be able to offer anything.

What I guessed had happened was that several matters, too trivial to specify here, had built up into a big resentment on his part. The shadow of Jessica from years before may have hung over the situation. The strains of that relationship had made my work and attendance erratic for a while (although never overseas, when it mattered most). Don had been insufficiently understanding at the time, and perhaps still was.

And then, in the manner of the freelance life, other possibilities opened up. I worked in the Caribbean for a new client, the British Government's Overseas Development Administration, and in Asia for two newspaper groups. Meanwhile, the Commonwealth Press Union continued to produce assignments.

I had an excellent working relationship with the CPU secretary, Terry Pierce-Goulding. He was a Canadian ex-military man whose father had been a senior Anglican clergyman. Terry was a convivial man in his upper sixties, but with a younger wife and a young family. He described himself as 'out of phase'.

I went to Tanzania again in 1986 for the CPU. This time is was on my own. I found the same economic deprivation as three years before. The beach at one of Dar es Salaam's main tourist hotels had been washed away. Most of the publicly owned long-distance buses were off the road through lack of spare parts – and there was even an acute shortage of beer because the brewery could not afford the imported ingredients.

Tanzania could not take full advantage of strong markets in some of her export crops, like coffee and cashew nuts. Modernisation and expansion of plantations was held back by the perennial problem – foreign exchange. For all the initial high hopes of President Nyerere's revolution, the government had been forced to swallow the International Monetary Fund's medicine.

It was the only Commonwealth country I encountered where 'Comrade' was the form of address. I found myself at a meeting with officials from Angola and the German Democratic Republic (East Germany). The chairman introduced us as follows: 'Comrade XXXX from Angola, Comrade XXXX from GDR and Mr Pulford from the UK.' When I asked why I wasn't a comrade, he said: 'Because you aren't from a socialist country.'

For me, the five-week journalism training assignment was a chance to get up close and personal with the leading newspaper group. The Daily News and its companion Sunday News had asked for help in upgrading their editorial operation and providing in-house training for the 40 or so staff journalists.

The recently appointed managing editor, 40-year-old Joseph Mapunda, set the scene by attending every one of the daily seminars conducted for editorial section heads. At other times of the day I ran classes for reporters and sub-editors, looked through copy and advised individual staff on stories, headlines and page layouts.

Somewhere along the way the newspapers' style book got revised for the first time since 1968 (when seven years after independence the expatriate-controlled staff were still absorbed with titles of the English nobility and how to spell the Caesarewitch horse race!!). Sessions were held with the advertising and distribution staffs, and a full report and recommendations were made and discussed.

A welcome breather saw me at a game lodge, where I watched animals trekking to a watering hole at sundown. They were engaged in the same activity as us. The zebras soon became invisible in the bush. It seemed to me that a creature with black and white stripes should stand out. But evolution is cleverer than that. It was effective camouflage.

Joseph and I made a four-day safari of 1,250 miles up and down the Uhuru ('Freedom') Highway that connects Tanzania with Zambia. I saw some of the country's problems at first hand, like main roads so shot to bits that Land Rovers were reduced to a crawl and firewood gathered from the bush in such quantities – and carried home by women on their heads – that soil erosion and 'desertification' were occurring. Firewood was used because peasants could not afford any other fuel, but the consequent destruction of land made their situation worse as they were even less able to afford fuel oil or bottled gas for cooking. This was an example of the vicious circle that three decades later still afflicts many in the Majority World.

In Mbeya, an up-and-coming regional capital, more than 550 miles from Dar es Salaam, the daily papers went on sale the morning after publication day. A distribution network was in place over the entire country, in itself an achievement, but there was no home delivery system outside Dar and few postal subscriptions within the country.

Another problem for the newspapers was the standard of English among reporters. The lingua franca of Tanzania was Kiswahili, English being more of a foreign language than in neighbouring Zambia or Kenya. Despite a previous intention to bury this part of the colonial legacy, government policy by then encouraged the use of English. Despite the reporters' shortcomings, what emerged in print was perfectly acceptable thanks to the efforts of the news desk and the sub-editors.

I reassured Joseph that we had the same problem of English, admittedly to a lesser degree, in the UK, and suggested that the solution was the same in both places: English ability should be a decisive factor in recruitment. We had found at Plymouth that remedial lessons (one of my experiments there) did not produce satisfactory results because by then difficulties were ingrained.

This second Tanzania assignment was a valuable opportunity for me to understand typical problems that afflicted the media and the people in the Majority World, and in many cases still do.

In 1986, I was on my sixth assignment in Zambia, most of them training workshops for all sections of the news media. I was well aware of the strengths and weaknesses. The media were relatively sophisticated, which I liked to think was something to do with the huge training effort poured into the country. At the same time, it was on a tight leash with all principal outlets controlled by the ruling party, President Kenneth Kaunda's UNIP, or the government (effectively the same thing in a one-party state). This situation had got worse when the Times of Zambia, previously owned by Lonrho, had been taken over by the state.

The system wasn't overtly oppressive, but freedom of speech was limited by self-censorship – arguably the severest censorship of all. It would have been impossible, for example, to challenge the idea of the one-party state or to dispute Kaunda's policy of boycotting South Africa.

Shoots of spring were to be seen, however. The private and irreverent Weekly Post appeared. Aware that journalists wished to turn the political climate to advantage, I decided to speak out in an article in the Times of Zambia (see Appendix Two for the full text):

Zambia had made a good start, I argued, but liberalisation needed to be speeded up if its news media were to take their rightful place at the centre of a free society.

The government owned both national dailies. I saw no reason why the government shouldn't own a daily paper, but to own both was one too many. The papers should be privatised, and a press council set up to guarantee standards.

The national news agency, which had a monopoly of incoming international news, could be handed over to the Zambian media. The system by which new publications had to be registered should be scrapped, with a press council set up to safeguard standards. The state still had to get its message across. ZIS (Zambia Information Services) should stay in government hands.

An unmuzzled media would be a step forward in Zambia's development, enabling members of the modern elite – civil servants, business people, white-collar workers – to communicate with each other and, equally importantly, with the government.

I was keen to acknowledge that the requirements of the media were different in advanced and emerging countries, and that there were reasons why well intentioned governments used the state control model, however deficient it proved to be in practice. I was equally keen to stress that the model should no longer be used to deny educated urban dwellers in a place like Zambia what they desired as strongly as their Western counterparts: a free press.

That article was a courageous piece to run. But the courage was not mine – as an expatriate consultant the worst likely penalty would be to be on the next plane out – but that of the editors of the Times of Zambia. It was an encouraging sign of Zambia's progress to press freedom that they felt able to do so after the long years of self-censorship.

In Zambia and over much of the Majority World, the dominance of the Big Four news agencies meant that international news was presented through Western eyes. Jeremy Tunstall, a British media sociologist, wrote an influential book titled *The Media Are American*. Two of the agencies, Associated Press and United Press International, were American; the two others, Reuters and Agence France-Presse heavily influenced by America.

This led to the phenomenon of agenda setting, in which newspapers and broadcasters around the world absorb and reflect the news values of the agencies without adaptation to their own customers. The agencies didn't set out to project a jingoistic Western or specifically American news agenda, but they were naturally focused on their primary markets.

Particularly in Africa, supplementary sources of international news were hard to find. The main issue, however, was the mindset of journalists in the Majority World. In country after country in Africa, Asia and the Caribbean, I urged editors to make their own judgements in terms of their readers, not blindly follow the priorities of the agency.

For instance, a coup in South America meant less in Asia than it did in adjacent Hispanic countries, so why run many paragraphs on a story whose local news value was three or four paragraphs? My special bugbear was saturation coverage of US domestic politics, which tended to be printed at a length that few readers wanted, just because an agency sent it that way. Sadly, most journalists lacked the confidence to decide for themselves. If AP puts a certain weight on a story, it must be so ...

TEN
BAMBOO CURTAIN

L ate 1980 saw the start of a six-month immersion in three
countries (Malaysia, Thailand and China) plus the colony
of Hong Kong. First came Malaysia, a federation formed
of Malaya and the separate states of Sarawak and Sabah (British
North Borneo). The federation originally included Singapore,
but this soon broke away to pursue a separate and very successful destiny.

Kuala Lumpur, the Malaysian capital, was a charmless mixture of the old settler town with the Selangor Club and the spacious Padang (common) and new buildings of the independence
era. KL would later sprout a forest of high-rises including the
prestige project of the Petronas Towers, for a time the world's
highest building. For the moment, however, modernity was
symbolised by an ugly elevated road slicing through the old
town.

With my two colleagues – Paul Cheesewright of the Financial
Times and Eric Hale, a warhorse photography lecturer – I stayed
at the Majestic Hotel. This was at Eric's urging: he remembered
it from the Second World War. It was the sort of experience that
one calls 'colourful' . With its tired furniture, ancient ceiling fans
and elderly retainers, it would have made a successful set for a
Hollywood horror movie.

The staff were attentive and kind, and the food was fine. We
lost some of it to monkeys, which would come in and out of
open bedroom windows with lightning speed.

The central fact of Malaysian life was and is that the Malays
control the politics and the Chinese control the economy. The
Chinese community was large enough for sectarian strife to be
a constant risk. To avert it, the main political party of each community formed a coalition, the Barisan Nasional, producing an
overwhelming political bloc. More than 30 years later the
Barisan continued to rule, although by then alternative political
parties had found their voices.

The main newspaper, the New Straits Times, was owned by
the Malay coalition party and the Star, then a newcomer, was

owned by the Chinese coalition party. This meant government control by another route. Nor did Malaysia's history of Communist insurgencies in both Malaya and Sarawak, with inevitable restrictions on information, help the emergence of an independent media.

The newspapers were full of politics, but where were the features, the human interest stories – the Daily Mail formula from Northcliffe days – that give British papers their fizz?

Our training courses in Malaysia were organised by the Malaysian Press Institute. The Kuala Lumpur programme was launched and closed with high ceremony, to which I responded in like style ('Thank you, Mr Director'. 'Thank *you*, Mr Course Director'.) The Malays are a ceremonious people, as addicted to titles – tun, tan sri, datuk and so on – as we are in Britain. The MPI had arranged for us to do further, short courses in the detached states of Sarawak and Sabah on the island of Borneo, collectively known as East Malaysia.

The driving force behind the Sarawak programme was an ex-Thomson Foundation student, Ashari (Nash) Manis. He was a locally born Malay who was working in his home state as a federal information officer. Later, he was posted, to his discomfort, to Peninsular Malaysia (Malaya) before retiring to Kuching, the Sarawak capital. Nash was one of the few to have won a place on two full-length Thomson courses in Britain. As an example of the Foundation's lasting impact on the sometimes isolated situations of Majority World journalists, Nash had kept his study material and used it in his own teaching sessions more than three decades later.

I was enchanted by Kuching, which had more than a whiff of the days when this independent jungle state was uniquely ruled by 'white rajahs' – the Brooke family. The ancient shophouses with their four-foot-ways (covered walkways) and goods piled high in colourful profusion evoked the east as it had once been throughout the region.

The politics of Sarawak was even more complicated than that of Malaya. The indigenous Dayak peoples were the majority in the state. They had little political or economic power compared with the Malays and the Chinese. Many still lived in the traditional way in jungle longhouses with rivers as their roads. Already this idyll was being eroded by logging, much of it illegal. Deforestation later became a major international concern, and later still palm oil plantations meant more clearances.

The state was served by its own daily paper, the Sarawak Tribune (the Borneo Post rose to prominence later). It was locally owned and not formally affiliated to a political party. This gave it somewhat more freedom of expression although, like the national papers, self-censorship had to be observed.

Our week-long seminar was a success except for one session where I 'crashed and burnt'. Deeply depressed, I made the mistake of admitting as much to Eric. 'Oh, I've just had an absolutely splendid session,' he countered, and proceeded to list why it was so splendid. It was a long time before I forgave him for this gross insensitivity.

The final leg of the Malaysian tour took us to Sabah and its capital, Kota Kinabalu (pronounced with the same stress as 'hullabaloo'). I was imagining another Kuching, but KK could not have been more different. It was on the coast, not up a river. The streets were straight, the land was flat. Above all, it was new with scarcely a building more than 50 years old. The reason is that the city was twice destroyed in the Second World War (when it was known as Jesselton) – once by the retreating British to deny it to the invading Japanese, and then by the retreating Japanese to deny it to the returning British.

The journalists of Sabah were touchingly grateful for our willingness to visit them in their outpost. We consultants completed the assignment, then went our ways. My destination was Hong Kong, for a course with another Thomson Foundation consultant, Barrie Harding.

We flew between high-rise buildings, seemingly within touching distance, into Hong Kong's extraordinary Kai Tak airport (since replaced). We landed to water on three sides of us: the runway was a finger projecting into the harbour. An aircraft ended in the water on no fewer than five occasions between 1965 and 1993 (wikipedia.org).

Although a colony, Hong Kong showed few overt signs of Britishness apart from policemen's uniforms and the ancient trams that rattled along the main street. The taxi drivers were remarkable for their inability to speak English.

One touch of Englishness was to be found in the frequent use of Western rather than Chinese given names, many people having both. Victoria Wong and Emily Lau were leading members of the journalists' association, which organised our six-week training workshop.

As the days went by, I developed an unexpressed *tendresse*

for Victoria.

'Vicky, how about a drink sometime?' I managed at last.

'With what raison d'etre?' she responded practically, unknowingly.

There was none I could bring myself to mention.

Hong Kong seemed to run itself in its myriad ways. The colonial administration was content to let the Chinese get on with what they did best – making money. This hands-off attitude included press freedom, which was extensive. Newspapers were mostly in Chinese. The main English papers were the South China Morning Post and the Hongkong Standard.

The extent to which Hong Kong took colonialism on its own terms is shown by the comparative circulations at that time of the Chinese-language Tung Fong Yat Po (half a million daily) and the South China Morning Post (about 50,000 daily). Beyond the big ones, Hong Kong was a little place with a lot of little newspapers (to borrow an idea from Lord Beaverbrook) – more than 100 dailies at a count of the 'mosquito' press.

Many of the Chinese papers were put out by a man and a dog, and often these had to work for other papers as well to get a living. Even the best Chinese papers paid poorly compared with the English papers, and these in turn did not match the Government Information Services. Typical starting pay for GIS officers was more than three times that for journalists in the Chinese press. Furthermore, GIS staff had a housing allowance that newspaper journalists lacked. This was a valuable asset in land-hungry Hong Kong with its sky-high rents.

The inevitable result was that many of the best journalists left the Chinese press for the English press, which in turn lost good journalists to the information services. GIS tended to be viewed by other media people as the fount of all wisdom. However, the story of the reporter with a flat overlooking Kai Tak airport who saw a plane crash and phoned GIS to see if it had happened is probably apocryphal.

Owners of the mosquito papers were well aware that when they trained someone they expected more money and could move more easily. Many owners were happy to jog along as they were. Journalists, however, argued that Hong Kong did not have the journalism it deserved, and training was the way to get it.

In fact, Hong Kong journalism was seen as something of a pinnacle by the rest of the region – but this wasn't the point: it merely underlined the low standards elsewhere. Printing in the colony was suberb, and the then-new technologies for composing type and receiving news material were widely used. The South China Morning Post had replaced news agency wire photos with the vastly clearer satellite pictures. TV stations made heavy use of satellite reception to provide immediate news.

In its commercial and technical life Hong Kong had the sophistication of a developed country, but its journalism didn't. Where were the follow-ups and human-interest stories? Why did most local items fail to make the 7.30 am radio headlines but had to be sought in the magazine programme? In all the media, local stories were discounted in favour of foreign stories – which, arriving ready-roasted, meant less time and effort.

Certainly, Hong Kong news media were among the most free outside the Western world, even with stories involving the tiger at the border (China). The two main English papers both gave big plays to a highly political story from London. Investigative reporter Duncan Campbell in the New Statesman magazine unearthed a Hong Kong official body called the Standing Committee on Pressure Groups. The aim was said to be to 'destabilise' apparently innocuous groups like the Conservancy Association to prevent opposition groups coalescing into a political party. This was at the behest of China, because Beijing could tolerate British rule but not politics on the doorstep.

The Post ran the story as a strap on page one with the heading SECRET PLAN FOR DICTATORSHIP IN HONG KONG – CLAIM. The Government's response was to admit the existence of the committee, but to insist that it carried out only normal public relations activities.

The SCMP carried the denial next day also as the P1 strap, while the rival Standard had a vigorous splash headline/strapline: THERE'S MORE DIRTY TRICKS – CAMPBELL – Newsman sticks by story of Hong Kong 'secret dictatorship'.

The secret committee story was run on the Government-owned radio station and, curiously, ignored by both English television channels (commercially owned).

The main feature of Hong Kong life was the crowds. High-rise buildings containing tiny apartments crowded in on each other. Government House – traditionally around the British Empire a place of spaciousness and sweeping lawns – was hemmed in and overlooked. The Chinese appeared indifferent to being jostled in the street. Not so Barrie. I had to restrain him from picking a fight with a stranger, reminding him that he wasn't in Oxford Street.

Shopping and food were what the city did best. Barrie was in awe at the jewellery, fashions and artworks on offer. He was beside himself at the keen prices for antiques. 'Look at that – and it's only XXXX!' he exclaimed. Or 'Goodness, that could fetch XXXX in London!' Barrie's wife was an antiques dealer, which gave him an awareness of prices at the cost, as I felt, of appreciating an item for its craftsmanship or beauty.

He tracked down Mr Chang, who was a famous tailor for the expatriate community, and we both bought safari suits. Barrie's was blue; mine was salmon pink. It was the only time I acquired a made-to-measure suit. It shaped itself to the body in a way I never knew was possible. I still have it, and put it on from time to time to assess my deterioration over the years.

Even in Hong Kong, total area 426 square miles or about the size of Greater London, it was possible to escape the crowds. This meant going to the islands. Lantau was the largest. It was then a charming, undeveloped place. Later, the airport was resited there and a road bridge built. I wondered where Hong Kongers went then for their antidote to the crowded city.

I was keen to see the New Territories. This was land that had been leased by Britain in the late 19th century to add to its original acquisition of Hong Kong Island. The colony's population soared with the development of Kowloon on the mainland side. The expiry of this lease in 1997 brought about the reunification with China. However, it was merely the trigger for the handover. The Chinese would have taken the territory back sooner or later.

I pictured the New Territories as a peaceful rural land of rice padis, duck farms and market gardens. The opportunity to find out arose when an ex-colleague arrived unexpectedly.

A message reached me at the hotel that a Mr Donald wanted me to call. I didn't know a Mr Donald, but it turned out to be Donald Wintersgill from the Guardian. He had sensibly given up trying to get across his difficult surname, and was sailing under his first name for the duration. Barrie and I were bound for China, but Donald had got there first. We met him on his way home from a training project for the International Press Institute.

Donald was keyed up and in urgent need of unwinding. For him, the challenge of living in China – in those days austere and alien – had been followed by the razzmatazz of free-wheeling Hong Kong. I knew well the difficulty of handling these extreme contrasts. He had several hours before his plane to London. To help him relax, Barrie and I poured several drinks into him.

I had the idea of a boat trip. We wound our way up the Pearl River towards the Chinese border. The New Territories continued to be densely settled. I waited for the countryside to begin. And then we were at the border. There had been no rural paradise. For that I needed to go somewhere like Surrey.

We were close to the political curiosity of Sha Tau Kok, a shared village where the China-Hong Kong border ran in the middle of a street. Villagers were able to cross over as they wished.

Donald was by then unwound and ready for his long flight home. It now became horribly clear that we'd lost track of the time. He had an excellent chance of missing his flight. Deep in the New Territories a taxi was hard to find. We located one eventually. The cost was fearful, but a successful scramble to the airport followed.

I was to do another course in Hong Kong later that year (1981). First, however, with Barrie, it was my turn to go behind the bamboo curtain for the Thomson Foundation. Our staging post was Thailand where we met up with Don Rowlands, the team leader.

The Thomson group had a newspaper there, the Bangkok Post. The main men, Michael Gorman and Ian Fawcett, were project-managing the China assignment. We were to help the Chinese launch their first daily newspaper in English, the China Daily (strictly speaking, the first since the Communist revolution).

Bangkok presented extreme contrasts: world-class hotels and the squalor of stagnant canals; fine Buddhist temples and Patpong Street, world capital of sex tourism. Even the ubiquitous putt-putts – three-wheeled passenger-carrying scooters – were unable to fight their way through the gridlocked traffic.

For visual fireworks it was impossible to surpass the Bangkok papers. Typographical colour – not plain old colour pictures, although they were unusual at the time – ran riot over the front pages: mastheads, headlines, panels, tinted backgrounds, all with the distinctive, curly Thai script. Massive white-on-black (WOB), or reverse, headlines added their portion to this in-yer-face effect.

On the news-stands the various titles, each tending to use a different)dominant colour, created a stunning effect. It was so exuberant that I loved it. A riot yes, but a disciplined riot.

The Bangkok Post, Thailand's most important English-language newspaper, had nothing to do with these pyrotechnics. It was a sober broadsheet in the Anglo-Saxon style. It had a nine-column format, meaning narrow columns that were good for advertising sales but difficult for editorial design. The Post made a virtue out of necessity by turning the last column of the front page into an institution and one of the main draws for the paper. Column Nine, as the space was called, presented humorous sidelights on the news. Who cares about the hard news? Many readers looked at Column Nine first!

From Bangkok, Don, Barrie and I went in a bound from tropical heat to the bitter cold of Beijing at the height of the winter (January 1981). We were immediately taken to an outfitters for coats, hats and gloves. The coats, which were very effective, had a heavy-duty, detachable wool lining (so the outer garment could be used in the summer). They were proletarian blue like millions of other coats in the city.

For the Westerner China at that time seemed as remote as the surface of the moon. Landing at the airport, I almost expected to breathe a different air. The country was reopening to the world after decades of seclusion. The Gang of Four, including Mao Zedong's widow, Jiang Jing, had only recently been overthrown – I watched their trial on live TV in Hong Kong – to make way for the economic liberalisation headed by Deng Xiaoping.

We were lodged in the Beijing Hotel, and gave thanks that we weren't in the Friendship Hotel, far from the city centre. That was the fate of many visitors. Our hotel was in the central avenue, which seemed to stretch for miles. From my window on an upper storey, I gazed at the remarkable sight of hordes of people on bicycles pouring along this road. It was a sea of blue. Cars were a rarity.

Central Beijing was a mixture of massive Communist-era buildings and streets, inspired by the Soviet style of architecture, and the remaining hutongs. These were narrow streets flanked by one-storey buildings facing inwards, so that the street side was not much more than a blank wall.

The main street intersections had hoardings placed diagonally on all four corners. For Deng Xiaoping and his liberalisers, the posters were clearly a work in progress. They made a bizarre mixture of the latest Hong Kong-style consumer goods and screeching slogans of the 'Workers of the world, unite' variety. The hoardings symbolised the change that China was going through.

Before the China Daily there was no newspaper in English available to visitors, just an unappealing duplicated daily summary of news. This was a lack that the government had to address with the planned increase in both business and leisure visitors.

The newspaper had not been launched when we arrived, but it was staffed and being produced on a dummy basis. Clearly everything was done in a methodical way. While we ran a training course for the editorial staff, fellow consultant Jon Lawrence of the Melbourne Age prepared designs for the paper.

The production arrangements were unlike anything I knew, although they made sense within that political setting. Elderly expatriates, British and American, were on hand as 'polishers' – to knock the English into shape. They were the true believers, who had chosen to live in China rather than their own countries.

This system of polishing was not a million miles away from the American concept of the 'rewrite man'. Given the problem of English standards in non-native-speaking countries, it would have made sense around the Majority World if managements could have been persuaded to adopt such a system.

The blue pencil came into play. Somewhere in the back sat a political censor, who was an extra layer above the editorial staff. This was belt and braces stuff. The journalists themselves knew what was expected of them. Presumably they had been chosen for their reliability or malleability.

Feng Xiliang was the deputy editor and effectively in charge editorially. He was an agreeable man of middle age. I suppose he had been picked not only for his excellent English but also his doctrinal soundness, although he didn't come across as an ideologue. I would have liked to know about his background, and was – wrongly – too polite to ask him. We struggled with the alien environment. It came down to nothing more than the blue workers' suits that everyone wore. They were enough to create a high mental barrier.

While the China Daily was directed at visitors to the country or readers abroad, the Chinese were not short of material in their own language. There were 1,690 newspapers and magazines with an aggregate daily circulation of 50 million.

Many of the newspapers were directed at particular sections of the community – cadres (people in leading positions), intellectuals, workers, youth and so on. I was told that the paper for intellectuals translated, rather charmingly, as Bright Daily News! I found myself an honorary intellectual. One of the culture shocks for a Briton or an American in China was to realise that when someone calls you an intellectual he is complimenting you, not insulting you

The best-known Chinese paper was for the cadres, Renmin Ribao (People's Daily), in whose compound the China Daily was based. In China a cultivated man is known by his calligraphy; to give someone an example of your brushwork is a compliment. Renmin Ribao's title-piece was supposedly from the brush of Mao Zedong. During my two months in the country I found little else by him on display. Apart from some poems, his books were nowhere to be seen (and certainly not that little red book so widely brandished during the Cultural Revolution). Works by the late Prime Minister, Zhou Enlai, were prominent.

Distributing a daily newspaper in a country as big as Europe had its special problems, and Renmin Ribao had the most widely dispersed printing operation in the world. Five million copies were printed daily, with about a third coming from the main plant and editorial headquarters in Beijing. The rest were run in no fewer than 21 other cities including Hong Kong, with plans at that time for Tokyo and San Francisco. It was an achievement to make the paper available throughout the 1.4 million square miles of mainland China, where population centres were unevenly spread and communications were sometimes primitive.

The same paper was produced all over China, with no edition advertising or local stories.

The paper went out with the mail because of the Post Office's monopoly of distribution. It even ran the news-stands. There weren't many. Casual sales amounted to only five per cent of circulation. The rest were subscription sales – a circulation manager's dream! Mainly they went to institutions like factories, offices and communes, but about half a million people had individual subscriptions.

As the official organ of the Central Committee of the Communist Party, Renmin Ribao was essential reading for cadres and for China watchers, both for what it said and what it didn't say.

Nearly five years after the fall of the Gang of Four, China continued to be racked by ideological struggles over issues like economic competition, development priorities, relations wit h the outside world, education and even the reputation of the late Chairman Mao. The pragmatists led by Deng Xiaoping appeared to be well in the ascendant, but there had been no complete purge of the 'ultra-leftists'. And, as I wrote in Media Reporter at the time, the pragmatists had clearly been applying the brakes for fear that the process of 'de-ideologising' China had been going too far or too fast. Perhaps this was an omen for the later trouble with the China Daily (see below).

Doubtless Renmin Ribao was valuable to readers in leading them through the ideological maze with its editorials and commentaries. It had plenty of staff: more than 100 in the international section alone. Twenty correspondents were based overseas. One of the most popular sections was Readers' Letters, with 2,000 or more letters received on a typical day, as I learnt during an extended visit to our next-door neighbour in the compound.

Many of these letter-writers were asking the paper to help them with complaints, explained the deputy editor-in-chief, Tan Wenrui. The letters were handled in various ways: they might be published, or referred to the government department *above* the one complained about (a good touch, that) or assigned to a reporter for following up as a news story.

In Shanxi Province, for example, a reader's letter was said to have been directly instrumental in stopping a rashly planned dam and river rerouting. The paper backed up the reader's letter with a commentary, and the construction was halted.

Renmin Ribao saw its function as educative, but I wondered what readers made of the following P1 news items on a typical day:

• Suzhou County Area formulates 10 solid measures to boost grain production;

• Leading cadres of' Leshan County Area go to the farms to help manage spring farming;

• 43 Shanghai middle-school teachers volunteer to travel north to serve in the border province of Ningsha;

• Population growth rate drops by 0.75 per cent in Wendeng County as a result of persistent family planning;

• Dongjiang cement works acts to solve problems resulting from reduced capital investment.

It was hardly 'hold the front page' stuff! There was, however, a single-sheet evening newspaper in Beijing sold by wandering vendors. It carried a lot of human interest material and sold like hot cakes.

Renmin Ribao's content priorities pointed to a problem for the China Daily. Staff had to try to produce a paper acceptable both to outsiders and to the regime. As Western consultants, we had somehow to work within those limits without betraying our own journalistic values or the interests of potential readers 'out there'. We were happy to be there because we felt that we were near the heart of the liberalising programme upon which China was embarked.

The China Daily had to assemble a staff able to work in English, the formerly bourgeois and imperialist language, after a long period in which the country had turned in on itself. By then, however, the whole nation seemed to be gripped by a mania to learn English – often from short-short-wave radios tuned to the BBC or Voice of America. Most of those who spoke no English could acknowledge thanks with a polite 'Not at all'.

Keenness for English had not yet manifested itself in an abundance of fluent speakers, so the China Daily had to give priority to speaking English rather than being a journalist. Some of the senior editorial figures were already journalists. It was our job on a six-week Thomson Foundation course to induct the rest – former teachers, translators, interpreters and so on – into the required skills.

In some cases people's obvious happiness at doing important and fulfilling work was reinforced by the fact that not long before, during the Cultural Revolution, they had been wasting away doing menial work in the country, following ox ploughs and trying to 'learn from the peasants'. One told us that even books had to be read secretly because it was felt you might be preparing to get away from the countryside. And in those days dancing parties and traditional Peking opera such as our hosts took us to were out of the question.

Another course member sketched for us how he spent his days studying at the height of the Cultural Revolution – half the time on revolutionary ideology, a quarter out in the fields learning from the peasants, an eighth insulting the professors for bourgeois reactionism and only the remaining eighth studying the subject in hand!

Little wonder perhaps that in the new climate our students

were more concerned with intros than ideology, design than doctrine.

The China Daily was to take the four main Western news agencies, Reuters, AP, UPI, and AFP, as well as the Chinese agency Xinhua. The newspaper was intended as a window on China for the outside world, but it escaped no-one that it would also be a window on the outside world for Chinese.

The China Daily staff were pleasant and agreeable to work with. We all of us avoided any mention of politics. We had a liaison person, an efficient young girl whom we nicknamed 'the General'. Eventually we learnt that she, in common with the others, could not choose her future career path. She would have to go where she was posted.

We discovered that the polite form of address for older people was 'Lao', affectionately meaning 'old', like the English 'old boy'. Younger people were 'shao'. Barrie, who was in his sixties and older than the rest of us, attempted a joke that showed spectacular cultural incomprehension. He said: 'I'll be Shao Harding then!' He had failed to pick up that in China, like the rest of Asia, it is age not youth that is reverenced.

We were not addressed as 'Lao', 'Shao' or 'Comrade' – just ' Mr' . The Chinese were too polite to risk embarrassing us with their ways of address.

Barrie had more of a point when we were invited for dinner in the home of one of the senior journalists and his wife. Such an invitation was an honour anywhere in the Majority World. Except at the highest levels, the occupants felt their homes shamed them compared with those in the West. We were served an excellent dinner in the tiny flat. When we asked what the meat was, we suspected from our hosts' response, a mixture of vagueness and suppressed amusement, that it was dog. Barrie, a dog lover, restrained himself with great difficulty.

The Chinese were fond of dog meat, but were well aware that it was distasteful to Westerners. If we were right in our suspicions, it was an abuse of hospitality to serve it.

We enjoyed many wonderful meals. They were prepared by elderly chefs who, as it was explained to us, had been unable to follow their 'bourgeois' calling during the Cultural Revolution. Now they rejoiced at being able to show they had not lost their skills. Sometimes, though, it was better to try not to taste, swallow and ask no questions. Sea slugs were a delicacy that looked as horrible as they sounded, but were less of a problem under the euphemism 'sea cucumber'. They could be usually slipped down the throat without chewing; prawns' brains could be disposed of without tasting if swallowed quickly.

Our hosts evidently considered that monkeys' brains, fresh and steaming from an animal whose head had just been sliced open, were a step too far for us. In other ways, we appreciated the Chinese mania for freshness. Once we had overcome our squeamishness, it was good to point to a fish in a tank and say, 'I'll have that one', and have it on the dinner plate 10 minutes later.

The Beijing Hotel provided a European as well as a Chinese breakfast menu. The local guests seemed to eat the same food for breakfast, lunch and dinner, but that suited few Western stomachs. Otherwise, the diet was resolutely Chinese. I sometimes yearned for variety. I found myself walking across the centre of Beijing in a successful search for the one restaurant that was known to serve potatoes.

We were treated to several course-dinners. Many of the dishes were meat and fish on their own, rice at these banquets being served only at the end. The purpose was to take away any remaining feeling of hunger. I needed to eat very little rice!

These meetings included multiple toasts while Don, as the team leader, would make short speeches. He had little direct experience of non-Western countries, and seemed to be anxious to give the Chinese what he thought they wanted to hear. This led him on several occasions to make disparaging comments about Britain. It became too much for Barrie and me. We told Don we thought it wasn't appropriate for him to run down his own country, and nor did our hosts expect it. Matters improved after that – and then he was gone, back to the domestic life that was so important to him.

I kept in touch with the world by short-wave radio. The stirring theme tune Lillubullero was a call to pay attention. However, I became disillusioned with BBC World Service, which I felt was fixated on the United States and perversely uninterested in news from Britain. To be sure, there was a programme specifically for news from Britain, but this should not have meant leaving worthwhile stories out of the main bulletins.

Day after day, these bulletins might contain not a single item from Britain. I said to myself, 'This is the *British* Broadcasting Corporation. Can there really be nothing worth mentioning in the whole country today!' The standard response to such complaints, that stories are played 'on merit', I regarded as a cop-out that begged the question of what merit was.

A quota system for countries to be mentioned in bulletins would be a negation of news values, and I didn't favour that. Yet news can be actively sought and found; I wasn't convinced that was happening at the BBC World Service.

It was the same situation that had influenced me when I worked for the Mirror training scheme. I asked a resident of Salcombe (South Devon) why he didn't read the Plymouth-based Independent, the regional Sunday paper for South Devon and Cornwall. 'There's never anything about Salcombe,' he said. 'I know there's plenty of stuff going on here.' He had a point. To a large degree, news is what journalists are prepared to gather.

The Chinese language is composed of ideograms, or symbols, each representing a word or a concept. Up to 4,000 such characters were in use in newspapers. I was keen to know whether Chinese could be read as quickly as English, with words made up from just 26 letters each standing for a sound. The opportunity arose when Lao Feng showed us the sights of Beijing. We came to an inscription on a stone tablet. I asked him what it said. He read it aloud as quickly as someone would read an inscription in English.

This wasn't a scientific test (he might have known the wording from memory), but it made sense that he could sight-read quickly. Chinese words consist of thousands of individual patterns – but so do English words. The reader in English sees words as a whole – ie thousands of individual patterns made by the letters.

I discovered a handy characteristic of Chinese writing: it can be read as easily from top to bottom as from side to side to side. Try that in English with its elongated word shapes and see how hard it is, apart from shop signs! Around the Chinese diaspora, some newspapers used top to bottom lines; others used side to side lines. Yet others used a mixture of horizontal and vertical lines: this was a neat form of layout variety that we lacked in English.

The Chinese treated us with great courtesy throughout the 10-week assignment. We were given all the visitor experiences – the Great Wall, the Forbidden City, Peking Opera and so on. Perhaps it was the standard tour, but it was no less fascinating for that. At the end of the assignment Barrie and I were flown to Shanghai for a quick look at that once-great commercial city.

We travelled by train to Hangzhou, the beautiful lakeside resort of emperors and the Communist elite. Our hosts pointed out the villa recently occupied by the fallen Jiang Jing.

We encountered an Australian girl who was travelling alone around China. I was astonished that the authorities had allowed it, but she said it was no big deal. She neither spoke nor read Chinese. Train information, bus destination boards and street signs were all a mystery to her. I didn't see how she could make her way on that basis, but she was getting on fine. She had more guts than I had.

Too soon our mission was over. I had never asked myself whether we should be helping the Chinese to make better propaganda. I believed – 'assumed' would be a better word – that freer media would be part of the great liberalising moves under way. In fact, China was embarking on a decades-long attempt to separate economic freedom from political freedom, of which the press is a part.

This had its parallels in the non-Communist world. Singapore and Malaysia were among countries to demonstrate that growing economic prosperity did not automatically herald growing press freedom.

For the authorities, the China Daily was a success both as a source of information for visitors to the country and as China's shop window globally. With satellite printing now readily available, it was produced in several countries.

And then came Tiananmen Square. The shots that killed protesters in the heart of Beijing made headlines around the world. The China Daily 'buried' the story as a tiny item. The devil of a controlled press is that, for all I know, the editorial staff had to argue with the censor to include even that – but it wasn't the paper I thought I was helping to launch. Yet would the interests of the journalists or of press freedom generally have been better served if training had been carried out by consultants from East Germany or the Soviet Union?

A Thomson Foundation training team was in China at the time of Tiananmen Square and the civil disorder that followed. What happened next challenged the identity of all of us involved in journalism training. The team went one way, out of the country, when reporters were going the other way, trying to get in to cover this huge story. To me, my fellow trainers were cutting and running. Every journalistic instinct should have been to stay (ignoring headquarters' orders to leave, if necessary).

Journalism trainers make great play of still being journalists, but are we? Is there a point at which we have ceased to be journalists and have become teachers?

ELEVEN
GLOBAL HEYDAY 2 – 1979-1987
(ASIA/CARIBBEAN)

Africa drew me to overseas work, but in the 'global heyday' years, 1979 to 1987, assignments also came my way elsewhere in the world. I came to cherish the many and varied experiences in Asia and the Caribbean as much as the African ones. I spent almost one third of those nine years on the road. No wonder my friends wondered where I was off to next!

An assignment in Sri Lanka in 1982 reunited me with my friend and former Yorkshire Post and Guardian colleague, Francis Ashborn. His situation was sad. He had retired to the island because his wife Renee wanted to go home. He would have preferred to stay in London. Then Renee died and, with no children, Francis was on his own in Colombo. He spent his days reading in the British Council library.

We first met in a splendid apartment at the Galle Face Hotel, with a picture window view of the Galle Face itself, a long expanse of greensward along the seafront. Francis must have thought I'd come up in the world. In fact, the management had given me the apartment for barely more than the price of a room. I thought I might as well be comfortable.

I had a strong feeling that Francis, not me, should have been running the one-month in-house training programme for the leading newspaper group. He had been a senior editorial figure in Colombo before he left for Britain. Who knows why the Sri Lanka newspaper industry did not make use of his experience? Maybe there was more to it, but I was reminded of the cynical saying that an expert is someone from out of town.

A programme of short seminars in Jamaica and Trinidad that same year was followed three years later by a longer assignment in Trinidad. I was to help the no 2 selling newspaper, the Express, to improve its editorial operations. I had hardly started on the project when I was called back to Britain. My father was dying. He had a brain tumour, but was not expected to go so soon. I made it with only hours to spare.

He convulsed and died in his chair at the nursing home. Our family's sadness was doubled by the fact that my mother lay in the same double room, in an advanced stage of dementia and unaware of his passing.

Owen Baptiste, the chief editor of the Express, had been very supportive of my need to return home. Now back in Trinidad early in 1986, I set about helping him with the paper. The plan was for me to work in with the staff and help them by example. It appealed to me as a way to do some real journalism. The trouble was it tended to make me just another sub-editor, albeit an expensive one and one who was much slower with the unfamiliar technology than the regular staff! It wasn't the best use of a consultant's time, an indulgence even – like a general choosing to fight in the ranks.

Owen was a strong personality. It wasn't clear how much external help he really wanted, or perhaps whether that help had been imposed on him. I felt the assignment overall was not very successful, although I transformed his Sunday magazine with an up-to-date design (including lashings of white space). He acknowledged the improvements, and was duly grateful.

Regrettably, I had to leave Trinidad days before Carnival, the big cultural event of the year. I was able to catch much of the run-up with tuneful calypsos and witty lyrics, many of them satirising the political scene. One of the most melodic and wittiest was 'Captain, my ship is sinking', referring to the government's problems. Free speech and a free press seemed to flourish in the island nation.

Guyana is Latin American by geography but Caribbean by temperament. It is one of only two former British colonies in South America (the other is Belize, previously British Honduras), a spectacular country largely of rainforest but densely settled along the coastal strip. I was sent there in 1984 by a new client, the British Government's Overseas Development Administration.

Politically, Guyanese voters at that time had a choice of left or lefter. The government of Forbes Burnham aligned itself with the Soviet bloc – and this was the party the West had initially welcomed as the better alternative to Dr Cheddi Jagan, a Marxist. Jagan had won pre-independence elections, but Britain refused to admit him to power. He was still around, 'cheated but not defeated'.

The parties represented a straight racial cleavage in the country: Burnham for the blacks, descendants of plantation slaves; Jagan for the Indians, descendants of the indentured labourers brought in to replace them when the freed slaves were no longer willing to work the land. The two communities were broadly equal in size.

Britain must have been delighted at the opportunity to run a potentially influential programme for government information officers. There were limits to how effective I could be in such a politicised environment, but the long (two-month) programme went off to everyone's satisfaction.

Guyana's economic problems didn't touch me at the leading hotel, the Pegasus. The capital Georgetown had many superb buildings all of wood, in an elaborate Victorian-Edwardian Gothic style, including the world's tallest all-wood building, St George's Cathedral. Much of the city is below sea level, drained with trenches and canals built by the Dutch – who continued to colonise Surinam next door after the British had taken over in Guyana.

I made a journey into the Guyanese interior in an 18-seat Shorts Skyvan ('flying shoebox'), surely one of the most comical-looking planes. Our destination was Kaieteur Falls, a solid wall of water up to 400 ft wide (120 m) dropping 822 ft (250 m) — more than twice as deep as Victoria Falls, five times as deep as Niagara.

Almost equally breath-taking as Kaieteur was our emergence from the vast expanse of rainforest to find ourselves over the cattle-ranching Rupununi Savannah, a great area of open space where you expect it least.

Perhaps distances best convey the thrill of the falls. You approach the edge across an open expanse of level rock. At first I didn't dare to go nearer than 10 ft (3m). Later, familiarity and a full (picnicked) stomach whittled that down to 4 ft (just over 1 m). In the end I was lying on my stomach and peering over the edge. From that position, the brain said I couldn't go over but the rest of me wasn't so sure – the pull was that great!

It was as if I was looking at the land below not from a high point but from an aeroplane – an extraordinary feeling of disconnection that even the mighty Vic Falls doesn't convey.

I left Kaieteur as chastened – and as satisfied – as a punter emerging from a fairground 'wall of death'. Returning to Georgetown, our plane flew below the level of the lip of the falls and then down the five-mile gorge of the River Potaro, which eventually flows into the Essiquibo. This is Guyana's biggest river but not its most famous. That honour belongs to the Demerara, which has given its name to some of the world's best brown sugar and rum.

Even harder to reach than Kaieteur (unless travelling by Skyvan!), from the Guyana side at least, is the spectacular, precipice-sided mountain Roraima. This is the setting for Sir Arthur Conan Doyle's novel about prehistoric monsters in *The Lost World*.

Three years later, I was to visit the country twice more. The 1984 programme had been well enough liked for the Guyanese government to want a repeat. This time the Overseas Development Administration partnered me with a Central Office of Information staffer and former African information officer, Don Dyment.

Our visit was jarringly interrupted by a street assault in which I was seriously injured. I dislike the term 'mugging' because it trivialises incidents that may have major consequences. In my case it took nine months to recover fully. As in so many Majority World countries, we were advised to be careful where we walked. Don and I judged it safe to walk in daylight to the departure point for the fare car (shared taxi) to New Amsterdam.

I lost the way and we were retracing our steps – doubtless looking lost – when the next thing we knew was that we were flat on the ground. We had been subjected to a classic Guyanese 'choke and rob' attack. This is carried out from behind at lightning speed so that the victim knows nothing until he is rendered helpless by being gripped by the throat while a second man picks his pockets. I kept the trousers I was wearing as a souvenir. The pocket containing my money was razored out so neatly that the trousers could have been resewn good as new.

Such was the power of gangs in Georgetown that a crowd gathered, but no-one dared to help us. One man pushed my bunch of keys towards me with his feet, for which I was disproportionately grateful. Nor did the government and the police seem to control the streets. The minister assured us that she knew who had done it, yet nobody to my knowledge was arrested.

'Choke and rob' gangs aren't out to kill you, but because the choking is indiscriminate victims sometimes end up dead. Don was shocked, nothing more; I was in worse case. My brain had been damaged. My consciousness was fragmented: I had two centres of awareness – within the head as usual and somehow a few inches in front. My intellectual functioning wasn't affected, and on that basis I struggled miserably through to the end of the programme. It was a frightening situation. It was so bad that I told myself life would not be worth living if it didn't resolve.

I was locked into this half-life, with no sign of the situation easing. Back in London, the ODA arranged for me to see a neurologist. He prescribed the beta-blocker Atenolol and assured me that things would return to normal by Christmas (nine months away).

Almost immediately, the two centres of consciousness dissolved into one. It seemed like a miracle! There followed, however, migrainous headaches so severe that sometimes I writhed on the floor in agony. A glimpse of a bright light – say, car headlights – made my vision fog. I was incapable of work for several weeks, but slowly I recovered. The neurologist's prediction was right on target. It took me until Christmas to get well.

I was saddened that, after doing their duty by referring me to the hospital, the ODA lost interest in the matter. They sent me a letter reminding me that under the contract they weren't responsible; I never heard from them again.

Later that same year (1987), I was back in Guyana for the Commonwealth Press Union. If they sold rear-view mirrors for pedestrians, I'd have bought one: the attack had left me feeling anxious when people walked close behind me, but the assignment passed off without incident. David de Caries had asked the CPU for editorial advice with his new newspaper, the Stabroek News. This was a welcome private sector production in a country where the media were heavily state-controlled.

Although I was able to help David editorially, we developed serious differences over how his newspaper was funded. The problem was capital. The Guyanese economy was so run down that plastic carrier bags had a secondhand value. No prospect of raising the necessary money within the country. David had therefore approached and received openly stated support from the National Endowment for Democracy. This US government agency was also engaged in covert funding elsewhere.

I suggested to him that the move was wrong because official funding – particularly by the United States, locked in an ideological struggle with the Burnham government – compromised the independence of the newspaper or, even if it didn't (as the lawyers put it) would easily be misrepresented. David was unable to see the point. Where else am I to get the money, he asked rhetorically. I suppose he was a desperate man; my objections probably sounded like airy-fairy theorising. But I remembered the damage to Encounter when the left-wing British magazine turned out to be funded by the CIA, or how Radio Free Europe was dismissed as a propaganda station because of its American government funding.

The Philippines was the location for one of my most unusual training experiences. This was a residential training workshop for Roman Catholic priests and nuns who worked as journalists on church publications around the Asian region. I joined my friend and former Thomson Foundation colleague John Cardownie for the short programme in Manila. Regrettably, it was the only time he and I worked together abroad.

The event got off to an embarrassing start when I pronounced the overnight accommodation not up to standard. The foundation expected its people to stay in 'the second best hotel in town', as it was neatly though unofficially expressed – ie not luxurious but of a good business standard. Our rooms fell far short of 'second best' or even third best. However, I hadn't allowed for the Catholic practice of lodging in each other's quarters, and I should have been ready to muck in. The organisers responded by transferring John and me to the luxury of one of the very top hotels, which wasn't what I wanted either!

It was obvious that the Philippines had been colonised by the United States and not a European power, at least in the decades since Spain surrendered it. Manila took after some of the worst characteristics of American life and few of the best. It was chaotic and violent. We were advised not to wander out at night. The many newspapers screamed their heads off, and – reflecting the American preoccupation with free speech – there seemed to be no curbs on what they could say.

Headline wording took me back to my days on the (Cleveland) Plain Dealer (although the PD drew the line at some of the more frantic words to be seen in Manila). Meetings were slated (scheduled) and people tapped (chosen), although someone else might nix (say no to) them. Heroes were lauded, plans were readied and victims were, inevitably, slain. I looked in vain for my favourites - slugfest (meaning the mother and father of a fist fight) and donnybrook (meaning more or less the same, and that one is in the Oxford English Dictionary), but perhaps I wasn't there long enough.

Manila's leading newspaper, the Bulletin Today, was so keen on a high page one story count that they even started news stories in the ears on either side of the masthead, 'jumping' or turning them from there to another page. This was a characteristic US practice taken to an exaggerated degree. It produced more stories on the front page but tended to be dysfunctional, many readers disliking turns and stopping where the story jumped.

The People's Journal Tonight was a punchy tabloid that sometimes printed the front page sideways. Even my old paper in London, the Sun in its IPC days, didn't do that, but I warmed to the way that, like the Sun, Tonight moved the title (masthead) around the page and varied its shape: top or bottom, at one of the corners or in the middle.

Some pages including the back were printed in Tagalog, the vernacular language for this part of the Philippines. This was presumably popular with readers. English is the lingua franca of the islands, but in general the people of Manila were less fluent at speaking it than I expected.

John Cardownie and I soon got to know the priests and nuns as people. They were a pleasant crowd, but neither holier nor wiser than the rest of us – just people. No one wore clericals and there was no religiosity in the air. This was a good thing, helping to focus the programme on the matter in hand – improving the journalism of the church media. And that was the rub. All the good that the Catholic Church did on the ground was, I felt, outweighed by the social consequences of its sexual doctrines, especially the ban on contraception – the spread of Aids, runaway population growth and the misery of unwanted children. Was it right for me to help the priests and nuns spread the church's message more effectively? It was a question I never asked myself, although I should have done.

My two assignments in Bangladesh were a decade apart. I was there in 1974 with my friend and colleague Tony Thompson on one of my first trips for the Thomson Foundation. Now, in the mid-Eighties I was back, alone, for the Commonwealth Press Union.

Bangladesh is a hard country to love, for all the friendliness I found there. It is ill favoured by nature – the frequent flooding of the Ganges delta – and by history. It won its freedom from Pakistan, but the Bengali people are split between the independent country and the Indian state of West Bengal. I was struck by the phlegmatism of the people, referring to the 'Indian period', 'British period', 'Pakistani period' and 'independent period', as if it was in the nature of things for them to be ruled by others.

My overwhelming impression was of crowds, not only in Dhaka, the capital, but also in the fields. In Europe we are used to empty fields with one man on a tractor at best; in Bangladesh it seemed we were never out of sight of people in the countryside.

In the teeming streets of Dhaka the cycle rickshaw was a good way to get around, if one overcame the dislike of treating a man like a horse. There were at least 80,000 of these rickshaws – bicycle at the front, two-seater 'rick' at the back, with one very hardworking human being as motive power. Rickshaw jams were common. In many Asian cities scooter-based taxis, or 'puttputts', abounded, but in Bangladesh the money for even this simple form of motorisation usually wasn't there. Cycle-rickshaws were to Dhaka what the tube was to London.

Other countries, other customs. At least the man no longer runs along the street between the shafts, exactly like a horse. And we the passengers are providing the rickshaw pullers with work. If the vehicles had been banned as degrading for a human being, what would have become of the pullers? Bangladesh had a huge labour surplus. Any sort of paying job was worth having. I was told that a hard-working rickshaw boy could earn more than a senior official like a permanent secretary. He was unlikely to live long enough to enjoy this wealth, however, commonly sickening and dying before the age of 40.

Weakened by the work and undernourished, some of the rickshaw pullers were barely able to move the vehicle. The slightest incline threatened to defeat them. I couldn't bear to sit there. I got out and walked alongside. Meanwhile, the midday sun was hotter than I had experienced it elsewhere in the tropics. It drilled into the top of your head. A hat was an absolute necessity.

There were good memories too. In the Chittagong Hill Tracts and on an extended river trip, I saw a less frantic side of the country. On the boat we were served simple but nutritious dishes of rice, dhal (lentils) and greens, and curried white fish. Both have been favourites ever since.

Both the 1974 and 1984 assignments were training workshops for all comers. In Bangladesh that meant a lot of potential course members. There was a vast number of newspapers, mainly in

Bengali, many of them tiny and most of them articulating the views of a political party or faction. Politics was strident and potentially violent. Two national leaders, Sheikh Mujibar Rahman and General Zia-ul-Haq, had been assassinated.

Many of the newspapers were primitive productions, including one typeset by hand with individual characters – a process Gutenberg would have been comfortable with. Yet the Bengalis are a sophisticated people, noted for their articulacy and intellectual interests. Bangladesh was also dirt poor. It demonstrated again, as I'd seen in Sierra Leone, that a country's economy not the cleverness of its people determines the sophistication of its news media.

In a 1974 article for the launch issue of the Bangladesh Times, I aired what I admitted was the 'gloomy idea' that the improvement of newspapers was tied to national development and would therefore be a long, slow process. My aim was to stress that journalists and publishers had a great deal of self-interest in promoting development.

Any journalist in a developing country at that time had heard so much rhetoric about national development that such stories were typically covered more out of duty than enthusiasm. Nor did much effort go into them. Development meant a strong focus on farming, but most of the articles in the press presented the paradox that those who could immediately benefit could not understand them (even when read aloud), and those who could understand them would not be interested! In other words, the articles were over the heads of farmers and boring for city-based business people and officials.

These articles often read like technical or academic papers – because that's what they were, lazily reprinted in the newspapers. I urged on readers of the Bangladesh Times what is an article of faith for Britain's 'red top' tabloids – that making complicated subjects accessible is not the same as oversimplifying, sensationalising or cheapening them.

The central problem was to get the interest of city-based readers. It would not be done with headlines like POTATO PRESERVATION BY IRRADIATION (an actual example seen in a newspaper). Instead of the lofty approach of writing about crop yields, growth periods and planting seasons, telling the story through people – how farmers are putting changes into practice; what it means for them and their families – would be more inviting. This, however, meant more resources in going out to see and interview the farmers, which was usually not affordable. Thus this small example illustrated the vicious circle: the media were poor and weak because of the level of national development while the level of national development was low at least partly because of the state of the news media.

Salaries were so low that journalists were forced to take second or even third jobs. This inevitably drove down editorial standards. Worse, poverty left journalists wide open to a range of corrupt practices, from extravagant 'freebies' to substantial gifts in exchange for favourable coverage to outright 'bungs'. While many heroically resisted temptation, others did not.

Corruption of journalists is an issue that has stalked the Majority World up to the present day. The lack of corruption in Britain and America, at least in a monetary sense, is founded on adequate salaries.

Tony Thompson, ever resourceful, discovered that an airline was offering weekend breaks in Kathmandu. It made an intermediate stop in Dhaka, and wanted to add passengers for the final sector. We were happy to be added. We were principled enough not to declare a day off for the course while we went on our jaunt. We took the long weekend consecutively so the course was covered at all times.

Kathmandu – even the name sounded magical – was a city of temples and surprisingly multi-storeyed brick houses. I watched a band of porters come in from a mountain trek, each with the sort of load that I could barely carry from the taxi to the airport check-in desk.

Back in Dhaka, I was invited to talk to the Dhaka Press Club about computerised typesetting, and I found myself thinking about cycle rickshaws. The connection? Jobs!

My subject was computerised typesetting, the technology that even then was widely used around the world – except in Britain!

Bangladesh had many small newspapers, often with precarious finances. For them the cost advantages of simple photo-typesetters – a technology that even then was widely used around the world, except in Britain! – might make the difference between survival and closure. The editorial advantages of photocomposition were great, too. But all of this would be achieved at the cost of printing jobs.

Mr Abdul Malek was the publisher the Bengali-language Daily Azadi, the biggest-selling paper produced in Chittagong,

the second city of Bangladesh. He was keenly interested in electronic print technology and frequently visited international
printing exhibitions. Yet he was re-equipping with secondhand
linotypes. He told me: 'One of the main reasons is that I don't
want to lose any of my loyal workforce who have been with me
since we started the paper 20 years ago.'

He was all too aware that Bangladesh had no elaborate social
security net for the jobless,

In Dhaka there were as many daily newspapers as in Britain,
yet the biggest, Ittefaq, sold only 200,000 copies. Low levels of
literacy and difficulties of distribution were among the
problems. The best-selling English paper, the Observer, had
only a quarter of Ittefaq's sales.

From Dhaka to Comilla is less than 50 miles. When I first
knew it in 1974, there were four ferries and the journey took five
hours. Two bridges had been built since then, but that still left
two time-consuming ferries.

I flew with the papers for Khulna, the third biggest city in
Bangladesh. The bundles took up the first few rows of the
Fokker Friendship plane. At Jessore they (and we) transferred
to a bus, and we all reached Khulna at mid-morning. When I left
the country there was a row going on because it was planned to
put back the flight by two hours, which would mean the papers
reaching Khulna only at lunchtime.

Probably no country in the Majority World has suffered a
worse image in the Western press than Bangladesh. It seems like
a place where little happens except earthquakes, cyclones and
political upheavals. It is associated with grinding poverty and
too many people.

Bangladesh was and is one of the most crowded countries on
earth. And yet there were positives, too. From the air the rice
paddies made an impressive picture of intensive cultivation. I
found that Dhaka could mushroom from a small provincial
centre in British India to a metropolis of four million people in
a generation, and still function.

I discovered in a memorable trip of 26 hours by river steamer
that there was still living room enough to travel for hours
through an uncrowded, almost empty landscape.

It was clear that relatively small amounts of spending would
promote development. The problem was symbolised on that
river trip. I must have seen two or three hundred fishing boats.
None had an outboard motor.

The fact that 'good news' stories about national development are often propaganda or non-events doesn't mean they have to be either. In reporting countries like Bangladesh, that is the challenge both for local journalists and for correspondents sending stories to the outside world.

Later that year (1984), thanks to my friend and former student Ashari (Nash) Manis I was invited to return to Sarawak for an in-house consultancy with the Sarawak Tribune. Once again, it was a pleasure to be in the quaint and attractive city of Kuching. I stayed at the Aurora Hotel, later sadly demolished, close to the Padang.

For 3½ months I worked enjoyably and fruitfully with the newspaper. I ran training workshops and also worked in with the staff. The editor, Raymond Adai, was big enough not to feel diminished by my presence.

The Tribune was locally produced in a state with a high degree of self-consciousness. It had been an independent country for a century under the 'white rajahs'. Many wished it still was. It had come into Malaysia by a questionable 'double shuffle' soon after the Second World War: first when the last rajah, Sir Vyner Brooke, decided of his own volition to hand it over to Britain, and then short years later when Britain bundled it with Malaya to form the federation of Malaysia.

Britain's interest in Sarawak was not helped by the assassination of one of the colonial governors. This was a rare occurrence anywhere in the British Empire (although a governor of Malaya was also assassinated). I was aware that in this exotic land of jungle, rivers and longhouses the politics was hot and heavy. I stayed well clear, believing my role was to develop the technical abilities of the staff.

The Tribune was a good paper within its lights, but improvement was needed. (Of what newspaper anywhere can't that be said?) It had plenty of competition. The newer Borneo Post was coming up strongly. There were Chinese and Malay language publications. We had to assume that many in the Chinese business community, a staple of our readership, could also read Chinese and were able to switch if it pleased them.

I hammered home the need for more and better feature articles to complement the news coverage. In an analogy that might not please all feature writers, I compared a newspaper without features to a meal without desserts or fruit to follow the meat and fish – incomplete! I was therefore delighted when the managing director, Haji Balia, told me that a distinguished London-based Islamic writer was visiting Kuching, and would write two features about her childhood in Afghanistan.

This turned out to be Amina Shah, a woman in her sixties from a prominent Sufi Muslim family who had been married to a highly placed Englishman. Her father and brother were both well known writers. Amina herself had written several books retelling traditional Afghani and Arab fairy tales in an engaging way. Despite this background, Amina had no airs and graces. She was the sort of person who would pack her few needs in a rucksack, and get going with an enthusiasm that would do credit to travellers 40 years younger.

Amina's two articles were splendidly evocative of another place and another time. They were unfortunately spoilt by care-lessness on my part, at least until we ran a correction. Several Afghani terms had been written with capital letters. This was against style so I stroked through each letter – the then-proof correction convention – to show that the word was to be made lower case. I neglected to check whether the typesetters knew about proof reading marks. They didn't; they took my marks to be deletions. Somehow it got into the paper that way, and many of the most interesting bits came out with a blank at the heart of them. 'We came home to steaming hot BLANK.' 'Another favourite delicacy was BLANK.' And so on.

I was mortified, but Amina was generous about it. Things happen in newspapers. A true professional. We became good friends then and afterwards, sharing several meals at the Holiday Inn, her base, which was nicely situated beside the broad and dreamy Sarawak River.

I made the Sunday Tribune look different from its weekday counterpart by the simple device of using sans serif for the headlines while the weekday paper continued to use serif type. Sometimes the simplest changes are the most effective. Derek Jameson explained how he transformed the look and the impact of the (London) Daily Express when he became editor. 'I just told 'em to make all the headlines and the pictures bigger,' he chortled in the Cockney accent he was at no pains to lose.

Christmas came and went. I spent it with Nash (a Muslim), doing the rounds of several homes. I was introduced to Michael and Dawn Kirton, an Australian couple who had fallen in love with Sarawak. We too became friends. Mike was a professional flyer who had been the personal pilot of the former state governor.

Nash explained that Christmas was one of four major festivals celebrated in Sarawak, the others being for the Muslim, Chinese and Indian communities. It was the tradition to pay calls on members of that community on their festival day. As someone with mixed feelings about Christmas, I found the idea of dutiful socialising four times a year not very appealing. Nor was I alone: Nash admitted that people were known to tactfully go abroad to avoid having to do just that!

Mightier by far than the Sarawak River was the Rajang, with Sarawak's second city, Sibu, at its mouth. This is the artery along which timber is floated to the warehouses and sawmills, having been logged in the jungle legally and illegally. Nash had arranged for a speedboat, and we set out up the river for Kapit.

All along the Rajang we saw Dayak longhouses and people fishing from their tiny boats. We landed a couple of times, which meant terrifying climbs up and down steps cut from a single tree trunk, with the ground many feet below. As I wondered how I could avoid falling off, the locals shinned up and down with ease. The scale of the river and the surrounding jungle was bigger than anything I'd seen (or imagined).

Kapit, an administrative and trading centre for the region, was at that time only accessible by river or air. There was no road out, while in the town the streets amounted to barely a mile. There were, nevertheless, many cars – mainly useless, but a fine illustration of how motormania spreads like knotweed.

I felt very comfortable at the Tribune and might have liked to stay, but it was time to move on. I hadn't seen the last of Sarawak, however. When the owner of the Borneo Post, Lau Hui Siong, heard about my consultancy, he wanted one too. So two years later, in 1987, I was back, working for him.

Mr Lau was a timber tycoon. This was a trade that depended on government permits. I suppose he valued the Borneo Post for the political influence it gave him, but he also seemed to enjoy newspapers. I found him pleasant and dependable – characteristics he passed on to his family. His son Philip, daughter-in-law Phyllis and daughter Josephine all worked in the business at that time.

Unlike the Tribune, which was produced and printed in one centre (Kuching), the Borneo Post put out semi-autonomous editions in Sibu, Kuching and Miri. Even in those days computers were advanced enough to allow sharing of content. However, each edition had its own editor and generated local content.

The papers required a certain commonality of approach and content so an elaborate liaison system had evolved to handle it. I was part of this for my four months' consultancy. I acted as pro tem chief editor, working for a month or so from each centre. This allowed me also to run training seminars at each place.

Once again, I preached the need for feature articles and 'dug out' news stories – ie news that the paper had found for itself rather than depending on stock sources like listed events or press releases. I'd spread this gospel all over the world by now. It was a key Thomson Foundation message. The foundation was right. These were among the weakest areas of Majority World journalism. They still were years later, albeit on an improving trend.

I was horrified to find that the Borneo Post sometimes filled unwanted pages by simply reprinting pages from an Australian newspaper. I pointed out to Philip Lau that this was a clear breach of copyright. Just as bad – since the Australians might have seen the funny side – it made our newspaper look amateurish. He agreed, and the practice was stopped.

At Philip's request, I put the Borneo Post into colour for the first time. This was mainly for the cartoons, with some spot (individual) colours for headlines, rules and panels. It stretched the expertise of the printing department, and mine, and was primitive compared with what followed. But it was a proud achievement at the time.

While in Sibu I made another trip up the Rajang, this time on my own. Travelling by public boat, I reached as far as Belaga. The local government information officer arranged for me to stay at a longhouse. Strolling along a jungle path, I turned a corner and was presented with an incongruous sight: a playground full of children neat in gymslips (the girls) and regulation shirt and shorts (the boys). I fell into conversation with the teachers, very articulate people, and I wondered what it was like for them to be posted to such a remote place.

A few feet off the track and I was already disoriented. I had no illusion that if I spun round I would be able to find my way back to the safety of the path. That was how dense the jungle was. A Chinese man I met in Belaga offered to be my guide on a cross-country trek to a mining camp, which would allow me to return to Sibu by another route. It would be an adventure and I was tempted; then common sense kicked in. I would be trusting my life to this man, whom I didn't know. If he abandoned me on the journey for any reason, I might well not have got out.

From Miri I made a trip by bus into Brunei and its capital, Bandar Seri Bagawan. The sultanate is a fragment of its former self. Brunei once ruled Sarawak; then as the ruling Brooke family gradually expanded their domains Sarawak threatened to gobble up the last of Brunei until Britain stepped in to stop it. The second rajah's final encroachment was the Limbang River and surrounding land. This cut Brunei in two – a situation that remains today.

Brunei might be tiny but it was no rural paradise. All along the coast were developments associated with oil, the drilling rigs themselves highly visible near the shore. The capital was a surprise. I knew about the 'water village', where the houses are built on stilts over the water with wooden gangways connecting them. I imagined the whole town had the quaintness of Kuching redoubled. On the contrary, thanks to oil it was highly modern with impressive public buildings.

Neither the Sarawak Tribune nor the Borneo Post was controlled by politicians, unlike the Malaysian national papers, but they were constrained in political matters. Self-censorship was underpinned by a licensing system where the government granted or withheld permits to publish.

This polite form of prior restraint became harder to justify as Malaysia made its journey from a backward economy to an intermediate developed economy. Years later, in 2006, the Tribune republished Danish cartoons lampooning the prophet Muhamad. The majority population in Sarawak is Christian, but it was still unwise. The uproar was such that the newspaper volunteered itself for the block and shut down.

It was a dreadful shock to return from abroad and hear about Terry Pierce-Goulding's sudden death. The news was there, in my morning post. He was in his late sixties. I attended his memorial service, feeling desperately sad and missing his cheerful presence. He always addressed me jokingly as 'Sir Cedric'.

Under Terry's direction, the Commonwealth Press Union developed a considerable reputation for journalism training on the ground through seminar-workshops and in-house advice. After he died, the momentum was lost. The Training Committee chairman, Arnold Raphael, soon reported that 'the emphasis had already switched from purely editorial provision to the important area of management expertise'.

This was a strategy I was unable to support. Only a fool would be against management training for the Majority World, and I wasn't that fool. I was against the downgrading of editorial training to the point of extinction. Moreover, few workshops of any sort were now done as the committee emphasised individual travelling fellowships and exchanges.

I had to do something and, two years after Terry's death, I spoke out at the CPU's 1989 annual meeting. These meetings were genteel affairs where business was taken on the nod before everyone adjourned for the important matter of lunch. The chairman, hurrying through the agenda, said: 'Any questions or comments on the item? No. Well, the next ...' He had missed my hand signal and had to backtrack to give me the floor.

I felt an unusual sense of power as I addressed the great and the good of the Commonwealth press. I complained that the training committee was squandering Terry's legacy of goodwill and expertise. Heads turned to where I was standing at the back. It had become obvious that this was not a normal contribution from the floor. The air of shock was palpable when I referred to the committee as 'supine'. I discovered that the idea of eyes coming out on stalks wasn't merely a metaphor. Many delegates really did look like that.

Arnold Raphael replied that there hadn't been many requests, an answer I felt was wholly inadequate. People don't request what they don't know is available! It is the responsibility of headquarters to let members know what is offered, and to work with them on identifying their training needs.

The CPU Quarterly later ran a long piece in which I set out my case in vigorous terms. I pointed out that newspapers did not sell on management excellence; it was for the editorial content that most people kept buying newspapers, keeping everyone (managers included) in work. So editorial might claim to be THE important area of expertise.

Any sensible editorial person acknowledged that managerial skills were vital. Indeed, their relative absence was among the most obvious characteristics of the Third World media scene. The CPU should certainly be involved in such training, but it should be as a complement to editorial training and not at the expense of it.

Seminar-workshops were the single most potent form of editorial training that the CPU could carry out. There was a large silent constituency around the world, managements as well as journalists, that would love this programme to be actively pursued again. Valuable as they were, individual travelling fellowships and exchanges could not match the worth of reaching much larger numbers of journalists within their own working environment. Workshops typically involved people several years into their careers. They were a form of skills upgrading usually not available from local resources in developing countries.

I stressed how isolated journalists were in many Commonwealth countries. Hard currency restrictions and high import prices might mean that they had little awareness of foreign newspapers and magazines. Perhaps there were harassment and press restrictions, such as those associated for so long with Lee Kuan Yew of Singapore, the CPU's chief guest of honour at its 1990 Hong Kong conference (and, I forbore to ask, what sort of irony was that?). An external tutor, by bringing the outside world with him, was a welcome breath of fresh air.

More than one editorial policymaker connected with CPU programmes had said privately that editorial workshops in the Third World had failed: they had been around for over two decades and journalistic standards were still dreadful. QED. My own response was – rubbish! In any particular country, compare newspapers of 20 or even 10 years ago with those of today (1991), and there was the proof. Zambia, for instance, had had lots of training aid, much of it by the CPU; Zambia was generally acknowledged to have one of the better and more independently minded presses. I doubted that this was coincidence.

I acknowledged that journalism hadn't improved as much as it might have done – should have done – in practically every Commonwealth developing country. Yet it was wrong to blame the journalists for this. Political restrictions on what could be said and economic constraints on the availability of newsprint, photographic film etc, etc. had often been damaging. Maintaining an English-language press in the face of a social policy of replacing English as the language of the country was a labour of Sisyphus.

From my own experience, I knew that many, many times journalists had emerged from workshops bursting with new skills and ideas, which they could not put into practice because of resistance by higher-ups. Managers with greater skills and awareness could break many of the log-jams that were holding back journalism in their countries. I ended by observing that here was where editorial and management training could join hands.

The article and my earlier remarks to the annual meeting had, I hoped, found their mark. But anyone taking a stance like mine can expect to pay a price. I never worked for the Commonwealth Press Union again.

I had lost the CPU and the Thomson Foundation, my two main clients for overseas work. I found myself in a waterless desert – but Africa and Asia hadn't finished with me yet.

Student magazine 1959,
proudly announcing our
celebrity contributor, actress
Jean Seberg

The beautiful but
tragic actress Jean
Seberg, seen here
in Les Grandes
Personnes (1961,
Zenith
International). She
wanted to be a
writer, and
contributed an
article to my
student magazine

With good friends Eric and Sue Frankland on the Staten Island Ferry
(New York) soon after arriving in the New World, 1968

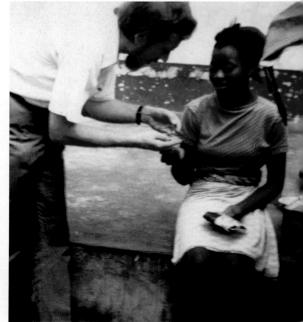

I bought more things
than I needed from this
pretty street vendor:
Nigeria, 1973

Meeting the oba (king) of Benin in Nigeria, 1973

With Thomson
Foundation colleague
Tony Thompson (left),
Bangladesh, 1974

If beards spell
wisdom, this trio is
worth hearing:
Bangladesh, 1974

At the Mirror training
scheme in Plymouth, lat
Seventies

Rainbow over the Victoria Falls, Zambian side. The flares
give the game away that this is the 1970s

Shades of Jack Vettriano in this shot of a couple enjoying a peaceful drink just above the Victoria Falls, Zambian side

Jacaranda trees in full glory: Lusaka, Zambia

Here's to the project! The Thomson Foundation team were hospitably received when helping to set up the China Daily, 1981

China, 1981. Our team leader, Don Rowlands, is behind me. Can't remember whether our side won

Village in Tanzania, 1980s

Pick your own was easy with this impressive mound of tropical fruit

Longhouse in Sarawak, mid-Eighties. Somehow I managed to get up there and back again (see also front cover picture)

Classic water village in Malaysian Borneo

Cyprus 1991: This airliner had been caught in no man's land between the two parts of of the island since 1974

Probably the favourite cover among my books – simple but expressive in both design and words

Autographing 'JournoLISTS' for Borneo Post journalist Lester Bingkasan: Sabah, 2009

The way we were: Borneo Post journalists in Sibu, Sarawak, 1987. Nicholas Lo is on my immediate left. He took another course with me 22 years later

Borneo Post journalists celebrate the completion of their course (2009). On my right (middle row, centre) are senior editorial manager, Sabah, Phyllis Wong and Sabah general manager for KTS Trading (parent company) Ngu Ngiong Hieng. Nicholas Lo is standing, extreme right [Picture Gordon Chin]

Enjoying a fish supper in Kuching, Sarawak, 2009. With me are 'Nash' Manis (left) and his uncle, Madon

Sunset in Sandakan, Sabah, 2009 [Picture: Phyllis Wong]

TWELVE
HOME FRONT – 1988-1990

I had not given up overseas work, but at the end of 1987 it had given me up. I was 49. It was to be four years before I did another foreign assignment. Meanwhile, the home front became my focus.

A chance meeting at the Ridgeway Hotel in Zambia led to work with the British government's Civil Service College. A consultant at the college, who was visiting Lusaka, thought they might want someone to teach media skills – that is, showing civil servants how to be effective when dealing with journalists.

When I approached the college, I found I was pushing at an open door. They were dissatisfied with their existing provider (whose identity I never discovered). Two members of staff, John Clarke and Elizabeth Chennells, put themselves through a module of what I proposed to provide; then, being satisfied, hired me for an initial one-day course.

This turned into a harmonious association that lasted for 26 years until the college, by then the National School of Government, closed in 2012. With the team I assembled, I was the sole media skills provider during that time, running numerous courses each year. I never had a formal contract. For much of the period everything was arranged by word of mouth alone. It was trust on both sides, a way of working I've always been comfortable with.

I wondered about the rightness of running with the hare and hunting with the hounds – training both journalists and those who deal with journalists; for example, showing journalists how to ask tough questions and showing civil servants how to answer, and possibly parry or block, tough questions! I countered metaphor with another metaphor: that of providing a level playing field.

Journalists tend to have all the forensic skills. It was – and is – astonishing how many public figures ruin their case through poor presentation. One of my favourite examples was the Eurotunnel spokesman, after a horrible fire in the Channel Tunnel, appearing on television in a dinner jacket, as if he'd been rudely interrupted on his way to a jolly. He sounded irritated, too. A simple suit (even if a dirt-streaked shirt and hard hat was expecting too much!) would have struck a more appropriate note.

Our courses typically had the generous provision of one tutor for every three attendees. This gave intensive hands-on training. A course worked best with two or three tutors and up to nine attendees. This allowed the tutors to combine plenary sessions with small-group work.

I therefore needed help, and I immediately thought about my former colleague, Donald Wintersgill. He was a current Guardian staffer as well as a journalism trainer for the International Press Institute. Donald, with an expensive house in South London and two boys to put through Dulwich College, was keen to join me.

We were both essentially print journalists. It soon became clear that we needed TV and radio people in the team. In these multi-media courses – which the college had rightly insisted on – print was rapidly eclipsed in popularity. After all, who wanted to practise plodding across-the-desk newspaper interviews or phone calls following up a press release when they could have the excitement of a three-minute, simulated broadcast interview, 'just like on TV' ?

Thus Donald and I were joined by a series of broadcasters: first Michael Meech and Brenda Ellison, then Andrew Boyd, Michael Dodd, David Golley and Simon Mann. We were ably assisted by technicians who worked our camera, among them Rick Ives, York Smith and Colin West. All the tutors and technicians were effective in their different ways and styles, but the bounciest was Mike Dodd. He was just on the right side of hyperactivity, and was invariably a huge hit with course members. People said: 'If he could bottle what he has, he could sell it for a fortune.' No one else delivered with the same razzmatazz, so it was an unfortunate fellow tutor whose session followed Mike's!

The head of media programmes at the college for many years was Carol Pedley. She left us to it, which suited me well. Carol could be hard to get hold of, but never objected to being run to ground at home outside office hours. A hard worker, she set a good example for managers of doing hands-on work herself – coaching in another area of communications.

The college was based in the beautiful setting of a country house at Sunningdale with about 60 acres of grounds including nicely kept formal gardens. The site had been expanded with various administrative and residential blocks. A jogging track – little used! – circuited the grounds. There was also a London centre in a drab office building for the one-day courses.

Mainly we worked in London, but it was always a pleasure to stay from time to time at Sunningdale and expose oneself to the whole country house training experience. This included slipping off the grounds in the evening for the nearby pub. On one occasion we mistimed it. Four ageing tutors had to scramble over the locked gates, when Michael Meech impaled himself.

The format of our courses was simple but effective. It was based on simulated interviews on material that the participant supplied. This was essential for providing realism. Interviews were recorded, played back and discussed in a group. Many attendees had never seen themselves on screen before. Once they had overcome the universal 'cosmetic effect' of seeing and hearing themselves, they could focus on the shortcomings of presentation.

These ranged from lack of eye contact (looking down – dejected; looking up – I don't know the answer but perhaps the Man Upstairs will help me!; looking past the interviewer or camera – struggling) to over-long defences of the weakest point instead of dealing with it briskly, and moving on to stronger ground (the switch technique): 'But frankly, the real issue is ...') Not only does a long answer on a weak point sound defensive but it also reinforces that point of weakness. People who 'protest too much' will be thought to have something to hide, even if they haven't.

Another difficulty was that, knowing so much about their subjects, the civil servants tended to 'talk it long' – hopeless for a TV studio interview of three minutes or a soundbite of 20 seconds. They had to learn to be less detailed.

I stressed the importance of body language, in which I included voice. The aim is to appear natural, as if one is having a conversation. A monotone voice shouts nervousness. I pointed out that, while nervousness was natural, being aware of its effect on the voice was the first step to overcoming it.

Almost always our course members' performance both in content and delivery improved as the day went on and interviews were repeated. Our customers were senior civil servants, from permanent secretaries or heads of quangos to technical specialists and office managers in the regions – anybody who thought he or she might encounter the media. It became clear that there was more contact between officials and journalists than was immediately obvious, particularly among the quangos and in the regions.

Print as a medium (newspapers and magazines) was generally in little demand on the media courses. It was discreetly dropped. We found a market, however, for dedicated courses on press releases. Releases are sent to all media, but their structure is similar to that of a news story for print. Done properly, the press release can be used unaltered, which for the issuer of the release is bingo! Not only does the organisation get mentioned but also it controls the way in which the message comes out.

It was uncommon for a substantial newspaper to use press releases unaltered, but frequent among trade magazines and smaller newspapers. However, even they drew the line at brash propaganda. The trouble was that government press releases with rare exceptions weren't written in a way the media could use; hence they could only be used as tip-offs, or just ditched.

It was usual for press releases involving government ministers to start with a quote from the minister, even though a verbatim quote is invariably not the best way to start a news story. There was a tendency to quote officials in order of seniority, although from a journalist's point of view – the one that matters if you want your organisation publicised – the interesting quote might have come from the most junior official!

I taught that websites had made a quantum difference for publicity. Press releases should be got up there quickly. Members of the public accessed these pages so they saw the information exactly as an organisation wished it, not as filtered by journalists. This was another reason for releases to be written to be read.

We also ran media workshops abroad, often through the government agency, UK Trade and Investment. I never wandered farther than Jersey, believing that the broadcasters were better equipped to do these projects. Mike Dodd was a stalwart of programmes for British officials in Dubai, Singapore, Tokyo and Rio de Janeiro among other places. These visits were invariably short, at the client's decision. Mike was out and back within a week – a far cry from my pattern of a month or more at a time on the ground.

In the later part of our long association with the Civil Service

College, we found ourselves in courses on appearing before parliamentary select committees and being an expert witness in court. This improbable extension of our range came about because someone perceived that these courses also involved asking tough questions. We were the people for it! Indeed, pretending to be an MP of the nastier sort wasn't very different from being a real journalist doing a mock TV interview.

The expert witness courses also involved asking journalism-style tough questions, with a few 'my lords' and 'your honours' thrown in. There were differences, however. Playing the part of prosecuting counsel, we could not ask the leading questions beloved of journalists ('And did you suspect that food poisoning might be the cause?'). We thought it wise to give ourselves advocacy training. The initial team of Donald Wintersgill, Michael Meech, Brenda Ellison and I trooped into a barrister's room in the Temple. He took us through a classic case of the great defender, Marshall Hall.

This was helpful because our difficulty lay in cross-examination of witnesses appearing for the authorities – the role the civil servants would often be in. Everyone on the course wanted a good show from the questioner, the tougher the better, but Marshall Hall himself would have been stumped with some of our scenarios. The VAT official who only had to testify that the fraudulent return had been received, stamped and passed up the line was never going to be cross-examined in reality. Somehow we had to make something of it for the sake of the show. It and other procedure-type testimonies could be torture.

Our torture came to an end when an incoming departmental team at the college had concerns about coaching witnesses. We had always told the course members that we could not deal with the actual case they faced. We would handle previous, decided cases or imaginary cases. As a further layer of protection, we were not lawyers, and could not be guilty of professional misconduct. I felt the college people were too cautious in their coaching fears, but nevertheless they dropped the course.

The select committee courses, in which I or one of my colleagues was paired with a committee specialist, continued to be a success. They were a lot of fun to do. Sue Rose, an experienced press officer and interviewer, joined us and greatly strengthened the team. By the early 2000s the market for media skills courses showed signs of saturation, but the select committee programme was in demand until the college closed.

The National School of Government was a victim of the spending cuts imposed by the Coalition government elected in 2010. The NSG model of mainly face-to-face courses was seen – wrongly, as I believed – as outdated in the era of internet-based distance learning. Money was also to be saved by departments and agencies carrying out more of their own training in-house.

My other clients at that time included the Central Office of Information, IPC Magazines and Uxbridge College. The COI was like a ministry of information but, being Britain, it was considered right to have a hand's-length agency arrangement for official information. I developed a programme in media law for them. In my Plymouth days I lectured on everything journalistic under the sun except shorthand, and I kept the habit. Eventually I gave up law as a subject when I found it impossible to keep up with a fast-changing field as well as dealing with writing and sub-editing subjects.

I was happy to be part of Jean Silvan Evans's team at IPC Magazines, based in Sutton, Surrey. This was the trade and technical end of the formidable magazine empire. Jean was an energetic woman, who developed a fine range of in-house courses. I dropped out when she asked me to take a fee cut along with the other tutors because of budget cuts. I was a touch intransigent in those days. Later in my career, or having just become older, I might have been more understanding of her problem.

Uxbridge College, on the outer fringes of London, has remained my only experience of non-adult training. I ran a media awareness course there one day a week for two years. The students were teenagers, and at first I failed to get through to them. Eventually I realised that I was lecturing to them in a way that even Oxbridge undergraduates would have found boring. When we started to put together a course newspaper – a practical project to which everyone could contribute – their attention and their interest were transformed. My weekly visits ceased to be an ordeal, for me and them, but I knew my work lay with adults.

The National Council for the Training of Journalists, the British newspaper industry's official training body, was another important source of work. I became involved with them in Plymouth days, when the Mirror training scheme ran one of their examination centres. Later, as a freelance, I tutored on sub-editing, feature writing and design courses.

The sub-editing courses were held at a conference centre in

Rugby – a location chosen as 'equally inconvenient from everywhere', as the director of short courses, Paul Hopkins, joked. The thinking was that a central venue was better than the previous system, where tutors and courses moved around between Torquay and North Berwick – finding that Scots turned up in Devon and Southerners turned up in Scotland. The dates were paramount.

I'm sure that participants from throughout the UK would have preferred the bright lights and the shopping of London. Nevertheless, in the palmy days of the 1980s, when companies were spending money on training, the courses were well supported.

They were held at the premises of the National Marriage Council, which became Relate National Marriage Guidance in acknowledgement that not only the married were having sex (and later, just Relate in acknowledgement of goodness-knows-what). The library where we held some of our meetings had many tempting sex books. It was good to know that, if need be, one could have one's marriage fixed and learn journalism at the same time.

The courses were long affairs – Sunday evening to Friday lunchtime. Students and tutors were all resident for the duration. Such a generous provision of time became unimaginable in later years, with the consequent loss of training in depth.

The Eighties in Britain were the last days of paper-based journalism. Opposition from the print unions delayed the switch to computers. Even the impoverished countries of the Majority World had gone over years before. Stories were edited on paper using hieroglyphics called subbing marks; headlines were written to what one hoped was the right length using a system called unit counting. Stories and headlines went to compositors, and in the case of headlines came bouncing back if the line was a 'buster'.

We simulated these operations on the course, which unofficially fell into two parts – before casting off and after casting off. Teaching this subject was a nightmare. Casting off is a method of judging the length of a story in type from the manuscript copy. With inaccurate casting off, time and money are wasted by producing type that becomes overmatter and is thrown away. This important skill is hard to imagine now when computers give a precise length or page make-up terminals show the space the story will take. Most subs' attempts at casting off were well wide of the mark, in the real world as well as on the course, not least because few were interested to get it right. It was therefore a great relief when this tricky subject had been got out of the way.

The number of participants was such that three or four tutors were needed, each with a group of four to six students. The arrangement had strengths and weaknesses. With an effective tutor it made for intensive learning; on the other hand, a week was a long time to be closeted with an ineffective tutor. A tricky situation arose when a group complained to Paul that they weren't learning anything. The tutor concerned was very old, and clearly had gone on beyond his time – an ever-present hazard for the teaching freelance.

Understandably, Paul felt unable to humiliate the man by dissolving his group. I was asked to go in and sort it out (as well as retaining my own group). But how to do it? We invented a title for me: I was the 'official recapper', who would drop in from time to time and provide condensed tuition in the subject to hand. I doubt that the tutor was fooled, but nothing was said and face was saved.

Although I kept my interest in newspaper and magazine design, I was losing interest in sub-editing. I felt I'd had enough of it by now, both as a practitioner and a tutor. I welcomed Paul's offer to oversee a freelance writing course titled Writing for a Market. This played to my conviction of the need for good features in newspapers – in press pioneer Lord Northcliffe's words, 'hard news catches readers, features hold them'.

The course was held in London over three weekends. Again, this was a duration that later became unsustainable. The (retitled) course ended up as a two-day affair. I even fought off pressure (not from Paul) to make it one day.

The main tutor was the popular Sue Teddern. She had started as an editorial secretary, and become a successful freelance feature writer. This was a not uncommon route into journalism. Sadly, she soon left the course, to be succeeded by the equally popular Barbara Rowlands. She was a college lecturer who practised what she preached as an active freelance in health journalism. Barbara and I were to have a professional association lasting many years.

Back in Rugby, the main tutor for the newspaper and magazine design course was unable to attend at the last moment. Paul's assistant, Don Wood, confessed that design wasn't his field, and could I do anything to dig him out of a hole? With no time to prepare and with a pre-announced programme, all Don and I could do was keep one handout page ahead of the class. But we made it, and the students were none the worse for the experience. I was soon invited to take over the design course. I called it my 'field commission'.

Another staple source of work in those years was the Guardian newspaper. Donald Wintersgill, whom I brought in to work with me at the Civil Service College, returned the compliment by asking me to join him on the newspaper's syndication service. I filled in for him on his days off and during holidays. It was good – and necessary – to be doing real newspapering again after my long spell of concentrating on training. This turned out to be another long-running connection, ending only in 2003 when I reached the official retiring age of 65.

Syndication in the British pattern is the system where newspapers re-sell their content, or a selection of it, to other publications around the world, offsetting their costs. I remembered the syndication sub-editor from my time at the Guardian in the 1960s. Jimmy Rowe would appear in the newsroom with his hands stained up to the elbows in a striking shade of purple. This came from the spirit duplicators that ran off copies of the articles to distribute to clients. Happily, by the time I came on the scene these Banda machines had been replaced by photocopies.

It was a live service: clients received material the day before and were able to publish it at the same time as the Guardian itself. The service was relatively primitive at that time. Mainly we passed our articles to the Washington Post, which distributed them around the world on its combined service with the Los Angeles Times. We had a handful of publications that we supplied directly at their London bureaux, while others had lifting rights – they could take content from the newspaper itself. In those days it might take several days for foreign clients to see the paper, but with features that didn't necessarily matter.

The raw material of syndication was paper copy sent to us from the main newspaper, particularly the foreign desk. The job became more interesting when in the late Eighties the introduction of computers meant that we could select material ourselves from the live databank. Selection was necessary because only part of the Guardian's content was syndicated. The clients preferred it that way: they were paying for a tailored service.

A profile feature that caught my interest concerned a stereotypical college lecturer, described as an eccentric bachelor with 365 cardigans – one for each day of the year. That seemed like an excellent idea to me. Always on the lookout for offbeat stories, I was delighted with this one. I knew the foreign clients would love this evidence of English eccentricity. Unfortunately, I'd overlooked the date: March 31. It was the Guardian's April fool story for the next day's paper.

To send out a spoof story flagged as such was one thing; to offer it abroad as a genuine article risked clients running it and looking foolish. I was mortified. I felt this was such a bad professional error that I offered to resign. Donald declined the offer. We never heard whether anyone published the article. The matter soon blew over, as things usually do in journalism.

The article I most regretted sending on the service was picked up from one of the feature sections. It was in praise of heterosexual anal intercourse. At the time, I felt this was 'edgy'. I realised later that it was simply crude. It was a mistake to have published it even in such a 'right-on' newspaper as the Guardian. It would have been particularly offensive in parts of the world where sexual matters were handled more discreetly. I doubt whether any of our clients published it.

Another important development was the Guardian's takeover of the Observer, which brought their syndication service into the fold. This enhanced our service in quality as well as quantity. They had a huge and valuable picture library. We learnt from their method of 'spot sales': in addition to their contract clients who received the regular service, they had a list of further publications whom they contacted for possible one-off sales of particular stories and pictures.

Observer syndication was partly a commissioning service. It went out daily, yet the parent newspaper appeared only once a week so there weren't enough articles to go round. The service needed to be bulked out. This was done with pieces specially written for the service, curiously known as 'servobs'. This terminology – a back formation from Observer service, and presumably telegraphese in origin – didn't survive the transition to the Guardian.

I became a frequent writer of servobs, which were mainly backgrounders on current news events. They were easy and enjoyable to do. It was the first step in a journey back to my original interest in journalism – writing.

THIRTEEN
ABROAD AGAIN – 1991-1995

By 1991 the mood in Zambia was that President Kaunda's government – in power since independence almost three decades before – had overstayed its time. With the economy on the floor and with the suffering that brought, the people demanded change. I returned to the country that year. The coming change was palpable. The flags of Frederick Chiluba's Movement for Multiparty Democracy were everywhere. Children flashed the MMD hand sign to cars as they passed by.

The MMD was swept to power in the election and Kaunda, to his credit, stood down graciously. I too was caught up in the mood for change. Of course, with hindsight it was naive to expect a new heaven and a new earth. The new government was a shaky coalition of business and labour interests. The new president – a tiny man in contrast to Kaunda, who was above average height – was the former trade union chief. The independent Weekly Post was later to describe Chiluba as 'a product of Kaunda's repression', a man whose 'credibility begins and ends with Kaunda'.

It was, however, significant that the new climate of free speech allowed the Post to make such a comment with impunity. For all that, the MMD was soon mired in difficulties – some produced by carrying out Western-induced structural adjustment programmes and others, like drug trafficking in the top reaches of government, defections and corruption, home-made. Crime soared as salaries failed to cover bare necessities and there was hunger in parts of the countryside. The average clerk earned the equivalent of only US$45 a month. But the government brought once-runaway inflation under control. Goods were in the shops for those who could afford them.

I was in Zambia for the Friedrich Naumann Stiftung (Foundation), having been recruited to run a one-month training workshop by the station chief, Hartmut Giering. FNF was the development agency of Germany's Free Democratic Party. This was the start of an agreeable five-year association that ended when Hartmut resigned and went to Zimbabwe to run a tourist lodge. He and I remained good friends afterwards.

By now I had trained a substantial chunk of Zambia's press corps. Some had risen to high positions, including Cyrus Sikazwe, editor in chief of the Times of Zambia, Josephine Mapoma, permanent secretary at the Ministry of Information and Broadcasting, and Patrick Nkama, an editorial executive at the Zambia Daily Mail. Others had left the profession, persuaded by the better money to be had in public relations or private business.

Returning to Zambia annually for five years in the Nineties, I found a very different country from the one I had known. Yet in 1993, two years after the MMD came to power, the country's state-controlled news media were still struggling to find a new role.

Expression was far freer than under Kaunda. Newspapers and television covered all political parties, and vigorous views not always to the government's liking were found in articles and readers' letters. But ministerial rhetoric and non-story ceremonies remained strongly in evidence on news pages and even more on TV and radio – the familiar recipe from one-party state days.

Discouragingly for supporters of independent media, President Chiluba's government seemed to be in no hurry to give up any of its media, which included the country's two daily newspapers. Nor did it show signs of ending practices like the registration of publications or filtering the output of foreign news agencies like Reuters and Agence France-Presse through the state-owned Zambia News Agency (ZANA).

The government's stance appeared to be that so long as anyone else could start a newspaper there was no reason why it should not keep the two it owned. And if the Times of Zambia and the Zambia Daily Mail were put up for sale it was not clear whether anyone would want to buy them. They had large staffs and obsolete equipment and a combined daily sale in a nation of 8½ million of under 50,000 copies.

Meanwhile, the independent Weekly Post, which started in the late Kaunda days, was believed to have overtaken the Times as the nation's biggest-selling newspaper. The Post was vigorous, annoying and stimulating. It linked Princess Nakatindi Wina, a government minister, with allegations of drug smuggling and financial corruption – the type of story that would have been impossible over much of the Majority World.

Managing director Fred M'membe received the attentions of

the police over a leaked cabinet document. It was one of several such encounters, but the paper continued to appear freely on the streets.

Low newspaper sales reflected the fact that for many Zambians – beset at that time by soaring inflation and the austerities of structural adjustment imposed by the World Bank and the International Monetary Fund – a newspaper had become a luxury. It wasn't always so. A striking feature of Zambia in the Seventies was vendors doing bumper sales in the streets. Yet for the would-be press baron underlying factors remained good: national adult literacy at 73 per cent and urbanisation at 56 per cent – both high for Africa.

Ex-President Kaunda was having difficulty in coming to terms with his loss of power after 27 years. He told a rally in his stronghold Eastern Province that he was giving the nation two months to decide if it wanted him back, and that Zambians did not 'have to wait until 1996' (the next elections) to change the government.

This was read as an invitation to unconstitutional action, but the MMD government, probably not wanting to make a martyr of Kaunda, responded only with words. And it soon became clear that voters did not need two months to consider Kaunda's offer. Public reaction was generally hostile.

A few days later Kaunda appeared to retract. He said he had been misquoted at the rally, and an accurate statement had been blocked. Then he repositioned himself by telling businessmen that centralist economic planning had outlived its usefulness. Africa should embrace free market economics. Bar-room pundits joked that Kaunda could come back under the government banner.

I turned road-going reporter to follow up the story for the Observer News Service, helped by the fact that everyone spoke English. On the streets of Lusaka it was hard to find anyone who supported a comeback by Kaunda.

Grace Phiri, a pavement vendor, said: 'He was a good president. He felt for the people. But his time has gone. Let him rest.' Student Bridget Phiri dismissed him with a sarcastic reference to his advancing years: 'He is my grandfather. If Chiluba has failed, there are others.'

Many Zambians blamed Kaunda for the ramshackle economy. The feeling that he had no right to question the activities of the present government underpinned many of the criticisms.

Electrician Jovito Jere said Kaunda failed to make things work in 27 years, and asked, 'What has changed?' Samson Chama, an airline worker, was more impassioned: 'He left a legacy of utter destruction. Now he wants to return, claim credit for it, and then destroy again what someone else has tried to rebuild.'

Zambians were puzzled about why Kaunda should want to come back at all, with his valuable retirement package – a pension, a new home in a location of his choice, transport, office staff and security – and continued international prominence. The impoverished nation was a small bottle of Mosi (the local beer) compared with the global stage, where Kaunda enjoyed the friendship of South African president Nelson Mandela.

Yet few politicians like to contemplate a career ending in failure, particularly those with the brio to say, as Kaunda did, 'I built this country and I can't destroy it'.

The long Kaunda administration was once widely popular for its progressive policies and commitment to welfare. But with a leader who was often preoccupied with African liberation abroad, it ended with food shortages, soaring prices, padded public payrolls, a disintegrating economy and a pre-revolutionary mood in the country.

Under the one-party state, restrictions on the news media were never total and bar talk flowed; yet the regime practised political repression and even torture – a point that President Chiluba was quick to pick up on. The tragedy of Kaunda is that he came to preside over a regime with a mixed record on human rights – the very issue that won him his international reputation.

Zambia's economic austerity programme spawned a growing army of street children. I interviewed a number of them. Agnes, aged seven, sold unappetising wares from a makeshift stand. The fruits, fried groundnuts and roast meats were covered in dust, with flies alighting here and there. She had no knowledge of food hygiene, but nor did her only customers – other street kids – so it didn't matter too much.

At 10, Katandula was already sexually experienced. Her customers were older street kids who had graduated to the status of 'mishanga' boys, the dubious characters whose activities ranged from hawking cigarettes to stealing them and anything else. If Katandula was typical, by the age of 14 she would have borne an unwanted child; at 20 she would be dead from Aids in a country where HIV infected at least a quarter of the urban population.

At least adult Zambians knew they were suffering the pain of structural adjustment in the hope of eventual gain. Street kids knew only that they suffered.

Boys as young as six were to be seen on the streets. Some just wandered around near restaurants in the hope of leftovers. Outside an eating place in Kamwala township a pack of boys squatted. Whenever a customer threw some food, it was snatched up by the eldest boy and the rest got none. Eventually all drifted away except the youngest, aged around seven.

Calling himself Jimmy, the boy told his tale. He said he had never seen his father, and his mother was out with men during the day and only returned at night. 'I usually pick my food on the streets,' Jimmy started to explain, 'because there is nothing to eat at home and my mother beats me when ...' Before he could finish, an Asian appeared from the restaurant and threw an eggroll at the boy. Jimmy snatched the food and retreated to the nearest gutter. He appeared again after a minute or so licking his lips and ran for home.

Unlike Jimmy, many boys and girls had no home except the streets. If there could be degrees of sadness in such a situation perhaps the saddest were those like Jimmy, who had a home of sorts, but who had to roam the streets to find the basics the home did not supply.

Of course, there were charitable organisations trying to help. But, lacking funds, they were like an army of determined soldiers without guns.

The Family Health Trust focused on orphans, whose parents in most cases had died from Aids. John Munsanjc, manager of the trust's Children in Distress department, reported surprisingly: 'Children, especially orphans, go to the streets because that is where they seem to get love and solace.' He and his colleagues tried to give that support in more benign ways, feeding the children and sending them to school until they had a chance to fend for themselves.

At the Zambia Red Cross Society's day centre in Lusaka's Garden Compound, children aged between five and 18 were taught carpentry, brick-making, tailoring and homecraft as well as school subjects. A spokeswoman regretted that a 'get rich quick' attitude among many Zambians was threatening the charitable support on which the centre depended. She said: 'No one is ready to share what he has with a neighbour. One would rather see his friend die than give a helping hand.'

The Human Rights Association of Zambia formed a club to teach street kids practical skills. Trustee Mrs Maureen Mainbwe said: 'It is painful to see innocent young children roaming the street with nothing to do when they should be in school. However, parents cannot afford the fees.'

Concerned adults wished more companies would follow the example of Armcor Security, which recruited more than 20 ex-street kids who had been rehabilitated at the Red Cross centre.

The government, meanwhile, was lacking in serious action. With growing unemployment, continuing though slowing inflation, a crumbling manufacturing sector and all-but-invisible tourism, it seemed to have no energy left for the street kids.

My final assignment for the Friedrich Naumann Foundation included a short course in neighbouring Malawi. It was my first opportunity to visit the country. External training courses were of limited use under the restrictive regime of Dr Hastings Banda, when every front page had to include a picture of the great man, and none was to be higher than his. By now the nonagenarian Banda had gone.

Hartmut had the inspired idea of holding the course at a resort hotel beside Lake Malawi rather than in Lilongwe, the capital. It gave me a first-hand look at some of the problems of this tiny country. The surrounding hills were progressively deforested as people, invariably women, ranged farther and farther for fuelwood. This triggered soil erosion, not to mention the ordeal for the women of having to spend hours each days walking to find fuel.

Cattle were herded to the lake at the end of the day to water themselves – an elegaic scene that would have appealed to the poet Thomas Grey. The cattle also relieved themselves in the lake, while human beings nearby used the water for drinking and cooking. Result: bilharzia.

The Central Office of Information sent me to Ghana in 1992 for a five-day workshop along with staffer Ian Carmichael. We were to go there and back in the week. This was a new experience for me, used to digging in for a month or more. Yet in the jet age there was no reason not to make short visits, and the course went well. For the participants it was a one-week course like any other. When we came and went was no concern of theirs.

I was surprised and depressed by the condition of Accra. I remembered it in 1973 as trim, clean and empty compared with

Lagos, which was run-down, dirty and crowded. Now Accra was like Lagos had been: run-down, dirty and crowded – a sad comment on unsustainable population growth and economic hopes unfulfilled.

Ian and I saw the massive public buildings put up by the former president, Kwame Nkrumah. These were derided in the West as 'prestige projects', but they celebrated Ghana as the first African state to achieve independence. At least at first, they must have been a source of pride for Ghanaians. We came across a large, older, white house with an armed guard at the gate. I should have known better, but I asked him: 'Who lives here then?'

Immediately the man was suspicious. He fingered his rifle (but did not actually raise it). I was clear that at this point we were not free to go. 'For God's sake keep smiling and don't argue,' I whispered to Ian.

'Who are you and what do you want?' the sentry demanded.

'We're just tourists taking a walk and looking at the fine buildings you have in Accra,' I replied.

'Where are you staying? What have you come for?'

Questions continued like this and I responded, doing my best to keep smiling. Ian seemed content to leave it to me.

Suddenly, without any obvious reason, the sentry broke into a smile. It was a 180-degree turn. He said nothing, but I took it as a sign that we could leave. 'Good evening then,' I smiled.

We turned and walked back along an uncomfortably long, straight road in full view of the sentry. 'Don't look round!' I urged Ian.

The building was Flagstaff House, the official residence of the head of state, Flight Lieutenant Jerry Rawlings. He had come to power in a coup, and sealed it by executing several of his predecessors.

As an old hand said, 'A smile goes a long way in Africa!'

Nearer home, I worked at a private college in Cyprus in 1991 and 1992 on courses arranged through Britain's National Council for the Training of Journalists. Kes College, somewhat incongruously, dealt with beauty therapy and journalism (not with the same students!). I took on some topics within longer journalism courses.

Kes was owned by Theo Stylianou, who was a headmaster in the state system. His entrepreneurship would have been unusual among teachers in Britain; it was less so in developing countries, as Cyprus was then. He and his wife also owned an orange grove. He gave me a bag of fine, fresh fruit from his trees.

The fundamental fact of Cypriot life was that it was partitioned (as it still is) between the Greek south and the Turkish north. Greeks and Turks could not visit each other's sector, although years later this restriction was eased. Tourists on the Greek side had very strictly limited access to the other side; from the other side, by the Greeks' decision, they had none at all.

I took the opportunity of seeing what I could of the north. It was perhaps 300 yards but it could have been three miles the first time you did it, walking alone along the road between empty and war-gutted villas, overlooked by United Nations troops cleaning their guns on the balconies of the Ledra Palace – the once grand hotel stranded in a Nicosian no man's land.

It was the only crossing point between the two Cypruses, and only foreigners might use it. You had to be back on the Greek side by 5 pm. No shopping was allowed while on the Turkish side.

The partition of Cyprus could not have been more bad-tempered. The ramshackle wall that bisected Nicosia Old Town was guarded by three lines of soldiers: Greek, Turk and United Nations. From the Greek side you could phone anywhere in the world except Famagusta down the road.

At Nicosia Airport, the hulk of an airliner could be seen. It was caught up in the 1974 fighting, and had been mouldering away ever since. The airport itself was out of use. Visitors to the Greek Cyprus had to use Larnaca on the island's southern coast while the Turks upgraded a small aerodrome near Nicosia – within easy reach of guns the Greeks did not dare use.

At Varosha, a suburb of Famagusta, by now an abandoned ghost town, giant cranes stood over partially completed hotels. They were just as they were in 1974 when they were overrun by the tide of war.

Tourists can be as nervous as impalas. Many, I heard, were afraid to cross to the Turkish side, although the same people would happily book a holiday in mainland Turkey. But I was in barely better shape as I walked through the Ledra Palace crossing, alone, under the guns, camera in hand and with visions of a Turkish jail before my eyes.

What I found over the wall struck me more forcibly than going from West to East Berlin in the Communist heyday (the Greeks' intention in allowing tourists to visit, I was told). It was like passing through a looking glass. I seemed to be in another city: in Asia, not the Europe I had left minutes ago. The place even seemed to have twice as much dust.

Eventually I discovered there were two reasons for this. Greek Cyprus had become wealthy – so rich that union with Greece, once a great political cause, was dead – on tourism and as a communications centre (a great and safe place for Middle East watchers); it showed in the size and glitter of the shops and buildings.

These developments had bypassed the 'Turkish Republic of Northern Cyprus', a state recognised by no one except Turkey and the target of numerous UN condemnations. This isolation declared itself in the run-down and ageing look of Nicosia on the Turkish side.

The other reason for the Middle Eastern feel of Turkish Nicosia was that since 1974 thousands of people had been imported into the island from a rustic part of the mainland to make up numbers. Although the Turks held nearly 40 per cent of Cyprus land, their people were originally less than 20 per cent of the population.

The presence of these Anatolian settlers added to the intractability of the Cyprus problem. According to reports, the settlers were scarcely more popular with the local Turks than with the Greeks.

Outside Nicosia, as a taxi drove me round on a well established tourist route, I found North Cyprus not so different from the Greek side, just less frenetic. Kyrenia was like the rest of the Mediterranean used to be, before mass tourism spoilt it. Direct international flights were not allowed, but plenty of British and German holidaymakers were to be seen. They benefited from the polite fiction of first landing in Turkey and then transiting to Cyprus in the same aircraft with a different flight number.

The Turks appeared to be comfortably settled in. Eighteen years of a de facto government was long enough for many of its people to know no other. For all that the invasion had been triggered by provocation from the Greek side, I could not rid myself of the idea that the Turks were making themselves comfortable in someone else's house.

Often they literally were. 'When you get to Famagusta please go and look at my house,' said a woman in Nicosia who had not seen her home since the invasion. It was just a pleasantry, of course.

The Turks had removed the crosses that surmounted Greek Orthodox churches, except in the two churches I saw that had become 'icon museums'. Neglect appeared to be a greater danger than desecration and vandalism to Greek churches because the Turks were too poor to maintain them.

I interviewed the Cyprus president, George Vassiliou, and opposition leader Glafkos Clerides for Gemini news agency. It was in the aftermath of the Gulf War, when many saw a parallel between the United Nations resolutions used to justify the Anglo-American invasion of Kuwait and those on Cyprus.

President Vassiliou, a 58-year-old businessman who was elected as a non-partisan candidate, insisted that the 'solution to the Cyprus problem would benefit Turkey more than anyone else'. He described the Turks' military occupation of northern Cyprus as 'Second World War, Maginot Line kind of thinking' in the rocket era. (Turkey had an estimated 35,000 troops on the island.)

' We aren't asking for General Schwarzkopf [the Gulf War commander] to stop over here, but there is now a world climate in favour of implementation of UN resolutions, which makes the search for the solution to the Cyprus problem more obvious.'

Alas, the president's hopeful interpretation proved wide of the mark! Two decades later there was still no end to the Cyprus problem, Meanwhile, street opinion was succinct: if Cyprus produced oil instead of potatoes, the problem would have been solved long ago.

Vassiliou would not be drawn on similarities and differences between Cyprus and Kuwait, but Clerides warned of the dangers of pressing the parallel. He said: 'What we can and should stress is that we are in front of a new situation where for the first time the Security Council is taking collective action (over Kuwait) to force obedience to its resolutions.

'But if you claim parallels and the Security Council says the Cyprus and Kuwait cases aren't the same, you have really stuck your face out for a punch – and as a politician for more than 30 years I've learnt to duck.'

The 72-year-old lawyer, who later became president of Cyprus, told me: 'I believe that in all the negotiations we have done, including when I was the negotiator, we have started from the wrong end of the stick. We began with the constitutional order, the inside, and we left this vital question of security unsolved. So everything either side suggests is put under a magnifying glass. If you solve the question of future security, the other things would be of much less importance.'

Both Vassiliou and Clerides wanted to see a federated, bizonal (Greek and Turkish) state. This was the solution finally accepted by the Turkish Cypriots under the Annan Plan in 2004 – only to be voted down by the Greek Cypriots. The latter were nevertheless rewarded with admission to the European Union.

Glafkos Clerides offered me a cup of coffee after the interview. 'Would you like a long coffee or Turkish coffee? Of course,' he added with a smile, 'we're supposed to call it Cyprus coffee now, but it's really Turkish coffee!'

Back home, the newscaster Martyn Lewis was making his own headlines with widely reported remarks about television dwelling too much on doom and gloom. Majority World journalists felt the same – it was one of their main impressions about Britain. Many were astonished at the negative tone not just of television but of all the news media.

Lewis was making a simple plea for more balance in the news, but the weight of conventional wisdom quickly descended on him. He deserved a more considered response than he got from Peter Sissons, Jeremy Paxman and other telly heavies who waded in. I wasn't aware of any celebrity journalist who publicly supported Lewis, but this didn't make him wrong.

Sissons said it wasn't the journalist's job to 'go in for social engineering to make people feel better'. Television, he explained, 'is about capturing and retaining the visual interest of a fickle, sensation-jaded multitude, and it is blood, mayhem, destruction, tears, fire and sword which do the trick'. I hoped Sissons was being ironical with this appalling piece of cynicism, with its emphasis on TV as entertainment. But I feared he wasn't.

Jeremy Paxman, just back from the Bosnian war, was equally appallingly frank: 'Those of us who spent last week in Tuzla knew what we were there for. We were waiting to see the thousands of refugees stream out of Srebrenica. We were waiting for bad news.' Hanging in the air seems to be the thought: 'What a pity it didn't happen.' But why regret it? That a bloodbath and uncontrolled exodus of refugees did not happen is itself real news — hard news and good news.

Paxman argued that the good news/bad news debate had been settled years ago, and was summed up as: 'Dog bites man isn't news, man bites dog is.' But he misunderstood the meaning of this excellent dictum. It refers not to good and bad news, but to unusual rather than predictable news. Nothing stops unusual news (the man bites dog type) from being good news. The BBC responded by loftily begging the question in its familiar way. A spokesman said: 'We treat our news priorities in line with other broadcasters around the world.' This told us nothing about whether the priorities were right or wrong; only that they were the same as other people's, by which was meant other Western people.

I felt that negativity affected all British news media, but was particularly an issue with television and, to a lesser extent, radio. In broadcasting, items must be taken in the order in which they are presented. The viewer/listener can't skip around to jollier matter. Sissons and Paxman lifted the curtain on television's secret: that bad news isn't more important or a truer reflection of reality than good news; it is simply more visual.

One after the other come tales of wars, famine, crimes, unemployment and crashes. Each item is true enough but, taken together, the world appears to be a worse and wickeder place than it really is. This news agenda distorts reality. The world is what the media tell us it is, as the authors of the important Glasgow University study *Bad News* were well aware.

I was shocked by the limited mindset displayed by the big names of journalism who commented on the Martyn Lewis affair. They were trapped within a culture-specific understanding of news. Arguably, Western journalism – now as then – suffers from being too event-oriented. Without more attention to the processes behind news situations, a subject breaks surface only as a series of particular events – frequently bad. There is an ongoing positive side to National Health Service hospitals in Britain as well as many lamentable failures, for instance.

Human interest stories – the individual beating the bureaucracy, the long-lost relative, the hill-climbing centenarian, firefighters rescuing a dog, and so on – are happy stories that the media prize. Yet on television they tend to be formulaically left to the end as an 'And Finally' item. They aren't integral to the bulletin.

In comments for the journalists' trade magazine UK Press Gazette, I pointed out that a concentration on gloom and doom was the most common criticism of Western media made by journalists and their managers around the world. These were not advocates of the North Korean style of propaganda journalism, just sensible people who found that negativity, triviality and sensationalism were the three deadly sins of Western journalism. And no country was more sinful than Britain.

FOURTEEN
ON THE ROAD – 1995-2005

In the mid-Nineties, my training work was flourishing but I felt the need to validate it with practical journalism. I was aware of too many teachers and trainers looking at their working experience in the rear-view mirror, ever receding as they became progressively out of touch. This especially applied in an era of technical change like this one, with computers, full colour printing and the internet transforming the news media.

So as well as my work with Guardian I started to look for more journalistic opportunities. Eddie Doogue was one of the pleasantest characters I dealt with in earlier years with the syndication department. He was the London manager for the Sydney Morning Herald, one of our clients. He had moved to Geneva to work with a religious news agency, Ecumenical News International.

I asked Eddie whether he would like some feature articles from London. Just as with the Civil Service College, the timing was fortunate. He had just fallen out with his UK correspondent. He needed news reports rather than features, but I thought I'd have a go. An initial piece – about a campaign to put the cross back into Easter – met with approval. I started to write for ENI regularly, aiming to produce one story a week.

The service was mainly sponsored by the World Council of Churches. It had a network of freelance correspondents around the world. I was happy to be part of the team. Articles were crisply edited, editorialising (the writer expressing opinions) was not allowed and in general the output bore comparison with that of the secular media. The same could not be said of all religious journalism.

The patch had to be built from scratch since in the circumstances I couldn't ask the previous correspondent for help. I made contact with the press officers of the main churches and the several 'ginger groups' within Anglicanism. The traditionalist Forward in Faith movement was a useful source as was, later, the liberal Roman Catholic movement We Are Church. I kept my eyes open for follow-ups from the national media.

Eddie and his colleague Stephen Brown originated many ideas themselves.

One of the main events on my watch was the death of Pope John Paul II after an historically long reign. Along with just about every other religious affairs writer, I failed to predict that Cardinal Joseph Ratzinger would be chosen as Pope. He was supposed to be too old – he was in his upper seventies – and too theologically conservative. We overlooked the long shadow cast by John Paul. Ratzinger had been closest to the late pontiff, at his elbow for years, and to the overawed cardinals choosing him must have seemed like continuing the reign by another name.

The Observer syndication service asked me to do a 'runners and riders' piece about the papal candidates. It was the type of article I hated to write: the odds against being correct were too great! By good fortune, I happened to mention Ratzinger among the outsiders. Honour was saved.

Leaders of the mainstream denominations in the UK poured congratulations on Ratzinger, even though he had traduced most of their churches in the Vatican statement Dominus Iesus as 'not churches in the proper sense'. (The leader of the French Protestants was impolite enough to mention this.) Such is diplomacy. The Catholic bishops in England rushed to congratulate their new boss, although privately most were horrified by the choice.

I was wrong too about Rowan Williams as Archbishop of Canterbury. He was perceived as politically and socially leftist. I therefore expected him to be a radical but stimulating leader. In fact, his public persona was neutral verging on the invisible. He seemed to be preoccupied – understandably – in holding together the Church of England and the worldwide Anglican Communion against the centrifugal forces of gay priests and women bishops.

There was another problem. I was in the press pen at Canterbury Cathedral for his enthronement as archbishop. His inaugural address was baffling in its lack of clarity. We looked at each other and asked, 'What is he saying?' Almost always the news point is clear in a speech. This time it wasn't. Next day's newspaper reports reflected this uncertainty with a variety of intros – for the speaker a public relations disaster. I felt that Williams was too intellectual to be the Chief Pastor of the country.

Where the Anglicans were battling with the issues of gay priests and women bishops, the Roman Catholics – Britain's second largest denomination – had the scandal of paedophile priests. I was in no doubt that the Catholic leadership, despite words to the contrary, was in denial on the issue. There were cases of priests being transferred to other parishes or jobs rather than being laicised and turned over to the authorities.

I was at a press conference when the speaker assured us that paedophilia was no worse in the Catholic church than in other churches, which was provably untrue. The root of it, I was convinced, was compulsory celibacy. If celibacy suits, say, 10 per cent of priests (a high estimate) but is required of 100 per cent, something bad is going to happen. Voluntary celibacy is a key demand of We Are Church.

One of the most interesting church leaders I encountered was Richard Holloway, the primus or chief bishop of the Scottish Episcopal Church. A charming and unassuming man, he agonised about Christianity in the modern world. His book *Godless Morality*, as the title implies, sought to develop a system of ethics that was not derived from God (Christian or otherwise).

I interviewed Holloway face to face at the 1998 worldwide Lambeth Conference of Anglican bishops. The press officers were anxious to prevent the press pestering the thousand or so prelates as they walked around the site at Canterbury. We were instructed to funnel all interview requests through the press office. This struck me as altogether too Stalinist and, taking advantage of an earlier phone encounter with Holloway, I approached him direct. At the appointed time the primus walked into the press centre, to the bemusement of the press officers, who knew nothing of the interview. Score one against bureaucracy!

Godless Morality appeared after Holloway's retirement, but he had chipped away at traditional faith in earlier books. For me, there was an issue of his doing so while still leading the Scottish Anglican church.

Another controversialist was Bishop David Jenkins of Durham. Years before he had called the resurrection a 'conjuring trick with bones'. I interviewed him well into his retirement when I wanted his comment on a report about hell. Like Holloway, he was a charming man. He was less categorical than I expected in saying hell did not exist.

Not all my stories for ENI were about heavy subjects. I gave a lot of attention to offbeat, 'talking point' stories. I spoke to a vicar who was a men's fashion expert – not normally a clergy strong point.

Another vicar was hugely successful with supernatural thrillers, and turned full-time author. I met G.P. Taylor for an interview when he was launching his second book, *Wormwood*. I found him at his publisher's office, autographing his way through piles of copies.

'You can ask your questions while Graham signs the books,' a publicity officer remarked.

This was a new experience for me, and a discourtesy I wasn't prepared to put up with. I explained that I needed the interviewee's undivided attention for a fixed time, say 20 minutes, in exchange for which I would finish on the dot. This was agreed. Graham Taylor readily put down his pen for the duration. I wondered whether the publicity officer was used to journalists talking with multi-tasking authors, to the detriment of the interview.

At least she left the room while I did the interview. I would have objected to her staying. I suspect I would not have lasted long on the film star circuit, where it has become common for press officers to be present at interviews (and to vet copy afterwards).

The saga of the Zurbarans at Auckland Castle provided material for several years. The castle was the official residence of the bishops of Durham. Since the 18th century a series of paintings by the Spanish artist Zurbaran, 'Jacob and his Twelve Sons' (representing the tribes of Israel), had hung there. They were valuable, and the cash-strapped Church Commissioners wanted to sell them. A furore followed.

I bequeathed this long-running story to my successor as ENI correspondent, Martin Revis (a former Guardian colleague). He was able to close it when a philanthropist stepped in to buy the paintings – and leave them where they were.

I wrote more than 500 articles for ENI. Like all news organisations, they had their quirks. Stephen was of the 'Paris is the capital of France' school of backgrounding (writing in unnecessary explanations). Once he explained to the Christian readership that the cross was a key symbol of Christianity. Eddie was obsessed with a bespoke comment on the event ('told ENI ...'). This was right and necessary to add a new element where the story had run previously in the general media; it was artificial and cumbersome where ENI was breaking the story at the same time as others, from a press conference, for example. It could be difficult to find someone who could usefully add a comment to

the hard news. Strange people were rung up in the quest for
'told ENIs'. Eddie's successor, Peter Kenny, took a more prag-
matic approach to bespoke comments.

More seriously, ENI's ban on editorialising – which I supported – extended to interpretation – which I did not. Interpretation was a horse of a different colour, and at the heart of a
revolution in newspaper writing. To describe a decision as
'stupid' is plainly an opinion (to some people it is sensible); to
describe the decision as 'controversial' is an interpretation upon
which both sides in the issue would agree. If both sides in a con-
tested situation agree with the characterisation, that's interpretation.

Interpretations help readers to understand the significance of
a story. Yet to write that liberals and traditionalists were 'on a
collision course' was off ENI's Richter scale, for all that the
colourful phrase was justified by the underlying facts. The
agency was throwing the paper out with the bathwater. In setting its face against the interpretative revolution in journalism,
it gave the articles a dated feel.

I got round the difficulty by planting the interpretation in the
mouth of an anonymous and invented source, by which it
became a news fact (someone else was saying it)! For example:
'Church sources indicated that strong opposition to the decision
was likely.' But I disliked being forced into this stratagem.

With a British general election looming, I wrote that the election was 'widely expected in May 2005'. This was hardly a
daring act of interpretation since the date was an open secret.
The statement emerged on ENI as the election being 'widely
expected by the British media in May 2005'. It was not enough,
it seemed, for the correspondent to make that judgement. When
others made it, that was all right. The election was duly held in
May 2005.

The line between opinion and interpretation isn't especially
hard to draw in practice, but can be intentionally overstepped.
I rarely watch the news on Britain's two main terrestrial television channels for this reason. Reports are full of correspondents'
personal opinions – a process encouraged by journalist interviewing journalist. Newsreaders conduct live interviews with
correspondents in the field, turning them into a source of news
instead of a conduit of news. The correspondents become 'personalities' . They may be interviewed for newspapers and magazines, be featured in the TV papers, progressively for the

viewer becoming part of the stories they are covering.

ENI correspondents were required to deal even-handedly with all denominations. I was never asked about my religious beliefs. Certainly I was no Walter Schwarz. He was the Guardian's religion correspondent who approached Christianity in the spirit of an anthropologist, as if it were a New Guinea cargo cult. I was sympathetic to religion and its achievements, but at bottom I was an 18th century deist – a believer in a created universe but not a personal god. My successor as ENI correspondent, Martin Revis, was an avowed agnostic. When he was appointed, he asked whether this mattered. He was told that his personal beliefs were irrelevant so long as he wrote stories objectively. Which he did.

My last story for ENI, in 2005, was one of the most offbeat. I did another version of it for the Observer syndication service. I visited Imber, a 'ghost village' in the middle of the Salisbury Plain military training area. The church was to be refurbished despite having had no regular worshippers since 1943.

This was a good example of worthwhile news features as follow-ups from a very short press release announcing that fact. I expected to be part of a media queue to visit Imber. It turned out that the local TV station and I were the only ones interested.

Stranded in the middle of a high explosive ' impact area' – at risk of being demolished by a stray shell but somehow surviving all those years – Imber church was a supreme example of the continuities of English life.

At the height of the Second World War, Imber was evacuated when the area was turned over to the Allied military in the build-up to the Normandy Landings and the invasion of Europe. The villagers never came back, but the medieval church of St Giles remained a place of worship and the graveyard was still in use.

I drove into the village with Lieutenant-Colonel Roger Fellowes, commandant of the UK military's Salisbury Plain training estate; just the two of us amid the vastness of the surrounding plain. The emptiness and the silence gave Imber a surreal feeling. The few original buildings that survived were bizarrely mixed in with new houses, windowless and empty, put up by the Ministry of Defence for mock battles and target practice.

A row of council houses had been built at Imber in the late 1930s. They still stood, having been used for their intended purpose for only a few short years. It was easy to imagine Imber as a living village with the pub (the Bell) and the manor house also standing. Both had been reroofed by the army in practical corrugated iron.

Imber was never a substantial place. With a population of 440 at its peak in 1851, it had about 150 inhabitants in the 1930s. Between 1927 and 1932 the authorities bought up tracts of land in the area, and most villagers became tenants of the military. That made it easier to extract them when the time came.

The few surviving villagers, or their sons and daughters, as well as the simply curious liked to visit Imber on the 50 or so days a year that the army allows access. The biggest event was an annual church service on St Giles's day in September.

'There are still many loyalties attached to Imber,' said Richard Trahair, property secretary for the Church of England's Salisbury diocese, which had responsibility for St Giles's church. 'Over the years it has come to be seen as a romantic place. Some people feel the villagers were misled by the army about being able to return after the war, but I've never seen any document to prove that.'

Colonel Fellowes acknowledged that there were still feelings about the 1943 evacuation and its aftermath. 'Inevitably though, they aren't coming back,' he said of surviving villagers or their descendants.

Trahair praised the army for the way it had cared for the church. 'They've looked after it since the war and they've done a good job keeping it going,' he explained.

By 2001, however, the church had become a problem. With major expenditure ahead, the Ministry of Defence indicated it could not continue its support. St Giles's was to be taken over by the Churches Conservation Trust – the story that brought me to Imber. This body was financed mainly by the Church of England and the British government to care for redundant churches.

'It's the best outcome for all who care about St Giles's because it ensures the church's future indefinitely,' said Trahair.

Ironically for a church stuck in a war zone, St Giles's turned out to have more 'hidden treasures', in Trahair's words, than had been supposed. It was uprated to Grade 1 in the British government's conservation categories.

Exposed 15th century wall paintings included a Doom (showing Christ sitting in judgment) and chequered patterns in the arches of the nave. More paintings lay underneath later plaster. There were bell ringers' tables painted on the wall in 1692, while letters carved into the stone of the porch were understood to be the initials of four 17th century church wardens.

All these rarities were set to make Imber even more popular as a place to visit, once the refurbishment had been completed. It was a twist that would have pleased the villagers of 1943.

I returned to Imber in 2011 for a Remembrance service at St Giles's. This time I was driven there in convoy with many others. Some 60 or so of us filled the little church – local people, military figures, well- wishers like me, even dignitaries like the local MP and the mayor of nearby Warminster. Wreaths were laid with due ceremony. I hoped coffee would be produced after the service but it wasn't. Then we all scattered back to the real world, leaving Imber to itself.

It was good to hear from my friend and former Thomson Foundation colleague Tony Thompson in Canada. He was a self-starter so I wasn't surprised to learn that he was now a successful publisher.

Tony had done this before. In the early days of free newspapers in Britain he launched community papers in South London, eventually selling them to a major group. He didn't especially enjoy his time at the Foundation or being a trainer. The Third World, which to me was exotic, was to him a boring place with limited facilities. He soon moved on, to Canada, which as well as its other merits got him away, as he thought, from a romantic entanglement. That didn't work. The entanglement followed him.

He worked as a freelance journalist, choosing the unglamorous subject of insurance because that was where opportunities lay. While at this work he fell into the trap of selling the same article to rival editors. It was accidental. He sold it to the Financial Times in London and also to a business publication in Chicago. He forgot that the FT might syndicate the article – which it did, to another Chicago publication. Soon Tony was fielding calls from two angry American editors. He told this story with relish, knowing it was a trap that any of us might have slipped into.

He then launched his own insurance newsletter under the grandiloquent title of Thompson's World Insurance News. That was similar to the American baseball championship being known as the World Series, and was typically Tony. At the time he contacted me, the newsletter had been running successfully for several years – a major achievement for an individual up against major companies.

Tony and I got on so well because we had similar temperaments. He was more overtly nonconformist than I was, but a strong streak of 'doing it my way' ran in us both. I was happy, therefore, to become his London correspondent. Not from my choosing, I had the portentous title of European Editor.

I was a better writer because of my long spells as a sub-editor. Anyone with subbing experience simply can't waffle with the same joyous abandon as before!

Waffly writing shouldn't be confused with colour writing. Waffle (also known as gobbledegook) expresses ideas at length for no gain: *adverse weather conditions* are simply *bad weather*; *in spite of the fact that* is a long-winded way of saying *although*; *seating accommodation* means nothing more than *seats*; *in short supply* seems innocuous but it doesn't earn its passage as *scarce* does.

Sub-editors dislike long, rambling sentences. Writers also benefit from knowing the impact of breaking many lengthy sentences into two. A useful idea is to look hard at any sentence that has more than two structural elements – for example, a relative clause introduced by *which* and a second statement following the conjunction *and*:

The Battle of Hastings, which was fought in 1066, was a turning point in English history, and added a new tier of overlords.

This can become

The Battle of Hastings, which was fought in 1066, was a turning point in English history. It added a new tier of overlords.

or

The Battle of Hastings was fought in 1066. It was a turning point in English history, and added a new tier of overlords.

Here's another example:

Even though it may not always seem so / shares tend to outperform bonds / although shares should be invested for the medium to long term.

Shorter sentences are one of the main yardsticks of readability. The other is the amount of long words – broadly, those of three or more syllables. We neither can nor should *eliminate/get rid of* all long words, but words that add nothing to the shorter alternative should be chopped. In the previous sentence, *eliminate* and *get rid of* mean the same. Impact and readability are greater with three short words instead of the one long one. So one word instead of three isn't always better!

There are hundreds of such words and phrases in English.

Sometimes it's one short word for one long one: *facilitate* means *help*; *initiate* means *start*.

My penchant for tight writing was honed afresh with the space restrictions of Tony's newsletter.

My father spent his working life of more than half a century in insurance so I had some sensitivity to the field. It was a restricted beat: Thompson's was strictly about property and casualty insurance (known in Britain as general insurance). This was a pity from the viewpoint of sexy stories because most of them were on the life side – the near-collapse of the blue chip life assurer, Equitable Life, and successive misselling scandals.

The one big story on the general side was the near-collapse of Lloyd's of London, then in full swing. This story was to run for several years. Tony's deputy (and successor as owner of Thompson's), Mark Publicover, told me I had transformed their coverage of Lloyd's. I did so through shameless borrowing and innate cunning. I came in in the middle of events, and was feeling my way in the dark. Later, I was able to drop the plagiarism, but a certain circumspection endured with this most complex of subjects.

Essentially, Lloyd's – which insured the biggest of man-made and natural risks around the world – had been hit by a series of disasters including asbestosis that threatened to swamp the resources of the market. This was made up of private individuals, the Names, who invested with unlimited liability but who had customarily enjoyed huge returns.

To contain the crisis, Lloyd's put through Reconstruction and Renewal, which reinsured the risks for 1992 and before in a separate company, Equitas. This allowed the market to be rebuilt for ongoing business. Many of the Names resented the cost of transferring their risks to Equitas. Over the years, diminishing groups fought stubborn legal actions in Britain and America, which they lost.

The new Lloyd's came to be dominated by limited liability syndicates, some of them owned by major outside insurers and others by Names who had set up such vehicles. Traditional Names found their share of the risks being underwritten, and therefore the profit potential, much reduced. However, the formula worked and profitability returned to Lloyd's.

Along the way, I discovered how if you were rich enough you could invest the same money twice. The investor was liable for the full amount subscribed (had to make that money available if needed), and took the profit from that. However, only a small part of these 'funds at Lloyd's' was actually handed over. The rest could be invested elsewhere, for a second profit on the same money. No wonder Lloyd's was popular with the wealthy!

Tony Thompson's flair came at a price. Despite his cheeky chappie persona, he was highly strung. This, I imagined, was a cause of his health problems. His bowel was removed and he had to use a stoma. The last time I saw him was when he visited London, and I hosted a dinner for him and our former Thomfound colleague John Cardownie. We made the mistake of getting on to the subject of the stoma over the meal.

Tony died, in his late sixties, not long after I started writing for Thompson's. The work was ably carried on by Mark Publicover and Jes Odam. A veteran in his seventies, Jes had been the technology editor on a Vancouver daily paper, and now ran Thompson's daily electronic feed.

This was sent by email, and had a simple but effective format. Every issue had three items of 200 words each plus a wrapping paragraph of shorts including funnies where they could be found. London – ie me – specialised in funnies. I copied this format for the Pulford Media newsletter, finding that the strict length limit produced crisp yet comprehensive items. I even used a version of the idea for an entire book (*Byliners: 101 Ways to be a Freelance Journalist* – see Chapter 16).

When the electronic service started, I had a problem of capacity. I was already on call daily for ENI on top of my training activities. I could not cope with another daily commitment. It was better not to promise what I couldn't deliver. I made an arrangement with Jes to file once a week as before (except for urgent hard news), and he would trickle the stories out through the week.

Mark was based in Toronto and Jes in Vancouver. As a reminder of how big Canada is, it emerged that although working so closely together they had never met. Both were delightful people to work with for nine years. I gave up the beat with sadness, handing it over to one of my former students, Louise Pevreal.

I placed half a dozen or so features in national papers, but mainly I preferred to concentrate on ENI and Thompson's. These and my training work kept me more than busy. An additional job I took on, as a volunteer, was to write a column for BAJ News, the quarterly newsletter of the newly formed British

Association of Journalists.

I produced around 50 columns before handing over in 2005 to Jane Furnival. She developed the column excellently and continued to write it until soon before her premature death from cancer in 2012.

The BAJ was founded by Steve Turner and a group of Mirror journalists as a breakaway from the National Union of Journalists. The NUJ had been well to the left of most of the membership for years, diverting much of its energy to political campaigns. Steve, a moderate, had been overwhelmingly elected as the union's general secretary. In a very short time he had fallen out with the National Executive Committee and was fired. A court action decided that he had been unlawfully dismissed, but he was not reinstated.

Partly because of my previous Mirror associations but mainly because of what I saw as the injustice of being wrongly dismissed but not reinstated, I resigned from the NUJ to join BAJ. It remained a mystery why more journalists did not do the same. BAJ was undoubtedly closer than the NUJ to the views of most journalists, yet it took years before membership reached four figures (the NUJ having a claimed total of 38,000 members [2012]).

Steve and his wife, Deborah, set about recruitment drives with huge commitment. He brought the same vigour to industrial relations. His great strengths were his encyclopaedic knowledge of employment law and his skill in negotiations. He represented aggrieved members in their battles with management, usually winning substantial compensation for them.

The column that I wrote was Freelance Forum. Members reported, anonymously as far as the readers were concerned, fees they received and any experiences they wished to share. The idea was to build up a picture, like a pointilliste painting, of conditions in the trade.

It emerged that the fees for articles were substantially higher in the mass circulation newspapers than in the so-called quality press, and were very low – commonly less than £100 – in small magazines. Both were to be expected, but we found that fees were disgracefully low in important regional daily newspapers, where a major article might command little more than £100.

Late payments were common although this could vary dramatically from desk to desk within the same publication, some being very prompt, others being very slow. Fees for articles and casual shift payments had in many cases been frozen for years.

One of the most striking findings was that fees in glossy consumer magazines were just as high as in mass circulation newspapers – but editors expected much more for their money.
Because of the tradition of active sub-editing in newspapers,
writers were rarely asked to rewrite; in magazines it was
common, sometimes more than once.

While some freelance journalists were commanding huge
fees, mainly for articles or pictures about celebrities or the royal
family, the situation for the full-time jobbing freelance was fairly
discouraging. Nevertheless, BAJ surveys repeatedly found that
most long-term freelances did not want a staff job. It's the independence, stupid.

Low fees didn't necessarily bother the spare-time freelance,
but they were a problem for someone wanting to be full time.
For that reason, many freelances bulked up their earnings with
teaching, public relations work or casual subbing shifts. Or else
they were freelances in name only, working for one publication
but without the security of staff status. To help the latter type of
worker, Tony Blair's government had legislated to give supposedly casual workers some of the rights of employment.

Thanks to Steve Turner, I was a beneficiary of the new law. I
had been working at the Guardian for one or two days a week
for years. At some point, we argued, this casual association had
morphed into part-time employment. This would entitle me to
a pro-rata pension. BAJ's lawyers pursued the claim on my
behalf. The company resisted stubbornly, and with their top-end
City lawyers must have spent more in fees than the money at
issue.

Steve said he had lost count of the number of cases that were
settled 'on the courtroom steps', metaphorically and sometimes
literally. Delay was the standard tactic to rattle the claimant into
giving up or settling for less. So it proved in this case, not once
but twice. At the very last moment the Guardian offered a lump
sum in lieu of pension first going back a few years and finally
to the date that we wanted.

I saw it as a famous victory. I said to Andy Badenoch, the editorial head of syndication: 'The good guys won!' 'I don't know
about that,' he answered non-committally. It was all he could
say.

Syndication, when done properly, was interesting and challenging. The combination of selecting stories and re-editing

material to suit foreign readers – adding explanation where needed and removing parochial references, for example – made the work a combination of copy tasting and sub-editing. It was a specific skill that newcomers to the desk had to learn.

The fact that the daily syndication service was a one-person operation was an attraction for me. I realised that I no longer liked to work in a team. I had been a loner for so long. I was also losing my tolerance for noise in a busy office – not the most useful state of mind for a journalist!

At one time the syndication desk was located in the Guardian features room. I was distracted by the constant chatter and personal telephone calls. Things were better when we were transferred to the newsroom one floor below in the Farringdon Road building. Here the atmosphere was quieter and more businesslike because people had more to do. The syndication sub-editor *always* had something to do because a substantial story count was expected from the shift. Best of all was when syndication shifted to our own quarters in an annex.

My desire for isolation was indulged further when Lis Ribbans, Donald Wintersgill's successor as syndication editor, asked me if I would like to be the regular Sunday sub. This meant I would have our floor to myself, and often the whole building. Being 'Mr Sunday' suited me in another way: it left the working week free for my stringer jobs (ENI and Thompson's) and training courses.

A snag was that the floor was reached by a tiny lift – barely more than a vertical coffin – which was operated by swiping a fob. (The fobs were individually programmed to allow access to particular floors.) Occasionally the fob failed to register the command, which added to the feeling of dodgy technology. To be stuck in a coffin in an empty building on Sunday night would be no small thing! For a while I phoned security back at the main building to say I was about to make the ascent; then I phoned them from the summit to say I'd arrived. I stopped doing it because it seemed so wet. I didn't allow myself to climb the four flights of stairs for the same reason.

The Guardian switched to a new operating system, Quark using Macintosh computers. It didn't make much difference to the syndication service, although we lost a useful feature of the former Atex system. This allowed a 'long directory': the first few lines of each file were exposed, meaning that you could usually tell whether the story was wanted or not without opening the file. With Quark all you saw was the file name: you had to open the file to find what it was about. The time added up over a shift – but I don't suppose the IT department thought to ask syndication what we wanted.

Quark was the sixth operating system I had to get my head round. I was a late user of word processors (the computer-typewriter hybrid). I had three in succession, each with a different operating system. For many years I did ENI and Thompson's work on the tiny Psion handheld computer (personal digital assistant). Then came Atex and now Quark. Finally I obtained a laptop and with it Windows for my seventh and (I hope) last system.

Other British national newspapers were occasional buyers of Guardian material, a useful type of spot sale. The Daily Mail had a particular liking for our features, which it reprinted a day or so later. It knew that the overlap of readers between the two papers was minimal, to say the least. These sales originally meant a great injustice for the freelance author of the article concerned. He or she made nothing from the further publication. Even worse, the Guardian got the article for nothing and more – selling it to nationals like the Mail for more than it paid the contributor.

I helped a National Union of Journalists working party to right this wrong. A freelance charter was hammered out. The proceeds of spot sales were now split 50:50 between the newspaper and the contributor.

I retired from my one-day-a-week job with the Guardian in 2003, aged 65, although I continued to write for the Observer syndication service. I was proud that in almost 20 years of shifts I had never missed a day through illness. Sometimes I had to call on the services of Dr Theatre, an able practitioner who gave the same prescription to thespians and non-thesps alike: get on with it! I might feel like death, then I'd forget about it during the shift, after which I went back to feeling ill again.

Two years later I gave up freelance journalism, including ENI and Thompson's, to concentrate on writing books. At 67, I was suffering from news fatigue. I had reached the point when I reacted to news with an 'Oh my God, I've got to do something about that!' No journalist should ignore such a signal. It was time for something else.

FIFTEEN
ENTREPRENEUR

Throughout my years as a road-going reporter I continued with my training work. The activities took up roughly equal amounts of the week. I was doing two jobs, with the hours to prove it. This was bearable because I enjoyed it and because I controlled my own workload. Every freelance is at the beck and call of clients, but within that limitation I could decide for myself when I worked, what I worked at and – thanks to laptops and internet cafes – even where I worked.

I didn't set out to organise my own courses, but the opportunity arose to do so. By the early Nineties the Writing for a Market course run by the National Council for the Training of Journalists (Chapter 12) had been reduced under market pressures from six days to two days. Then the NCTJ announced they were closing it. The economics of short courses, then and since, were difficult, but as the course leader I reckoned it was rescuable. I offered to take it over myself with a company I had formed, Pulford Media Ltd.

All the NCTJ had to do was to refer future applicants to PML, receiving in return 10 per cent of the gross fees from these and our own direct enrollees. We would bear all the costs and take the profits. This offer, which was accepted, betrayed my financial inexperience. It was a potentially expensive way to buy into their client base. Their return was guaranteed, but I was taking all the risks and might make a loss. The sensible route would have been to share the net profits after income and outgoings were taken into account.

Nevertheless, I was delighted that the course had been saved. Now titled News and Feature Writing, it was unique so far as I knew in bringing these two key strands of journalism together under one roof on a short course. The pairing echoed what many of the course members did in their jobs.

The London hotel where the course was housed changed its tariff, and it was necessary to move. I rented space at the London Centre of the Civil Service College, where colleagues and I were tutoring media skills courses. Barbara Rowlands continued to work with me on News and Feature Writing;

later, Chris Howe, a Daily Telegraph sub-editor, also taught sessions.

An attraction of the short course business is that profit rises steeply after a certain number of enrolments is passed. The main direct costs are tutor fees and hire of the venue. These are the same whether the course is run with three or 30. However, the NCTJ had not planned to close the course without a reason. We ran the course three or four times a year, but enrolments rarely rose above four per course. This meant that News and Feature Writing washed its face, but did little more.

My philosophy was that if a course covered its costs it was worth doing. It was a shop window for the more profitable in-house courses, a number of which came my way. I did training for Protestant newspapers in Northern Ireland and Catholic newspapers in the Irish Republic, concluding from the experiences that the Irish north and south weren't as different from each other as they thought.

Short courses, once important enough to have their own department, were becoming seen as peripheral at the NCTJ. The focus was firmly on running the reporters' proficiency examination and accrediting the colleges that taught it. When Rob Selwood, the chief executive, decided to drop the Design short course (which I tutored), Pulford Media took it on.

My former schoolfellow Roderick Thomson joined me as company secretary. Together we created an ambitious slate of short courses that included Proof Reading, Press Releases and Freelance Journalism as well as the staple writing and design courses.

By the late Nineties full colour was coming in strongly in newspapers. It was obvious that the various colours were being used editorially without much awareness of what they signalled, or how they could be used effectively in page elements beyond pictures (like borders, panels, drop-in quotes and headlines). I spent much time and effort preparing an Editorial Colour course. It was a party that few came to, and sadly it had to be dropped. Meanwhile, colour continued to be used to nothing like its full potential.

The joint venture with the training council, helmed on their side by the short course manager, Jan Alder, proved harmonious and long-lasting. But I was determined that PML would be more than their operating arm. I insisted that course certificates of attendance were issued by Pulford Media in our own name 'in association with the National Council for the Training of Journalists'.

No one got rich from the short courses, but they brought benefits to both sides. PML had a place in the market that we couldn't have obtained by ourselves; the NCTJ had a range of courses that they continued to brand as their own, with minimal effort and at a time when they had financial concerns.

Together we delivered a series of courses for Amnesty International. We agreed to share the net profits 50:50. We had won the contract in a competitive tender. I'm sure the NCTJ brand helped, but Pulford Media had the tutor resources to put the programme over successfully. The star, however, was a tutor from the training council side – Fabian Acker, idiosyncratic, lovable and a grammatical purist.

AI staffers for whom English was a foreign language couldn't help warming to Fabian on the uses and misuses of the comma. Soon they were immersed in the correct application of 'that' and 'which', which even Shakespeare and the Book of Common Prayer didn't always get right, at least by our current understanding. This nugget was invariably praised in the course feedback forms.

The NCTJ was rocked to its core when death claimed two chief executives in quick succession. Rob Selwood died in hospital of generalised organ failure. His successor, Sally Mellis, was in post only a few months. She had no chance to make a mark before she had to stand down with the cancer that soon killed her. Both were in their fifties.

I hardly knew Sally, but I was deeply upset by Rob's premature death. He was always positive about our joint venture and, more importantly, he did so much to save the NCTJ from its financial near-collapse. He was always cheerful, one of life's most important qualities. I wrote obituaries of them both for the Guardian, and attended their funerals. Both occasions were packed with professional associates, family and friends – a happy affirmation that they had lives outside journalism training.

Sally's successor was Joanne Butcher. She was a young woman brought in from the outside. She stabilised the organisation by serving for years. She was always cordial towards me, but short courses did not seem to be a priority. We never developed the professional closeness that Rob and I had enjoyed.

Pulford Media put much effort into developing our own

client base for in-house programmes. We created a course for witnesses in court, and ran this for a government agency. My friend David Brummell, a senior government lawyer, was among those supplying the legal input.

The influential Fairplay shipping magazine (later Lloyd's Register-Fairplay) was an important client for our journalism training. Any technical magazine faces the issue of whether to recruit people who know the subject or people who know journalism. Is it more effective to train the specialist to be the journalist or the journalist to be the specialist? At Fairplay, editor Paul Gunton and his colleagues believed that maritime experience and knowledge were vital; hence the editorial staff contained a good few sea dogs as well as youngsters learning the ropes of journalism.

I ran courses for both groups, and found that the middle-aged ex-mariners were well able to adapt to the demands of journalism. With sufficient motivation, people of many ages and prior backgrounds can become successful journalists. The point was proved in a different setting when Pulford Media was invited to train former printers at the Evening Post, Bristol. They were to be become sub-editors.

The age-old craft of composing type for printing was finally superfluous in Britain. Now material was typed only once, mainly by reporters, with all other operations – newsdesk vetting, sub-editing, page make-up – performed on screen. This was 'single keystroking', which made the compositors who reset type from edited paper copy redundant. The make-up comps, who assembled galleys (trays) of metal type into pages, were redundant, too. Some printers and assistants were still needed to operate the printing presses.

As I discovered as I went around the Majority World, the computer revolution came very late to the British newspaper industry. I saw things in Zambia that were unknown in Britain. This was because of determined opposition from the printing unions, the National Graphical Association and SOGAT. Their resistance was broken, amid bitter disputes and angry scenes, first by Eddie Shah and then Rupert Murdoch. From there the revolution became general.

Eddie Shah was a small-town newspaper owner who was gripped by the potential of the new technology. From his provincial base he went national in 1986 with a daily newspaper, Today. It was produced by non-union labour.

Rupert Murdoch, the owner of the Times and Sunday Times, circumvented the NGA and SOGAT another way. An alternative workforce from the electricians' union was trained at a secret plant in Wapping, in London's Docklands. When the new workers were ready, the surprise was sprung and production was transferred, also in 1986. Sections of British opinion hadn't forgiven Murdoch or the electricians more than 20 years later, and probably never would. Many of us realised, however, that the Gordian knot had to be cut.

The displaced printers were compensated in a variety of ways. At the Evening Post the small group of volunteer compositors were retrained as sub-editors as part of an agreement with the unions. The EP editor was the affable Brian Jones, ex-Guardian deputy editor and one of the ablest men not to have edited that newspaper. He took a great interest in the experiment.

I found the former printers took to the work easily. They were bright, and I wondered what circumstances had put them on the wrong side of the blue collar/white collar divide. It would be too simple to say lack of educational opportunities, although that was very likely part of it. Perhaps it was choice, or family tradition, or the job openings available at the time.

A pleasantly different assignment for me was to judge the entries in the Association of Free Newspapers design competition. For several years I took on the substantial chore of looking at hundreds of pages from a visual point of view; then – the easier part – picking the winners in the various categories.

It could throw up conundrums, like the newspaper that was excellent in all departments except the front page, which was terrible. How do you rate that in the category for the paper overall? I felt it wasn't right to disqualify the newspaper for a bad front page, and gave it the prize. It was nevertheless an embarrassment to see that front page displayed on the winners' board.

The design of the free papers was generally competent, but with few examples of real flair. This was not surprising given the constraints of time and limited staffing under which they were produced. It was hard to be brilliant in pages dominated by advertisements.

Because the newspapers were free, income came only from advertising rather than the classic mix of advertising and circulation. It varied widely from title to title, but the proportion of ads in the paper could be as high as 80 or 90 per cent – compared with the 50 or 60 per cent typical of paid-for titles.

It seemed for a while as if free newspapers would become universal in the local press. One of the attractions was said to be that you could guarantee how many copies were distributed: the paper was put through people's front doors whether they wanted it or not. Paid-for sales could not be so precisely gauged.

But it never worked out that way. A hybrid local scene persisted, with some titles free and others paid for. Many factors were at play. One of them was that verified free distribution didn't mean verified into everybody's home. Piles of free newspapers left in public places or, worse, bundles of them dumped over someone's hedge did nothing for advertisers' confidence.

It took me several years to rid myself of the idea that at a certain level of reputation, business would come of its own accord. Eventually I realised that by and large there is no such level. The world's must successful corporations must constantly refresh the public's awareness. I've never been a networker; have never wanted to be. Looking back over my career, I see that so many jobs both in training and in journalism have flowed from prior contacts. Even more might have done if I'd been ready to network.

By 2007 Pulford Media and the NCTJ were still living together, but we were destined never to marry. The short courses weren't going anywhere much even with the training council's brand and marketing resources behind them. PML added its efforts with an attractive quarterly e-newsletter and mailshots, again without great success.

I decided to try to grow our way into bigger profits by increasing the number and range of courses one year. One of the apparent attractions of short courses is that they incur no upfront charges if they are called off in sufficient time. Neither the tutor nor the venue need cost anything (depending on agreements with them) if a course has to be cancelled through lack of support.

The snag is that the reputation of the company is on the line if it keeps announcing courses and cancelling them. With that in mind, we sometimes ran courses for two people. The result was that the top line shot up and the bottom line went down – it was costing PML money to put courses on!

The NCTJ had other courses that we weren't part of and that were good profit earners: a law course and refreshers for the reporters' proficiency examination. I therefore proposed in 2007 to buy these courses from them without any money! I suggested that we would relieve them of the courses in exchange for an equity stake in an expanded Pulford Media. My pitch was that, with our single focus on short courses, we could develop their potential better than they could. The idea didn't get beyond square one, which was an opportunity lost for both sides.

With the avenue of open courses blocked, I decided that Pulford Media's best prospects lay with tailored training for companies and government departments. At a meeting with Joanne Butcher and Jan Alder, I explained that we wished to give up the short course partnership. They were taken by surprise – because they were on the point of telling me the same! They also were dissatisfied with the uptake for short courses, and wanted to manage them themselves in order to build them up. Since they were already marketing the courses, it was unclear what they could do for themselves that they weren't doing for the joint venture. So far as I was concerned, though, they were welcome to try. We amicably went our separate ways.

It was good to see that News and Feature Writing continued to be offered under the NCTJ flag. This was the course that I saved from their decision to close it all those years ago.

Pulford Media had plans for the future, but it was to be one where I was no longer 'out front'. I had long earmarked 70 as my age to retire from teaching. This was in 2008. By then it would be three years since I had plied the journalism trade. I had always felt that journalism teachers should keep doing it for real. Even more importantly, I had seen too many trainers and journalists going on into their seventies when past their best. I didn't want that for me.

We had an established team of tutors and technicians to continue the work. I remained active with 'back room' tasks like accounts, invoices, payments and statutory returns. Liz Tayfun joined as training manager, taking on the operational management that I gave up.

Since then, I haven't missed teaching. 'Glad to have done it, glad not to be doing it' has been my attitude.

Liz happened to be my sister. She was the first choice for the job not because I wanted to build a family business but because of her substantial training experience, albeit in the different area of personal development. We told our team of trainers about the relationship, but we neither concealed it not proclaimed it to the clients.

A hard worker like her brother, Liz put enormous energy into PML, which was a part-time job that she combined with her own slate of activities. She was based in Geneva, having spent much of her career with the United Nations and where many of her clients were to be found.

We calculated, correctly as it turned out, that having the training manager out of the country would not be a problem. In the days of emails, wi-fi and Skype, location had become largely irrelevant. There was also the upside that through her contacts she might land us some international NGOs.

Pulford Media, through Liz's efforts, won a competitive tender for media skills courses with a major United Nations agency. Our tutor, Michael Dodd, delivered the programme in Geneva, Nairobi, Kinshasa and Budapest, with either Rick Ives or York Smith as the technician. In Kinshasa the team was joined by Isolda Agazzi as the Francophone tutor.

Working in the Democratic Republic of Congo was not for the faint-hearted with 'continuing tension and insecurity' following a civil war, according to the British Foreign Office. We were aware of the responsibility of asking a team to go there. However, the UN agency judged the situation in Kinshasa stable enough to gather two dozen or so of its representatives from across French-speaking Africa and beyond to take part in the training. Mike and his colleagues bravely decided to follow that lead.

The sessions – in English and French – took place in what turned out to be an oasis of calm, the Memling Hotel, in the centre of the city. A fellow guest was a representative of the former colonial power, the Belgian minister of foreign affairs (despite Belgium not having had a government all year).

Outside the Memling the city was abuzz all hours. The DRC is one of the poorest and most populous African countries, with more than 70 million people – at least a tenth of them crammed into sprawling Kinshasa.

Commercial activity, or attempted commercial activity, happened on all fronts at all times. The team's drives from and to the airport were along a highway with huge numbers of people amassed on both sides – doing deals, transporting goods or just being part of the throng. The central market places were much the same although with far more sellers than buyers, underscoring the tough economic times.

Kinshasa wasn't yet geared for tourism. Visitors were advised not to walk near the banks of the Congo because of lingering instability after an attempted coup when the president's riverside residence came under fire. And yet the energy, dynamism and general cheeriness of the ordinary people promised a valuable foundation upon which to build tourism and more.

Our UN contract was a heartening achievement as the world battled the worst recession since the 1930s. Training is always one of the first casualties of companies looking to cut their spending, so inevitably training providers would suffer. It was reported, to no one's surprise, that in the UK 'companies involved in professional services and in travel and tourism were the worst hit' for critical financial distress – ie heading for the rocks. Even the survivors wondered whether editorial training as a business had a worthwhile, long-term future.

SIXTEEN
AUTHOR

The void left by freelance journalism was filled by book writing. For years, like every journalist, I'd wanted to write a book. Most never do. As I approached 60, I looked likely to stay in that club.

I had made desultory attempts over the years. In my twenties I entered a novel-writing competition run by the publishers MacGibbon and Kee. When the manuscript was returned, I looked at the story again and agreed it was dreadful. I put it in a drawer and left it.

A supposed journalism textbook was nothing more than a collection of my lesson handouts. It didn't add anything to the existing range of textbooks. I produced expanded synopses – mini-books but not of commercially publishable length – on the menace of the motor car and the menace of the United States. By the Eighties, however, these subjects were looking dated.

I proposed a triple biography of Kwame Nkrumah, Julius Nyerere and Kenneth Kaunda, with the common thread that these three were radical African leaders who with the best on intentions had run their countries into the ground. It failed to interest the publishers, Fourth Estate.

With hindsight, I find these subjects embarrassingly all over the place. I had ignored two of the basic rules of authorship. I was not writing out of my own experience. They were simply subjects that interested me, but in none apart from journalism was I a specialist. Publishers, naturally, are interested in authors with specialised knowledge and with a record of newspaper and magazine articles in the subject.

My second failing was to give up too easily. Each of my ideas was offered to only one publisher, where it was offered at all; yet many books that went on to be huge successes have been initially rejected, sometimes by publishers queueing up to say no, from *Pride and Prejudice* to Harry Potter.

Several factors came together to enable me finally to produce my first book. Work for Ecumenical News International had given me confidence in writing about religion. I was struck by a tiny section in Thomas Pakenham's monumental *The Scramble for Africa*. He described how deep in the interior and three months' march from the coast, Anglican and Roman Catholic missionaries hurled insults at each other from opposing hilltops in what became the city of Kampala, Uganda. This episode was so bizarre that I immediately thought, 'I can do something with this.'

As I looked into the subject, I found that the British colonisation of Uganda was carried out in three unusually clearcut stages – Henry Morton Stanley's visit of exploration produced an appeal for missionaries, to which the Anglicans responded, and the presence of the Anglican missionaries, through the enormous publicity that was generated in the home country, led directly to Britain's military conquest. These stages would give a book a worthwhile overarching theme.

I spotted an obituary of a writer who had produced an 'unpretentious' historical book 'entirely from secondary sources'. An unpretentious book, making use of my African experience, was all I wanted to produce. That chance item gave me a green light. I had neither time nor access to study primary records in London and Kampala, but I could dig into the subject with published books. Thanks to the London Library, I studied the writings of those who were there at the time as well as modern commentaries.

The result was *Eating Uganda* (1999). The title came from the African expression, 'eating the country', meaning to take control of it. It was of modest length, 70,000 words. Writing it was harder than I expected. Having acquired a facility with 1,000-word articles, I assumed that the book would be no harder than writing 70 articles, which given time was not hard at all. It wasn't like that. The difference of scale made it a different job. So did the need to maintain a theme.

It was true, however, that if you write 1,000 words a day, an easy quota for a writer, you will complete the book sooner rather than later. I found it essential to keep trudging on. It was no use waiting for inspiration: the mood came from the writing, not the writing from the mood. My philosophy was, and is, to get something on paper or screen, even if it appeared to be rubbish. The writing probably wasn't be that bad, but even if it was the juices were flowing by then and the passage could be revised or rewritten.

Eating Uganda had a hostile review in the Journal of African History and a favourable review by a bishop in the Church Times. Academic Richard Reid in the JAH accused me of peddling Victorian stereotypes of explorers and missionaries. The bishop, on the other hand, liked the vignettes in the book and the way the story was left to tell itself.

Reid was scarcely more enamoured of the spin-off *Casualty of Empire* (2007), a shorter book (50,000 words) but a more ambitious research project. I had the benefit of the comprehensive library at Rhodes House, Oxford (part of the Bodleian). The book was, according to the reviewer, worth 'perhaps a couple of short commutes, or a slightly delayed sojourn in an airport'. I countered this dismissive comment with a website posting pointing out that commuters and air travellers were choosy about their reading matter, and I would be happy to be included among their choices.

The books could not be fitted into any of the usual boxes. If the Journal of African History implied that I was too warm towards the British Empire, *Casualty of Empire* was attacked from the opposite flank in a journal for former empire officials. Here I was accused of denigrating the colonial enterprise. Being attacked from both sides is usually the sign of being well positioned in the middle!

Certainly, I liked to think I was taking a cool look at the heated subject of colonialism, driven by what I'd seen for myself in Africa. I admired the work of the missionaries, while not being blind to their cultural insensitivities towards African societies. I was aware that the thoughtful among Britain's colonial administrators believed they were taking part in the development of the countries in their charge.

The words of the colonial administrator Sir Harry Johnston, as expressed in *A History and Description of the British Empire in Africa* (undated but around 1910), can serve as the credo of generations of imperial civil servants.

'It is only by maintaining [Johnston wrote] a perfectly honest administration of these lands assigned – perhaps only temporarily – to our control, that we shall merit the distinguished position in which we have been placed by circumstances, and that without recourse to mere force we may be able to maintain ourselves as rulers in Africa, with the full consent and fraternal co-operation of the Negroes, negroids, and other backward coloured peoples, for whom we are doing what the Romans and the Normans did for us.'

It is easy to mock the idea of Britain doing for Africa 'what the Romans and the Normans did for us'. We may call it a mask for exploitation or, patronisingly, say that the administrators were themselves being exploited by imperialism and failed to realise it. The difficulties, however, may lie with us, not them.

Interestingly, Johnston saw the definition of white and non-white as developmental rather than racial – in other words, white and non-white are synonyms for developed and undeveloped. Hence the Japanese are counted as white; the backward are only *mostly* coloured [original emphasis].

For Westerners of the late 19th and much of the 20th centuries it was commonplace to say that nations evolved towards the highest forms of civilisation. Few dare to express it in that way today, but much of the difference is in language, not content. *Eating Uganda* and *Casualty of Empire* were written from an evolutionary perspective, to the dismay of some readers.

Yet social evolution, properly defined, is about technology and institutions, not about 'higher' and 'lower' human beings. The very idea of *development* depends on evolution, and not just of an economic kind. Twenty-first century concepts like *good governance* and *civil society* involve changes to political and social structures.

The ability to choose your government, the separation of executive and judiciary, the setting up of individual titles in land and emancipation from religious superstition – these are not purely Western concepts. They speak to all people, everywhere. My view is that a society with these arrangements is more civilised than one without them.

Evolutionism in its Victorian form became discredited because of its erroneous assumption that Western society had arrived at the pinnacle of human achievement, in the same way that human beings were seen as the crowning achievement of biological evolution. A glance at the West's selfish individualism, rampant consumerism, corporate giantism, moral bankruptcy and spiritual barrenness makes clear that we have in no sense reached this pinnacle.

Relativism has now become the general guiding principle. It holds that societies differ in their social and political arrangements but none is 'higher' or 'lower' than others. It encourages us to help to save weaker cultures from a one-size-fits-all, Western approach. Yet it remains as much an article of faith as evolutionism. Neither offers a full explanation of the facts on the ground.

Present-day Africa poses an impossible challenge for cultural relativists. They cannot recapture the optimism that prevailed in the 1960s and 1970s, when independence was young and that blissful dawn was alive with prospects. African countries seem to have an inexorable tendency to slide back into 'Big Man' rule. This alarms relativists. Some of course will meekly defend the Big Men, simply because they are African. Others will attack them – but hold back from criticising their predecessors, the equally autocratic kings and chiefs of the pre-colonial 'golden age'.

A special headache for relativists is when the colonised take the part of the colonisers. The Ugandan-born Dr John Sentamu, Archbishop of York and the second-ranking bishop in the Church of England, told Sarah Sands of the (London) Daily Mail in an interview (November 2006): 'While the empire was there, the British thought they were doing some good in the world. For me, the vision was what made the missionaries go out, made the empire what it was: the sense of education, better roads, infrastructure, the separation of the executive from the legislature.

'All these fantastic values which, as someone who was a recipient of them, I can look back on and say: what a vision!'

With *Eating Uganda* I did not repeat my earlier mistake of offering it to only one publisher. Sheelagh Killeen, a friend and neighbour in South London, where I lived at the time, took on the job of offering the book around. She was very industrious in making contact with publishers and agents.

Fourth Estate had earlier warned me that general readers had little interest in Africa these days, and therefore it was tough to publish a book successfully. Certainly, for all the phone calls, emails and sample chapters, Sheelagh was getting nowhere.

It never occurred to me to go to a 'vanity publisher'. This derogatory terms refers to an arrangement where the author pays the publisher to produce the book rather than the conventional model where the publisher pays for the book in exchange for most of the profits. The description is not wholly accurate. A book may be privately produced and worthwhile, just not commercial enough to be conventionally published. One of the most valuable books I examined in my research was like that. Vanity publishers, however, don't do much marketing – which is vital for the successful selling of books.

It wasn't the route for me, but I formed another idea: I wanted to be my own publisher. With my knowledge of editing and interest in design, I reckoned I could do it. Thus I was in the paradoxical position while Sheelagh continued her trawl of publishers of hoping that my book would be rejected.

I got my wish. After 20 or so approaches, we accepted that no one had the faintest interest in *Eating Uganda* and I was free to do it myself. This was the origin of Ituri Publications. The name was coined by Sheelagh after the Great Congo Rainforest, which features prominently in the book. None of my later books has been offered to an external publisher. I enjoy controlling the entire process from writing through production and marketing to invoicing for sales.

The classic difficulty for the small publisher is marketing. This was even cited as a reason for the venerable mid-size house of John Murray putting itself up for sale. Ituri is no exception. My books have sold in top bookshops, but probably not in the numbers they would have enjoyed if produced by a leading publisher. I've traded bigger sales for control (including the freedom to publish what I want) – a deal I haven't regretted.

The Pulford Media company secretary Roderick Thomson and I agreed at the start that Ituri books must be produced to good trade standards. They had to pass what we called the 'Waterstone's test' – ie be able to hold their own on the shelf with the products of mainstream houses. Patrick Armstrong of Book Production Services was the key to fulfilling this aim. He has designed and typeset all the Ituri titles with much flair. Another invaluable helpers was Jude Brent-Khan, my secretary/PA from Mirror days in Plymouth, who came back on board to handle distribution of the books.

As Ituri developed, it published some books by other writers. We also moved into ebooks (see later in this chapter)

My second book, *JournoLISTS: 201 Ways to Improve Your Journalism*, has sold the best. It was published in 2001 and remained continuously in print. It is a simple book of practical tips, covering the waterfront from interviewing to page make-up with the various stages of reporting and sub-editing in-between. The tips were drawn from those I found most useful in the courses I taught.

The trick, it seemed, was to keep the advice short. Many journalism textbooks are wordy and tediously overloaded with examples, which often look dated by the time the book appears. *JournoLISTS* kept examples to a minimum, and chose those that would not date. The 201 tips made a book of no more than 30,000 words.

The book's continuing appeal is due to the fact that basic journalism skills don't change – how to ask questions, how to write clearly and grippingly, how to produce visually appealing and impactful pages, and so on. When *JournoLISTS* was written, use of the internet was fragmentary and limited. Fortunately, I had a clear enough view of the web for my comments to hold up a decade or more later.

Keith Waterhouse, author, playwright and columnist, kindly agreed to write a foreword. Keith, whom I knew from Mirror days, understandably hadn't read the book in deep detail. He opened his remarks by saying that there was 'more to the job [journalism] than avoiding hanging participles'.

A hanging, dangling or unrelated participle is a bit of an obsession with grammatical purists, for all that its use (or misuse) goes back centuries. It is a verb form that is not properly linked to the main part of the statement, as in 'Enjoying a challenge, skydiving was Jane's favourite sport'. Grammatically, the sentence says that skydiving enjoyed the challenge, but the participle *enjoying* is intended to relate to Jane.

Having written warmly about the topics I covered, Keith added with a flourish: 'And yes, the hanging participle does get a look-in.' The trouble was that it didn't. I had forgotten to include the point, which had to be hastily added when the book was in proof.

I used the same format eight years later with Byliners: *101 Ways to be a Freelance Journalist (2009)*. This time, however, each practical tip was expressed within strict length parameters. None was to be less than 200 words or more than 400 words. The idea was to give the book an especially tight framework.

The discipline proved valuable for the writer and, I liked to think, helpful to the reader. Here was a chance to deploy the journalistic skill of covering any subject at any required length. In practice, 400 words proved ample. Sometimes the item had to be cut back to that length, but the loss was in details not core matter. Occasionally, an item had to be 'bumped out' to make the minimum 200 words. Discreet padding is another journalistic skill!

I felt the writing experiment was a success, but *Byliners* (also around 30,000 words) didn't match the sales of its companion volume. This was a surprise when so many people dreamt of being freelance journalists. Others had no choice but to try their fortune as freelances. The book was published during an economic recession when journalists were being made redundant.

If *JournoLISTS* traced its roots to my abandoned collection of lesson handouts from years before, my next two books also brought discarded projects back into the light of day.

The idea of a book about the environmental downsides of motoring was 'still dead'. This subject, I realised, had been done to death. Then I had a eureka moment. The growth of aviation – the shocking price of binge flying – was an equal or even greater environmental concern. The trebling of commercial flights that the government was in the process of greenlighting meant not only more carbon dioxide and other polluting emissions but also noise nuisance for hundreds of thousands of homes in the UK. There were safety implications as ever more aircraft were shoehorned into the sky. Meanwhile, corporate jets, helicopters and sport flying all showed slow but steady increases.

Environmentalists pointed out that on present trends flying would consume all the UK's allowable CO_2 emissions without a couple of decades, leaving nothing for industry, heating and running of homes – or motoring!

The nub of the situation was that the growth of aviation was – and continues to be – essentially unconstrained. That was the policy with the motor car that had led us into the present problems of pollution, noise, safety and environmental tranquillity. It was clear to me that if policymakers of, say, 1910 had had a crystal ball they would have regulated the growth of motoring. The desertion of freight from rail to road, motorways and the preference for cars over trains for inter-city journeys, car commuting into cities with a single occupant, multiple household car ownership, a relaxed official stance on causing death by dangerous driving and other characteristics of current motoring would not have happened or would have appeared in more benign forms.

It occurred to me that aviation was in the same situation as motoring in 1910. If the same policy stance continued to be taken now as was taken to motoring then – even though we had the crystal ball – the social outcomes would be even more damaging.

To look at aviation in the mirror of motoring experience was the idea behind *Air Madness: Road's Mistakes Repeated*. It was, I hoped, an innovatory perspective on a vital subject. The first two editions appeared in 2003 and 2004, respectively before and after the appearance of a government white paper broadly endorsing the aviation industry's 'let it rip' approach. These were concise to the point of barely getting off the ground as a book. The third edition of 2008 was a more ambitious affair at 55,000 words. It followed the appearance of influential climate reports from the Intergovernmental Panel on Climate Change and Sir Nicholas Stern.

In a case study, I discovered the heights of absurdity in plans to turn a modest flying field more than 50 miles (80 km) from its intended market, sited next to a nuclear power station and a nature reserve (with the risk of birds fouling aero engines), into a major airport.

Undeterred, the Department of Transport in its 2004 white paper identified development possibilities at Lydd in Kent. The airport owners picked up the baton, seeing the all-but-invisible 3,000 passengers per annum growing initially to 300,000 ppa and ultimately to two million ppa – a breathtaking 9,900% expansion. A runway extension to accommodate largish jets like the Boeing 737 and Airbus A320, and a terminal with a capacity for 500,000 ppa, were planned.

Lydd, which is on the coast, was built in 1954 for cross-channel car ferry services. It enjoyed strong levels of traffic in the Fifties and Sixties, but competition from roll-on roll-off sea ferries saw it decline in the early Seventies. Budget travellers could fly from Lydd to Le Touquet in France – destinations equally inconvenient for their respective national capitals, but at least the flights were cheap. Then came another wave of cheapie ways to get to the Continent: Eurotunnel, Eurostar, Ryanair and Easy-Jet.

In the cosseted aviation industry, no-one ever said a facility has outlived its purpose, let's close it. A new use must be found. Lydd reinvented itself as Lydd-London Ashford Airport, despite being near neither London nor Ashford.

London was 53 miles, with no railway. The nearest rail station was Appledore, 7 ½ miles away. That would leave 70% of passengers getting to and from the enlarged airport by car by country roads, according to consultants retained by airport opponents. The consultants projected that just 10% of passengers would use the bus and another 20% taxis.

Lydd was located amid the isolation of Romney Marsh, described by Louise Barton of the opposition Lydd Airport Action Group as 'one of the last remaining tranquil areas of the

South-east'. It was less than three miles from the Dungeness nuclear power complex, raising fears of an air accident or a terror strike. It was also on top of a major reserve operated by the Royal Society for the Protection of Birds (RSPB) and the Dungeness conservation area – more than 7,400 acres including what is described as the most diverse and extensive examples of vegetated shingle in Europe, with special forms of broom and blackthorn, together with a large population of great crested newts.

Lydd's managing director, Zaher Deir, insisted there were no safety concerns. 'We have a fully upgraded and licensed air traffic control system, and we are confident there is no danger posed by our proximity to the plant or the military firing ranges [at Lydd and Hythe],' he told the Daily Telegraph.

'There are nuclear facilities all over the UK close to aircraft movements. If there is a danger it exists everywhere, not just at Lydd.' He had a point there although not the one he intended.

As for birdstrikes posing a danger to aircraft in flight, Deir added: 'We have a bird management scheme and we have efficient methods of keeping birds and the aircraft apart.' That sounded like getting rid of the birds. Kent Wildlife Trust said control measures at the expanded airport might include degrading the birds' habitat over a radius of up to 10 miles.

From both safety and environment points of view, it would be hard to find a less suitable site for a major airfield. That did not prevent the plans going forward and condemning local communities to years of uncertainty.

The Conservative-Liberal Democrat coalition taking office in 2010 cancelled a third Heathrow runway – a centrepiece of the now defunct white paper – but showed no sign of gripping the aviation issue as a whole. Expansion was still on the agenda, just somewhere else. Determined campaigning by those who denied the existence of man-made global warming fuzzed the need for pollution control. Noise nuisance, safety risks and loss of amenity remained as great concerns as ever.

My next book was also a reinvention of a project abandoned years ago – the menace of the United States. I had long realised that there was an enormous existing literature on the subject, and that people had complained about America for almost as long as the country had existed; often using the same terms, too, like loudness, arrogance, inwardness and the sense of exceptionalism (uniqueness).

Everything I could say had been said already ... on the other hand, the sheer number of books suggested that there was always room for one more! I found my way into the subject by interweaving the personal narrative of my three years living in the US Midwest as a journalist and student with my descriptions and comments about American history, economic and politics.

The title of the book, *Siren Society* (2005), was meant to convey that just as sirens lured sailors to their destruction so America as an example to the world was both fascinating and fatal. Once, this was the book I most wanted to write. When I came to do so, I had little enthusiasm for it. At less than 30,000 words, it fell short of the intended length. I struggled with the thought that the subject was a worked-out seam.

Sales were lacklustre, which probably proved the point. Even so, I was happy to put some points into the public marketplace of ideas. For example, I underlined that there was nothing new in the United States invading other countries. It had done so continually since the mid-19th century, starting in neighbouring South America.

I called attention to the American obsession with giantism and prodigality, with consumption unremittingly ahead of countries with equal affluence, like Norway. I felt that the explanation lay in immigration. The United States was a nation of immigrants. There was no point in tearing yourself away from your roots in order to live no better than at home – in other words, lavish consumption was needed to validate the decision to emigrate.

As I wrote it, I began to wonder whether I was writing the wrong book. Was my target really America as such or its effects on my country, Britain? Perhaps an exploration of why Britain had turned itself into the world's largest satellite state – economically, politically and militarily – would be a better subject. In one graphic example, I realised that American forces were exempt from UK law even if offences were committed off-base: a soldier could kill a Briton on a public road, and be beyond the reach of British courts. But whose fault was all this – Britain's or America's?

There were echoes of British dependency in the book. Much of the fault lay with the news media. In example after example, I showed how America was held up in the press as the benchmark for success or acceptability. Favourable references to America far exceeded those to France, Germany or any other nation. The format was always the same. The British situation/action/policy/arrangement was described, to be followed by how things were better in the US. I called it the 'whereas in America' syndrome. It was, I believed, immensely damaging to national self-esteem.

Sadly, nothing has changed in the years since I wrote *Siren Society*. Fast-forward to 2012, and the cultural cringe continues:

> *There has often been talk of 'workfare', a scheme used successfully in America where benefits are paid in return for state-sponsored work. The main obstacle to such a system in Britain ...*
>
> *New targets are needed. American reformers realised this two decades ago.*
>
> *It is a very different picture in the US where banks, firms, and families have been chipping away at debt ...*
>
> *Sir Mervyn could have done anything with his magic money – lent it to companies, for example, as his American counterparts have done.*
>
> *I asked a BBC drama executive why it [the TV show, 24] was so much better than anything on British television ...*

I pulled together concerns about the United States, the European Union and the Blair government's attitude to civil liberties in a three-part pamphlet, *Our Vanishing Freedoms*, published in 2006. While concerns about the overweening power of Washington and Brussels were well known, the steady erosion of Britain's civil liberties by its own government, I felt, was less familiar than it should be.

A string of measures were introduced with the best of intentions to combat terrorism, but they were quickly misused. They included a woman arrested for reading out the names of the dead at the Cenotaph in London, councils examining residents' bins for the wrong sort of rubbish, businessmen sent to the United States under a one-sided extradition treaty and a secret body that would have made Henry VIII proud – the Special Immigration Appeals Commission. In the name of protecting Britain's intelligence sources, the accused were not allowed to be present at the tribunal, nor to know the case against them or hear the evidence.

At the same time, terrorists and would-be terrorists as well as others were able to use the Human Rights Act to thwart the decisions of government and in some cases common sense

I was shocked too at the casual way in which 800 years of legal practice was swept away when the common law of double jeopardy was repealed. Henceforth, an accused could be tried more than once for the same offence even if previously acquitted – ie he or she could be put in jeopardy twice. Repealing the law of double jeopardy made every acquittal provisional, although anyone acquitted in court and with the exhaustion of any appeal is entitled to a final assumption of innocence.

Hard cases make bad law. While undoubtedly tempting to have another go in the event of a perverse acquittal – as it had been for 800 years – the downside risk was enormous. The move was accompanied by the usual assurances about significant new evidence being needed. However, it was easy to imagine the ratchet effect of ever-more-common second trials, a gradual lowering of the threshold of new evidence. The same process had already occurred in sentences for murder, where once life meant life.

Bookshops are not interested in selling pamphlets. If they are placed on a shelf like books, they can't be identified because they lack a spine. They have to be stacked flat on a counter, taking valuable space. With one exception, no bookshop would take *Our Vanishing Freedoms* even though it was available on sale or return. (Bookshops normally pay upfront, with the facility to return unsold books for credit.)

I was grateful to Blackwell's, Oxford, for displaying the pamphlet. One of their copies was stolen. For the statistics, I counted this as a half-sale on the basis that someone thought it worth stealing!

Two Kingdoms of Uganda (2011) united my earlier books, *Eating Uganda* and *Casualty of Empire*, which focused respectively on Buganda and Bunyoro, in order to heighten the contrast between the fates of these traditional kingdoms. This was my first book to reach 100,000 words. (The present book is of similar length.) I hold no brief for doorstopper books where several hundred thousand words have become commonplace. This is especially so in fiction, where length often has more to do with lazy writing than deep detail!

The title *Two Kingdoms of Uganda* was chosen to echo that of one of earliest works of African historiography, Robert Ashe's *Two Kings of Uganda*. Ashe was a Church Missionary Society pioneer who was present at many of the events he (and I) described.

The tales of the two kingdoms complemented each other

most dramatically. Buganda co-operated with the incoming British while Bunyoro resisted – fateful choices with consequences to the present day.

I didn't take the easy publishing option of slapping the two books together like pieces of bread to make a sandwich. They were woven into a single narrative – an editing job that was almost as hard as writing the book from scratch.

Thanks to the excellent resources of Rhodes House, I located a verbatim text of Dr David Livingstone's 1857 'Senate House' speech in Cambridge, and reprinted it as an appendix. It was one of the most important speeches ever in the history of Christian mission. Among its effects was to influence Henry Stanley, whose appeal was the direct cause of the CMS sending the first missionaries to Uganda.

The Uganda story touched those of two traditional kingdoms elsewhere in Africa: Asante (now part of Ghana) and Barotseland (now part of Zambia). I added chapters on both to give what academics love to call 'a comparative perspective'.

Like most Ituri titles, *Two Kingdoms of Uganda* is available as a Kindle ebook as well as a printed book. Ebooks exploded into the public consciousness around 2010 with the success of Amazon's Kindle reader, but their roots stretch back several years. Sony was among those offering ebook readers before Kindle arrived; before that, electronic texts were available to universities internationally from content distributors. Ituri has had a contract with one of these, ebrary, since 2002, and has signed with another, EBSCOHost, more recently.

The seemingly permanent breakthrough lay in taking ebooks out of academe and putting them into trains and boats and planes. Ebooks are supremely practical. We can buy what we want, when we want and where we want. No longer do we have to weigh down our holiday luggage with half a dozen printed books.

Ebooks are also supremely attractive to publishers. With distribution costs almost zero and typographical make-up not far behind, they can be priced at less than a printed book and still produce a thumping profit. The danger is that publishers, not the public, will drive further demand for ebooks. For readers, there is room for both formats.

Much will be lost if the printed book is driven to extinction or near-extinction. Even the humblest paperbacks can be attractive objects: striking, glossy covers, variety of typefaces, crisp printing with well judged margins and other white space and a pleasant feel in the hand. No one ever said a computer file, aka an ebook, is a thing of beauty!

The present book is my eighth. From the start, I learnt that the scale of a book made it a qualitatively different experience from writing articles. It is essential for non-fiction books to have a central idea or theme, or else one will be overwhelmed by the size of the task or lost in the labyrinth of information.

Because the task of writing a book is so huge, the only way I can tackle it is to sit down at a set time in the day and start writing. Sometimes the words are sticky to begin with, but once underway I invariably achieve my usual pace. I find it necessary to have a daily quota. Mine is around 1,200 words – not especially large. Writers' quotas can be anything from 500 words a day (several famous novelists) to 4,000 words or more. On the other hand, I turn out more or less finished copy. The material rarely needs more than tweaking and tightening here and there.

The chapters in the first book, *Eating Uganda*, were produced in a mixed-up order, depending on what I felt ready to write at the time. As I became more experienced, I found it better to write in chapter order from first to last. This, I think, is more likely to provide a smooth narrative. However, I'm not rigid in this, and will write a chapter out of sequence if necessary.

My main device for speeding up the job is to deliver factual content in three stages: (1) absorb the information from notes or web searches; (2) write it up from memory; (3) check and infill by returning to the notes and website transcriptions. The work will take a lot longer if we verify every last detail as we go, and the flow of the writing will probably be lost.

For me, these book-writing experiences have been a satisfying journey, a learning journey, that started late in life. The journey, I hope, isn't over yet.

SEVENTEEN
BACK TO BORNEO –
2009-2010

In 2009 I found myself in Malaysia working with the Borneo Post, a newspaper I had previously helped in 1987. I owed this resurrection to my friend Nash Manis, who reminded the paper that I was well placed to meet their training needs.

It was flattering to receive this invitation, but at 70 + was my health up to the project? The legacy of my years of work in the tropics was skin cancer and diverticular disease, the former triggered by overexposure to the sun and the latter a colon condition prompted by abrupt changes of diet and climate. The cancer was of the superficial, non-life-threatening kind (basal cell carcinoma) and would not be made worse by returning to the tropics. The diverticular disease was another matter. It would be no joke to have bowel problems throughout the month-long visit.

More importantly, a few months earlier I had had successful surgery for bladder cancer. Careful diet and the avoidance of stress are among the main ways to inhibit the return of cancer. There would be no guarantees for either in the rush-and-tumble of the Malaysia project.

My concerns, although not without an objective basis, were ultimately a form of hiding in my tent. So what if a change of diet elevated the cancer risk fractionally? Yes, it would be a tough programme, but hard work stress doesn't damage like anxiety stress – the opposite, in fact. I told Phyllis Wong, who was in charge of the Borneo Post's editorial operations, that I was on my way.

My destination was Sabah, one of the two Malaysian states on the island of Borneo (the other is Sarawak). The flight from Kuala Lumpur descended along the coast, giving me a lingering, luxurious look at the sharp tropical colours of sea, sand and palms. A ribbon of development stretched along the shore with the buildings, too, standing out brightly.

Phyllis greeted me warmly at the airport. The faces had faded, but we remembered each other from 22 years earlier, when I worked for her father-in-law, Lau Hui-siong. Then she put me into quarantine. By this was meant that I couldn't enter the office for a week under company policy for arriving travellers. It was the time of a bird flu epidemic. Strangely, only half the staff at Kuala Lumpur airport chose to wear face masks.

The Borneo Post had recently started the Sabah edition, and needed to overcome a public perception that it was 'a Sarawak paper'. I passed the time in my hotel room writing a report for Phyllis on the edition's strengths and weakness and those of its competition. Two other dailies were produced locally; the New Straits Times and the Star came in from West Malaysia.

I also had time to explore Kota Kinabalu, the state capital, where we were based. This time around KK, as it was universally known, seemed a much nicer place than it had on my previous visit in 1980. In the compact city centre just about everything was in easy walking distance of my hotel. The seaside location meant that breezes tempered the tropical heat, which in any case wasn't as severe as I remembered. The Upper Star bar had a balcony with a wide view of the sea and offshore islands, best enjoyed with a glass of wine as the sun went down. The stuff of dreams.

Above all, the street life of Malaysian Borneo seemed comfortingly familiar although more than two decades had passed – the four-foot ways (walkways), the open shopfronts, delicious cooking smells wafting everywhere, the faces of Malays, Chinese and the indigenous Dayaks. Unlike West Malaysian women, few here wore headscarves.

The hotel guests were mainly locals. A minority were tourists who would head off to climb Mount Kinabalu, the highest peak in Borneo, or see the orang-utans near Sandakan.

I'd thrown a couple of light jumpers into my suitcase, but in the office I wished I'd bought half a dozen. I was amazed at first at how high the air-conditioning was set. I spent the whole visit wearing three layers – vest, shirt and jumper – while everyone else was comfortable in one! It is, of course, understandable that in an unremittingly hot climate cold is valued where it can be found.

Phyllis was a famously hard worker. After early morning gym – where she persuaded me to join her, there being no other takers from among her colleagues! – she worked through until late in the evening. It was especially tempting to do this because she occupied an apartment in the same company-owned building as the newspaper.

I couldn't match her pace, but my days were long. The entire editorial staff went through my training workshops in two groups, reporters and editors. The reporters were joined by some of their counterparts from the Malay-language sister paper, Utusan Melayu. Phyllis, to her credit, sat through both programmes as a participant. Nash Manis and his uncle, Madon, came over from Sarawak, and Nash joined me in teaching the groups.

Nicholas Lo, chief reporter at the Borneo Post's Sibu office, was among several staff from Sarawak who joined the programme. Nicholas had taken my course in 1987; now he was back for more. Naturally, I was delighted. I had with me a picture from 1987 for comparison – from which he emerged the winner!

At the same time as the courses, I continued my analysis of the printed media, which produced a further report and recommendations for Phyllis, the Sabah head of the KTS holding company, Ngu Ngiong Hieng, and the 'big boss' in Sarawak, Dato' Henry Lau.

English usage was heavily stressed in the workshops and in individual tuition. The language was often shaky in the Borneo Post as it was in the other Malaysian papers because English was not part of the air people breathed. It was just one language among many.

In streets and homes, many people used the varied languages of their own communities (Malay, Chinese and Dayak). To speak with someone from another ethnic group, Malay (known as Bahasa Malaysia) was widely used. Nor could it be assumed that the top tier of professional and business people would read an English newspaper. Most were Chinese. The Chinese-language press was well established, and was a viable alternative and competitor.

I made many specific recommendations for the Borneo Post. I also called attention to a characteristic of the entire Malaysian press: too much politics and too few lighter, 'human interest' stories. Political announcements and speeches were an easy way to fill space. Besides, most of the newspapers, including the two nationals, were controlled by political parties or politicians. The BP was an exception, although like the others it had to exist in a restrictive political environment. That environment had caused its competitor in Sarawak, the Tribune, to shut down after it reprinted Danish cartoons about the Prophet Muhamad.

As the Sabah project drew to a close, I was glad I hadn't allowed health considerations to leave me earthbound. I was able to keep, more or less, to my special diet. Everything was available, at a price, even health freaks' favourites like muesli, liquid soya (soya milk) and St Dalfour sugar-free jam (strictly, sucrose-free fruit spread).

One of my concerns was to eat meat only once a week. The Chinese have difficulty in understanding vegetarianism. To them, meat equals prosperity. Why should someone who can afford it not eat meat? For vegetarian one needed Indian but Sabah, unlike West Malaysia, had only a tiny Indian community.

A favourite meal for me in Chinese restaurants was plain tofu (beancurd), rice and green vegetables, which were available in remarkable variety. Inevitably, the dish never came out like that. Bits of meat and fish were lovingly dropped in to create a sort of pilau.

After the training workshops in KK, I made a tour of the Borneo Post's 'out-stations' – the charmingly dated term by which they were known. I ran short seminars in Sandakan and Tawau and on the island of Labuan (the last a contiguous federal territory, not part of Sabah). Flying across the state to Sandakan, we enjoyed a spectacular view of Mount Kinabalu. I was shocked at how little forest remained apart from on the foothills of the mountain. From coast to coast, under that flight path at least, the forest had been cleared for palm oil plantations. I thought about the displacement this meant for the forest-dwelling Dayaks. Where were they now? In the towns presumably, the longhouse life gone for ever.

Palm oil is stunningly profitable. I learnt from someone in the sector that a mere 100 acres would yield a net profit of £20,000 a year. Nor was it necessary to work for this. One employed workers from Indonesian Borneo (Kalimantan) for tiny wages, and pocketed the net. New strains of palm tree bore fruit after just four or five years. They were low so that they were easily cropped from the ground.

Few plantations were, in fact, as small as 100 acres. Most were huge affairs run by huge corporation extracting huge profits from palm oil. It was easy to see why the jungle was in peril. It already was when I stayed in Borneo in the Eighties. Now the process in Sabah seemed to have reached the end-game. Elsewhere, the process must conclude either with serious and effective conservation or the complete clearance of the rainforests.

The old Sabah, then British North Borneo, is vividly evoked
in a trilogy of books by Agnes Newton Keith. This is known by
the title of the first book, *Land Beneath the Wind*. Sabah adopted
the phrase as a marketing slogan. Newton Keith was an American writer married to a colonial official. Her books are no nos-
talgia-fest. The second deals with the ordeals of the Japanese
Second World War occupation, and the third with the hard times
after the war.

I visited her house in Sandakan. It was a typical house of its
period – built on stilts so that cooling air could pass underneath,
with large, airy rooms. It was not as old as it looked, having been
rebuilt after the war (when much of Sabah's 'built environment'
was destroyed). Near the house were the English Tea Rooms,
serving delicacies like scones.

On Labuan Island I was taken to see a water village, built
over the water. Here, too, the houses were on stilts although for
a different reason: to make fishing easier. The most famous
example is at Bandar Seri Bagawan, or Brunei Town (see Chapter 11), but others like this one remain on Borneo. I passed along
planked walkways as one would a village street, looking – but
trying not to stare – at the homes to either side. A narrow pier
projected farther out to sea. I vertiginously picked my way to
the end, with nothing to hold on to.

To people outside the region, the island of Borneo is often
thought of as a country. In fact, three countries each possess a
part of it. The biggest part by far is the Indonesian state of Kalimantan, which was a Dutch colony. Brunei is a tiny, independent
– and very rich – sultanate. Sabah and Sarawak, the two states
of Malaysian Borneo, both have unusual histories.

Sabah until after the Second World War was owned by a chartered company. This was a commercial company that, by charter
from the British government, ran the territory with powers of
life and death over the inhabitants. The concept, extraordinary
to a modern understanding, has echoes of 21st century private
finance initiatives. It was once a common way for Britain to
develop its empire on the cheap. The East India Company and
Cecil Rhodes's Chartered Company in Southern Africa are the
most famous examples.

The East India and Chartered Companies were long gone but,
perhaps because Sabah was small and far away, the North
Borneo Company drifted on. When it took possession of the territory again after the Japanese, it was plainly an anachronism.

With little or no fuss, North Borneo became a British colony and, after a few years, joined the Malaysian confederation as the state of Sabah.

Sarawak was even more of an oddity constitutionally – ruled for more than a century by three Europeans in turn, not as colonial officials but as monarchs. These were the 'white rajahs' that fascinated the outside world. The authority of the Brooke family derived originally from the sultan of Brunei. He possessed a swath of southern Borneo, a portion of which around the Sarawak River he gave to James Brooke in exchange for clearing the area of pirates.

Brooke became the first rajah, to be succeeded by his nephew Charles and his great-nephew Vyner (Charles's son). At a point that moralists can debate, the rajah's legitimacy became self-validating as an expanding Sarawak started to threaten its original patron, Brunei. Britain finally stepped in to prevent the rump of the sultanate being swallowed.

The Second World War changed everything for Sarawak as it did for Sabah. The third rajah, Vyner Brooke, had for years been a part-time ruler. He spent much of his time in Britain, with his nephew Anthony running Sarawak in his place. After the Japanese had been expelled, an ageing Vyner Brooke lost interest even in his limited commitment. He handed the territory to Britain in 1946, presenting its people with a fait accompli and depriving Anthony of his inheritance. The cession was approved in the Council Negri, or parliament, only with the 'payroll vote' – the rajah's officials.

Beneath its surface calm, Sarawak has suffered an undercurrent of disaffection ever since. The second colonial governor, Duncan Stewart, was assassinated in 1949. Independence came in 1963, not as a separate country but as a constituent part of Malaysia along with Malaya (independent since 1957), Sabah and Singapore. (The last later left the confederation.)

In both Sarawak and Sabah, old ethnic roles continued to be played out. Malays dominated politics and government, Chinese dominated commerce, and the original inhabitants, the Dayaks, even when settled in the cities, struggled for a share of the cake. Religion added another complication. Malaysia as a whole was heavily Muslim, but in the Borneo states Christians were in a majority over Muslims (Sarawak) or nearly equal with them (Sabah).

In Sabah in 2009 and in 2010, when I was invited to Sarawak,

I was reunited with these issues for the first time since the Eighties. On the surface not much seemed to have changed. My sight wasn't sharp enough to know what emancipation the Dayaks had achieved; it was clear, however, that in religion careful tolerance still prevailed. However, Christians were concerned about access to public sector jobs; they also worried about the future as Malaysia, like the rest of the Muslim world, experienced an expansionist Islam.

Word of my Sabah courses reached the Borneo Post journalists in Sarawak, who decided they would like them, too. Hence the following year (2010) I found myself in Kuching, the state capital. Phyllis Wong, whose duties took in both states, was again on hand to welcome me; so was Nash Manis, whose home was in the city.

Almost my first question to Nash was 'Are the old shophouses still here?' I was delighted to find they were. These picturesque streets had been recognised as a tourist attraction – business that Sarawak now wanted although it had been indifferent to it in the past. A few high-rise buildings were to be seen here and there, but the main sign of the passing years was the riverfront. This had been developed into a handsome promenade, which was still being lengthened during my visit.

Kuching was often troubled by 'haze' – a smog of timber particles drifting across from the Indonesian state of Kalimantan. The haze was distressing for asthmatics. It was produced by illegal forest fires, which were lit to clear the jungle.

The workshops followed the same pattern as the Sabah courses the previous year: separate groups for reporters and editors, with an additional small group for senior reporters. One of the subjects that attracted the greatest interest was press freedom. It arose in answer to a question, which led me to explain the idea of 'prior restraint', and how this limits a free news media.

I heard how in Malaysia newspapers continued to be licensed by the government. Without a licence an offending newspaper cannot publish. It was truly disappointing to find that in an advanced and generally tolerant country, huge economic strides had not been matched by the removal of this restraint.

The lack of prior restraint is at the heart of press freedom as understood in the 'Anglosphere' of the United Kingdom and the United States. It had to be fought for and won in the UK during the 18th century. The American colonists, in their successful revolution later that century, took up the battle and wrote press freedom into their constitution – to be honoured in fact as well as on paper.

An interesting sidelight on those ancient struggles is that to this day in the UK there is no value added tax (sales tax) on newspapers, magazines and books. This flows from the decision to end stamp duty on publications, derided by opponents as 'a tax on knowledge'. This is surely one of the world's great political slogans.

No prior restraint is the concept that the news media are answerable in law for what they publish, but only *after* publication – ie no external body or person exercises 'prior restraint' of publication. Courts, press councils and ombudsmen are institutions that properly call the media to account post-publication. Defamation (libel), privacy, confidentiality, contempt of court and national security are examples of laws that limit the media, aiming to ensure that they don't abuse their freedom. A court that imposes an injunction against publishing particular information clearly breaches the principle of no prior restraint, but these are exceptions that prove the rule.

A censor sitting in the back office, self-censorship because of fear of reprisals and licensing of newspapers and magazines, as in Malaysia, are all forms of prior restraint. The last is the least severe of the three, but this still means that some publications won't or may not be licensed. Licensing by a parliamentary body or independent commission is an improvement on licensing by the government, but it remains prior restraint.

There is no licensing of newspapers and magazines in the Anglosphere, although both the UK and USA have found it necessary to license TV and radio channels. This is because the airwaves have a finite capacity and a broadcasting free-for-all helps no-one. In countries fortunate enough to enjoy no prior restraint, freedom is rarely total. Content may be controlled by a political party, an individual proprietor or, informally, a major advertiser.

Supporters of licensing argue that it is a safeguard against scurrilous publications that deprave and corrupt politically, religiously and socially. This is a line of argument that tends to appeal more to those in power than to those without it! Those who hate the news media and those with axes to grind also deploy this argument.

During the Sixties and Seventies, as waves of countries became independent from the colonial powers, the argument was heard that a free press, with its tendency to criticise government, was a block on national development and would stir up sectarian strife. The trouble with this argument is that it assumes the government has a monopoly of wisdom. Emerging countries, it was added, had not reached the developmental level where the luxury of a free press could be enjoyed.

This patronising argument overlooked the fact that every country in the world has its 'first world' sector, whose inhabitants desire the same free media as anywhere else. It has been found in country after country that economic development does not automatically produce political development, including a free press.

Unfortunately, the British colonial authorities (other colonial powers may have been worse) declined to allow the same press freedom that Britons expected for themselves at home. Successor regimes have been able to say that they are merely using the powers they inherited. The argument wears thin several decades on. There is nothing to stop independent governments from dismantling these laws – but politicians the world over are loath to give up powers!

No country can claim to have perfected the relationship between press, government and public, and probably none ever will. In the Anglosphere, for example, extremely permissive American legal reporting leads to 'trial by the media', while US libel restrictions have been watered down to vanishing point, effectively denying justice to aggrieved parties. In Britain, the same common law of libel has gone in the opposite direction, tending to favour the claimant over the defendant media, while judges have introduced through case law the previously unknown tort (non-criminal offence) of invasion of privacy.

For all its imperfections, no prior restraint with the media answering after the fact of publication is the only route compatible with democracy.

The training courses were of special importance because the Borneo Post faced new competition. The Tribune was allowed to resume publication after its disappearance with the Danish cartoons affair (see this chapter, above). The national newspaper, the Star, started a local printing, and promised to increase its editorial capacity in Sarawak. (It was expected that the New Straits Times would launch a local edition in Sabah.)

The 'new' Star got off to a shaky start from its point of view. We were surprised at the scantiness of the Sarawak content, some of it old material reheated. I urged the BP journalists not to be complacent, quoting Goethe to the effect that the fortunes of war go this way and that, and no prudent fighter despises his adversary! The Star had larger resources overall, but the Post had more journalists locally, which should translate into continuing superior local content.

I pointed to the several successful regional dailies in Britain, which survived head to head with the national newspapers. Foremost among them was my own first newspaper, the Yorkshire Post. The regional paper has to provide some local value that the nationals cannot match while giving sufficient coverage of national and international news. It must be able to stand alone, to be the only paper that the reader takes or at least needs to take. When it is seen as a second or supplementary paper, it is potentially finished.

The Borneo Post was already strong on national and international news. With Phyllis and the Kuching staff, I set about charting the expansion of its local strengths.

The 'big boss', Dato' Henry Lau, whom I met several times, took a close interest. The newspapers in the group, which included Chinese and Malay language titles, were a small part of the business empire. KTS Holdings had all the marks of a very rich company. It was involved in the two big industries of Sarawak, timber and palm oil. Although KTS was not primarily a publisher, I assumed the newspapers were valued for the influence and access they brought as well as involvement in what continues to be seen around the world as a romantic industry.

Dato' Henry was a relative but not of the immediate family of Lau Hui-siong, from my days with the paper in the Eighties. Control had shifted within the Lau clan, displacing Philip, formerly the heir apparent, who nevertheless still worked with the firm. Lau Hui-siong had been absolutely straight-dealing with me in financial and other matters. That characteristic of the company hadn't changed. It was exactly the same with Dato' Henry.

To mark the end of the Sarawak courses, Nash and Madon took me on a long road trip. Our destination was Sibu, timber town and the Borneo Post's home before it transferred to Kuching. The Indonesian border was close as the road made its way from east to west, reducing the state to a narrowish strip in places.

Unlike Sabah, Sarawak has plenty of jungle at least for the moment. Dayaks from the longhouses brought fruit, vegetables and fish, all in dazzling abundance, to the roadside markets that dotted the route. Chinese merchants kept shops to sell goods from the city to the locals. These were classic trading stations (although ones where no one looked twice at a mobile phone).

In Sibu, I met again Philip Lau, Phyllis's husband and the man with whom I worked in 1987. The first he knew that we were in town was a phone call from Nash that morning. I would have settled for a meet and greet and a sandwich, but naturally it couldn't be. With almost no notice, Philip procured for us a fine Chinese course dinner.

Finally, it was back to Sabah for a short follow-up of last year's programmes. I was delighted to be warmly greeted by the girls and boys. The office was as cold as ever. This time I brought more jumpers. The Yummy Chicken, a popular eatery with Borneo Post staff, had gone. Otherwise KK was the same. The Upper Star was still enticing, with its spacious view of the tropical sea bathed in yellow as the sun went down.

EIGHTEEN
LESSONS FROM A LIFE

Much of my professional life has been spent in editorial training. Therefore I would like this book to have a double purpose. I hope it has told an interesting tale. Now, in this final chapter, I want to explore what resonances my five decades at the rockface of journalism have for the industry today. Inevitably, the book has focused on newspapers and magazines because they have been my main field; yet much of what emerges applies also to broadcast and web journalism.

From Nigeria in 1972 to Borneo in 2010, and in Britain too, a consistent theme in my teaching has been the importance of feature articles in newspapers. In my role of reader, I want content that explains things in greater depth than a news report either can or should. I want this material to look attractive and different from news, using all the tricks of the designer's trade. I'm far from alone: in fact, the mix of news and features – and a clear distinction between them – is the key to successful newspapering. To repeat the words of Lord Northcliffe, founder of the Daily Mail: 'Hard news catches readers, features hold them.'

Time then to tie up the ends and pin down this animal called a feature. It can be easier to recognise one than to define it! In a sense, a feature is any editorial material that is <u>not hard news</u>. The news backgrounder, the editorial/leader, personal column and the gardening notes all look at a situation in a different way from the news report, which primarily aims to *describe* in neutral terms. The news backgrounder *explains*, the editorial/leader *guides*, the personal column *stimulates* through the expression of strong, amusing or unusual views, and the gardening notes *instruct* us how to achieve certain practical outcomes. So a feature takes a perspective other than that of the news report.

The news backgrounder, or 'news feature', is concerned with a process rather than an event – the trend in non-natural births (Caesareans), using the publication of the latest figures (an event) as a peg. The best news features have strong topical pegs. We can identify eight ways in which a news feature, the most important type for the improvement of newspaper content, differs from a news story:

It will usually be (1) *longer*. It should be 'meaty'. It should (2) *look different* through design effects like alternative headline typefaces, standfirsts (introductory material separate from the main text), drop letters and drop-in (pull) quotes (both ways of breaking up text) and wider text setting. It can be (3) *more individual*. And for the writer that's good! The news report is supposed to be strictly factual, but in a news feature interpretation or even comment is wanted. It will be (4) *multi-sourced*. This type of feature can't be hung on a single source ... several are needed for a rounded picture and for authenticity.

Features of all sorts are (5) *structured differently*. The news story makes an 'inverted pyramid', with information presented in descending order of importance. A feature, on the other hand, is like a classical stone pillar or column – the top, middle and bottom are identifiably different but all essential in their separate ways. (6) *Intros are more varied*. A feature typically starts softly, seeking to tease or amuse us into reading the piece. There is therefore an almost limitless number of ways to begin a feature. (7) *Endings are strong*: the news story should dwindle to its end, but the feature must go out with impact. It follows from this that *cuts for length in a feature should be taken from the middle (body) of the piece, not from the end*. The belief that stories are to be cut from the bottom is a myth: it applies only to inverted pyramid news stories.

An effective feature is (8) *thematic*. It is more than a ramble around a subject. It takes a particular aspect of that subject, and develops it. That is a theme.

Although journalists are widely told that a feature must have a beginning, middle and end, they do not always learn what this means in practical terms.

The newspaper or magazine feature article typically makes a T shape. Picture a character with three distinct parts: at the top a horizontal stroke; then the vertical shaft; at the bottom a shorter vertical stroke like the 'foot' on many sorts of type. This letter T corresponds to the three parts of a feature article, like this: ·

- The <u>intro or lead</u> is often indirect, with the aim of inviting readers into the article rather than informing them baldly about the subject – a quote, an example, a scene, even a question. Unlike the summary news intro, the feature intro does not have to be a single paragraph. It may run to several.

- The <u>body</u> of the feature is where the theme is set out and the material presented.
- The <u>ending or outro</u> is almost as important as the intro in a feature article, hence it needs a distinctive 'foot'. To round out the piece satisfactorily, the ending needs to be strong – a conclusion firmly stated, a quote, a question pointing to the future, an example that refers back to the intro example (thus tying up the package).

Writers tend to give much less attention to outros than to intros – big mistake!

It is vital to make a clearcut distinction between news and features – and for the journalist to know what type he or she is writing! However, some forms of advanced news writing employ typical feature techniques:

<u>Colour pieces</u> may use an intro that paints the scene or some other indirect start, and finish with a strong outro. Colour pieces may be sidebars to the principal, hard news story or standalone items, among them human interest stories.

<u>Narrative treatments</u> relate the story in chronological order. This is far removed from the inverted pyramid approach of hard news. It is a story-telling approach that may be the best way of getting across longer, dramatic events.

<u>News analysis</u> requires the writer to get behind the hard news to explain what it means or what is likely to happen next. Unlike a standard news feature, there may be no quoted sources. News analysis may shade into the writer's opinion – again a feature technique

HOME ...

First steps (Chapter 1)

HIDDEN AGENDAS. When I wrote a hostile review of a school play, I was working off an unstated personal grievance. I wanted to be in the play, and I was particularly sore that a friend was given a main role. Without realising it at the time, I acted in bad faith. Older hands, and professional hands, have done it too, but that doesn't make it right. Two local newspapers ran reviews, one of them mine. A teacher observed, correctly, that one reviewer was determined to find everything right about the play (the standard approach for am-dram) and the other (me) everything wrong. Journalism has a place for prejudice – columnists live off it – but not for hidden agendas.

LIBEL IN ONE WORD. One little word, and in the real world of professional newspapers it might have cost thousands. Fortunate that it was a school magazine, and my own father was involved. I published a joke poem that began 'Whisky made my father tight'. I meant an imaginary father, not mine. I didn't mean to suggest that my father had a drink problem (he didn't), but readers, including parents who knew my father, might have thought 'Out of the mouths of babes and sucklings ...' It was plainly libellous – and unnecessary. I could have written 'Whisky made his father tight ...' and no one could say it referred to anyone in particular. I was the editor of the magazine, and there was no one to check my copy. An alert sub-editor might – should – have sounded the alarm. This is the value of a second pair of eyes.

GROW WITH CARE. As editor of the student magazine, Oxford Opinion, I presided over an evolutionary expansion, including four issues in the term instead of three, a visual rather than plain text cover and distribution in Cambridge. A later, 'shock and awe' expansion – many more pages, glossy paper, changed format, distribution throughout British universities – was followed by the expiry of the magazine. Over-expansion destroyed a successful magazine that – rarely among student publications – was solvent without subsidy. It could have continued indefinitely.

SHORTER IS BETTER. Amateur writers usually want to say it too long – 2,000 words when 1,000 will do, or a series instead of a single article. That said, longer articles and series are sometimes right. I proposed for the Reading Mercury a series of articles on the distinctive Edwardian architecture to be seen along the Thames – boathouses, chalets, mansions, bridges and so on. The editor, Mr Hobson, agreed to a series against the objections of the news editor, who wanted just one or two articles. The editor was right: here the material justified a series.

UNSUBSTANTIATED INFO. When later on I urged Reading Mercury readers to visit a house that had burnt down years before, I received a hard lesson in the dangers of using unsubstantiated information. I had simply copied the material about Coleshill from an old guidebook. I fell into an elementary trap. Without corroboration, if the information is wrong, we'll be wrong; if it's out of date, we'll be out of date. We can make the information safe by confirming it with personal contact or from a second, reliable source, or by attributing it to a source (in which case the source will be wrong, not us). In the internet age, however, a second website source needs to be treated with caution. Sites frequently recycle information – which may make it wrong many times over!

BYLINES OR FEES? I received no payments for the Mercury articles, perhaps because I was too naive to ask. But it got me into print, and greatly boosted my confidence. What matters in the early stages of freelancing are writing credits (bylines). Sometimes it's good, despite Dr Johnson's dictum that nobody but a fool works for anything except money, to work for nothing except the bylines.

Periodical press (Chapter 2)

FALSE PRIDE. After my graduation from university, the Reading Mercury offered me a job as a trainee reporter. I turned this down out of false pride: I had written feature articles for them, and the drudgery of general reporting seemed like a loss of face. It was nothing of the sort. Mr Hobson's offer would have turned me from an amateur contributor into a professional journalist. I was hopelessly unrealistic about where I was.

AT THE DEEP END. I was lucky not to find myself in a career cul-de-sac. In the early Sixties, journalism training consisted of day-release and block-release courses for indentured trainees. Pre-entry courses for those yet to be employed in journalism were not available. I found myself by a circuitous route on a weekly news magazine for family doctors, Pulse. It started as soft public relations, but evolved beyond that. This job was outside the scope of the indentured training scheme, so I received no formal training. The philosophy of 'being thrown in at the deep end' has its limits. It took me years to discover what I would have found out in months with systematic training. I believe that every employee is entitled to appropriate training.

The corollary is that when employees fail, it's usually not their fault. If I didn't fail at Pulse, I certainly wasn't a shining success. Maybe the failing employee has not received adequate training; perhaps he or she is in the wrong job. In fact, short of a drink problem, a family crisis or a nervous breakdown, failure is the management's fault, not the individual's.

PRIORITISING. The boss, Alan Huet Owen, liked to think that he gave his people good on-the-job training. In reality, the training came with substantial amounts of harassment and bullying. He was fizzing with ideas, which he threw at me in indiscriminate amounts. I was too inexperienced to sort the urgent from the non-urgent, the important from the optional. I had yet to learn to prioritise ideas and activities.

TECHNICAL COPY. I was often at sea with the meaning of the copy I was handling. Editors and sub-editors on specialist publications like Pulse face the problem of processing technical copy they don't fully understand themselves. The newspaper dictum of not putting into type anything you don't understand can't apply with technical magazines. If it did, everything in a medical magazine would have to be edited by doctors. Unaffordable! Like others in the same boat, I developed an intuition for what was safe and what needed to be checked. Sometimes, however, the only resolution of the dilemma is to clear the edited version with the contributor. The sub-editor is well advised to check points individually. If the contributor has sight of the whole piece, the changes may prompt a row – even if they are journalistically necessary!

SPEC LETTERS. I got my break into daily journalism by a speculative letter. This approach worked for me again with my American newspaper (see Chapter 5). Nine out of 10 letters will fail and most won't even be answered. But the 10th may land you the job. It may even be the job you wanted most, as my experience with the Yorkshire Post showed.

Yorkshire (Prologue and Chapter 3)

TENACITY. In all the years since, I've believed that my tenacity in getting to Leeds in the worst of the weather got me the Yorkshire Post job, allowing me to cross over from the periodical press to daily newspapers. Perhaps there were other factors but, never mind, tenacity is a key quality in journalism. We can all go a long way with it.

HORSES FOR COURSES. Sidney Burton of the Yorkshire Post was the first copy-taker I saw in action. It is one of the toughest jobs in newspapers, requiring the ability to cope with a never-ending flow of material and to take instant decisions on which stories to use and at what length. The always cheerful Sid was an impressive performer, but the job doesn't suit everyone. That would include me. Nor did I like my temporary stint as a leader writer for the opposite reason: a whole day to generate 300 words wasn't my idea of action! The joy of journalism is that it has jobs for every temperament, from the scholarly introvert to the gung-ho extrovert.

WORK FLOW. The working environment in the YP subs' room was a revelation to me after the difficulties in my previous job. Sid fed us one story at a time; then waited until we were clear before giving us the next one. Later, I was to find that this is usual practice in properly organised subs' desks. Having worked on several, in Britain and America, I've never been told 'Hurry up' (although at one place I was discreetly asked to slow down!). It is the way to get the best results. People work at different speeds, but malingerers are rare to non-existent among subs on major newspapers.

UNFLAPPABLE. Another impressive performer was Bernard Dineen, the features editor. He declined to flap when interrupted on deadline. The telephone caller would think he had all the time in the world. Bernard's secret was that he was on top of the job and, sensibly, had a bit of capacity in hand as the deadline neared.

HOUSE STYLE. Reporters are famously free and easy about house style, but sub-editors have to believe it matters whether we write 7 kg or 7 kgs and say 'the council has' or the 'the council have'. The Yorkshire Post had an elaborate style book, understood to be inspired by that of the Daily Telegraph. As well as preferred usages, it gave helpful advice about common grammatical and factual pitfalls. Readers notice inconsistent usages and grammatical mistakes, so an office stylebook is an essential part of professionalism.

UNSOCIAL HOURS. Sub-editors on morning newspapers give up a lot of their social life – anything that involves regular evenings and weekends. The typical shift begins mid-afternoon and continues until late evening. In my case, amateur dramatics and cricket were out, not to mention crippled chances on the dating scene! The job isn't for everyone, especially younger people.

STIRRING UP THE READERS. Lack of letters to the editor doesn't mean that the newspaper isn't being read. The Yorkshire Post in my day often had surprisingly few letters to publish. However, it does suggest that the content is not stimulating enough. That's why newspapers run columnists with contrary views to their own. And for the columnist, it's more important to be interesting than right.

HIDDEN LIBELS. If we call someone a thief and he isn't, that's plainly defamatory and needs to be punished. But the law of libel is trickier than this. One of the toughest parts is innuendo. I wrote that a Yorkshire landowner 'only rarely' visited his estate. I didn't mean to suggest that the landowner was neglecting his estate and his tenants, but that was what he claimed. The newspaper's lawyers agreed there was an innuendo (hidden or extended meaning) to that effect. For journalists, innuendoes are more of a problem than plain statements because like the rocks below the water they often aren't seen until too late. It's often forgotten that truth is a complete defence in libel. The law gives us more protection than we may think. My statement about the

Yorkshire landowner was true, but we didn't think we could prove it in court.

TRITE INTROS. Ever since Yorkshire Post days, I've hated feature intros that use corny sayings or quotes. I used a familiar line from Shakespeare to begin a profile of a Leeds worthy. It was rightly put into the dustbin. This sort of cliché is just as much to be avoided as threadbare sayings like 'a red rag to a bull'.

APPLYING FOR JOBS. Twice in my career, I've applied for two jobs simultaneously – when I wanted to move to Fleet Street and when I wanted to leave it. By applying for two jobs you can take your first choice if it comes up, but if it doesn't you've saved a lot a time in locating an alternative. I applied to the Guardian and the Telegraph from Leeds, and had offers from both. I wound up working for both – the Guardian during the week and the Sunday Telegraph on Saturday. Four years later, I had to decide between jobs in Tanzania and the United States. I chose America and stayed there for three years. Turning down the offer of a job that you've applied for may leave noses out of joint, but they have bigger things to worry about and the noses will soon come back into shape.

Fleet Street (Chapter 4)

FINDING OUR METIER. Journalism has satisfying jobs for people of all types, but we need to find our metier. I was slow to recognise that my metier in sub-editing was on the stone. I was good at progress-chasing the pages as they flowed through the composing room, making quick cuts for length and rewording 'bust' headlines. On the other hand, the grind of text editing and headline writing night after night, combined with an impracticable commute, led to a nervous collapse. My Guardian colleagues Arnold Kemp and Donald Wintersgill in different ways identified their metiers, and changed course. Arnold, a Scotsman, left London journalism for Edinburgh and later Glasgow; Donald became an antiques correspondent.

ON THE ROAD. Work as a sub-editor has its own, quiet satisfactions, but is better done when we have had our fill of being 'on the road' as writers. Further on in my career, I was happier at the subs' table. Sub-editors have been described as the people who *make* the newspaper. Later trends to reduce or even abolish the function are to be deplored, resulting in a loss of quality. Few writers realise the importance of sub-editing, although Clare Hollingworth of the Guardian graciously acknowledged that she owed a major award to the subs.

DESIGN CRUCIAL. Publications that depend heavily on 'the look' – mass circulation newspapers and consumer magazines – also need layout artists or graphic designers. They are the powers behind the throne because they make us want to read the words. This was my big lesson when I went to work at the pre-Murdoch Sun, and encountered them for the first time. The Sun's design was highly innovatory. The look could not have been achieved to the same standard by journalists without graphical training.

CAREER LADDER. The Guardian of my time had many people who were still there 40 years later. Many of these lifers by then occupied the summits. Experience on a variety of publications is good in career terms only up to a point. Beyond it, we become rolling stones. This may be personally satisfying, but it isn't a path to the top. The rule for those who want to be editors is not to change ships except for a promotion. Otherwise the better course is to stay on board and hope to climb the internal ladder.

SPECIALISTS. Specialist writers are among those journalists who have found a niche and have no wish to be editors. Probably the most erudite at the Guardian, and certainly the most obscure, was Victor Zorza, the Kremlinologist. His articles on the never-ending ins and outs of Kremlin policy, derived from the meticulous research, were absorbing for a handful of readers but of doubtful interest to most. Material of this degree of specialism is treating a general newspaper like a club noticeboard.

SATURDAY SHIFTS. My regular Saturday shifts with the Sunday Telegraph were among my most satisfying jobs in journalism. Sunday newspapers, with their small core of full-time staff, need more help one day a week. Saturday subbing shifts were and are a useful source of extra income; Saturday reporting shifts were and are harder to come by. I was often chosen to handle front page running stories at the Telegraph because I could cope with the pressure of fast moving events and could collate material raining down from different sources.

SUBBING STANDARDS. I warmed to the strict sub-editing standards at the Telegraph. I was impressed by proprietor Lord Hartwell's attention to detail, working his way through galley proofs and making suggestions for improvements (a method also followed by the editor of the Yorkshire Post, Kenneth Young, who was a former Telegraph man). Resetting of type in galleys was time-consuming and costly, but Hartwell was a perfectionist. His method, however, remains relevant, and works better today when type can be changed in a computer quickly and at zero cost.

BUSINESS NEEDS. The Telegraph group's priority in those days was journalism without enough regard to the business side. This led to its forced sale to Conrad Black, later to serve time in an American prison for offences connected with his newspaper empire. The Guardian, protected by its special trust status, has constantly put itself under financial pressure because of its easygoing approach to editorial spending, leading to the sale in later years of capital assets.

'POPULAR' v 'QUALITY'. In a paradox that outsiders find strange, it is harder to hold down a job on mass circulation ('popular') papers than it is on the more prestigious ('quality', or 'unpopular' !) papers. This is particularly true of sub-editing, but it is also so with reporting. Both subbing and writing have to be tighter; ideas must be expressed more clearly – although not necessarily more superficially. I struggled on the Sun where I hadn't on the Guardian. In recent years, the quality-popular divide has narrowed as the upmarket papers chase circulation by making themselves more popular. Disregard different layouts, and it can be hard to tell in which type of paper a news item and even more a feature has appeared. Popular journalists find it provoking that they have superior technical skills and less prestige than their counterparts on upmarket newspapers. However, they can console themselves with the better money!

Plymouth (Chapter 8)

GRADUATE TRAINING. The Mirror graduate training programme when I took over was attracting far fewer applications than a national scheme of its stature ought to have done. This was easily put right by determined publicity, mainly to the universities. Within three years we had increased applications five-fold. The iron law of marketing applied here as everywhere else: if you don't tell it, you can't sell it. No organisation, however huge and whatever its reputation, will succeed if it sits back and waits for people to come to it.

MOTIVATION. One of the crucial qualities in journalism is motivation. It's a competitive business, and in many ways a difficult business. The half-hearted are unlikely to succeed. I paid special attention in the selection process to the question 'What other training programmes have you applied to?' The opportunistic answer might seem to be 'none', implying a single-minded wish to work for the Mirror Group. In fact, I eliminated anyone who wrote 'none' because either the answer was untrue or the applicant was insufficiently motivated. Someone who was truly keen to get into journalism would try every possibility.

TYPES OF TRAINING. The Mirror training scheme was highly successful in producing journalists who worked all over Fleet Street. Several more became best-selling authors. Much of this was due to the unique pattern of training that evolved at Plymouth. (I'm not claiming credit for this model, which existed before I arrived, although I like to think I improved it here and there.) Elsewhere in the country, journalists were trained in a variety of ways: pre-entry courses, block release courses or day release courses. It was a matter of debate which was the most effective method. Mirror trainees experienced all three.

The trainees attended a full-time course before starting on their newspapers, then a 'top-up' block course some six months later. Throughout their two years with the scheme, trainees came back weekly for day-release training. They were posted to two, sometimes three newspapers – a weekly and then the Sunday Independent. We were able to pursue this Rolls-Royce approach to journalism training because the Mirror had bought the local company specifically for the training scheme.

COPY CLINICS. I was proud of an innovation I called copy clinic. Trainees made an additional copy of everything they wrote, and passed this to me. I returned these articles with my comments, good and bad. The clinic system helped to address issues of English as well as the structure and impact of articles. The system had value for the trainee because I was able to give a piece more attention than a hard-pressed sub-editor could in the rough-and-tumble of production. A problem for the trainee journalist was that an article might be changed before appearing in print but with no explanation. With my training orientation, I would not only suggest a change but also give the reason why. I was careful not to appear to be competing with or second-guessing the editors and sub-editors. For this reason copy was usually critiqued after the stories had been published.

SHORTHAND AND TYPING. We taught touch-typing and shorthand (using the Teeline system), although the National Council for the Training of Journalists qualification examination tested only shorthand. The British newspaper industry is obsessed with it. I continue to believe that typing is a more important journalistic skill than shorthand. My reason is simple. Shorthand is tested to 100 words a minute – but no one speaks that slowly in the real world. The 100 wpm note-taker will be left behind after a sentence or so. He or she might as well jot down key names, facts and phrases, and reconstruct the passage from that – as journalists in most other countries do.

Home front (Chapter 12)

TOUGH QUESTIONS. Working with the Civil Service College (later the National School of Government), I trained civil servants in how to handle the news media. I was also training journalists for other clients. I asked myself about the rightness of showing journalists how to ask tough questions and showing civil servants how to answer, and possibly parry or block, tough questions! I answered myself with the idea of a level playing field. Civil servants tended to lack the skills to put their case effectively to journalists. We the public benefited when cases were properly presented.

DRY-RUN INTERVIEWS. The biggest demand for many years was for help with TV and radio appearances. My colleagues and I ran simulated interviews using attendees' own material. The interviews were video-recorded, played back and critiqued. This type of training is effective but time-consuming. Our courses typically had one tutor for every three attendees. A course worked best with two or three tutors and up to nine attendees, allowing for plenary sessions as well as small group work. If the training is to be effective, there is no way round this expensive, hands-on approach. Presentational skills can't be learnt properly from a computer programme.

'COSMETIC EFFECT'. All of us seeing ourselves on screen for the first time are obsessed with how we look or sound – the universal 'cosmetic effect'. It's invariably different from how we imagine ourselves. The reaction is curious since we are well used to seeing ourselves in static photographs, not to mention bathroom mirrors! Once we have got over the cosmetic effect, we can get down to business.

PRESENTATION FAULTS. The most common faults of presentation are lack of eye contact (looking down – dejected; looking up – helpless; looking past the interviewer or camera – struggling), talking too long – hopeless for a TV studio interview of three minutes or a soundbite of 20 seconds – and speaking in a monotone, which comes over as either nervous or over-rehearsed. Defending the weakest point at length is a tactical error. It should be dealt with briskly before moving to stronger ground. This is the switch technique: 'But frankly, the real issue is ...')

PRESS RELEASES. For both civil service and public relations officers on my journalism courses, I gave the same message about press releases – that if we want them to be used (and otherwise what's the point?), they must be produced in the form that the media want. I was aware that trade magazines and smaller newspapers often used press releases unaltered – and sometimes bigger publications could be tempted – but they drew the line at crude propaganda. The language of the effective press release is not that of the advertisement.

DIRECT TO THE PUBLIC. Generally, what is needed is for press releases to be written and headlined like a news story. Another reason for press releases to be written to be read is that they will appear on the organisation's website. This direct access to the public amounts to an exciting new channel of communication, which is there to be used.

KEY QUOTES. Government press releases were usually unimpressive because they were formulaic. They don't appear to have improved over the years. It was common for press releases to start with a quote from the minister, even though a verbatim quote is invariably not the best way to start a news story. There was a tendency to quote officials in order of seniority, although journalistically the most worthwhile quote might come from the most junior official!

INTRANSIGENCE. I dropped out from courses with Reed Business Publishing because along with other tutors I was asked to take a temporary fee cut. The department's budget constraints were genuine. Such intransigence on my part was self-defeating. Sometimes it's right to bend a little.

PITCHING THE MESSAGE. I wondered why I failed to get through to teenagers on a media awareness course at Uxbridge College that I ran one day a week for two years. Then the penny dropped: I was lecturing them as I was accustomed to do with adults. When we started to put together a course newspaper – a practical project to which everyone could contribute – their attention and their interest were transformed. Adapt your material to your audience and – for all groups – keep it active!

COURSE LENGTH. One of the most enjoyable courses for me was the National Council for the Training of Journalists' residential sub-editing programme at Rugby. This ran from Sunday evening to Friday lunchtime. This length was unimaginable in later years, with the consequent loss of training in depth. Editors and managers started to want in one or two days what had previously been done in four or five. The NCTJ's Writing for a Market course was good while it lasted. This was held over three weekends – again a length that had to be cut back. Recessions come and go, but training budgets have been affected by what looks like systemic change – falling sales of printed newspapers and magazines, and the uncertainties of making money from web-based publications.

EDITORIAL SYNDICATION. Syndication is a handy way for a newspaper to offset some of its editorial costs by selling its material for republication by others. The Observer was a good example of how to run a syndication service. It had an impressive system of 'spot sales'. As well as clients who received the regular service, it had a list of further publications to be contacted for possible one-off sales of particular stories and pictures. I became involved with Observer syndication when the Guardian bought the parent newspaper. The Guardian's syndication service survived into the era of the online newspaper. Although clients could have picked stories off the website, they preferred to continue to pay for a tailored service.

Reporter (Chapter 14)

KEEPING IN TOUCH. It was stimulating to work again as a road-going reporter for a decade up to 2005. This was partly from a desire for a new challenge; partly to revalidate my training work. I was aware of too many teachers and trainers looking at their working experience receding in the rear-view mirror. They became progressively out of touch, especially in an era of great technical change like the present one.

READABILITY. I was a better writer because of my long spells as a sub-editor, when tight writing becomes second nature. Shorter sentences are one of the main yardsticks of readability. The other is the amount of long words in a passage – broadly, those of three or more syllables. We should aim to reduce (minimise), but not get rid of (eliminate), long words.

BACKGROUND. Ecumenical News International news agency was marked by careful attention to detail. Backgrounding might be written into correspondents' reports. Generally, this was helpful, but sometimes it was over-zealous. A churches readership doesn't need to be told that the cross is a key symbol of Christianity.

INTERPRETATION. ENI's abhorrence of interpretation – which it saw as editorialising – I found dated. The two aren't the same. Editorialising is expressing an opinion; interpretation is drawing out the meaning of a news situation. The line between them isn't especially hard to draw in practice, but can be intentionally overstepped. I rarely watch the news on Britain's two main terrestrial television channels for this reason. The reporting style is self-indulgent. Reports are frequently more recognisable as correspondents' opinion than as interpretation – a process encouraged by newsreaders doing live interviews with correspondents in the field, turning them into a source of news instead of a conduit of news.

BAD NEWS AGENDA. Broadcaster Martyn Lewis's widely publicised call for television news to dwell less on doom and gloom deserved more than the kneejerk rejection it received from some of the luminaries of British TV journalism. I agreed with Lewis. The issue is not about injecting happy, non-news stories but about balance. The present news agenda produces a 'false Gestalt': wars, famine, crimes, unemployment and crashes – each item is true enough but, taken together, the world appears to be a worse and wickeder place than it really is. Journalists from the Majority World are amazed at the Western media's obsession with gloom and doom – nowhere more than in Britain.

PROs. Public relations officers sometimes tried to call the shots more than I was used to or cared to accept. When I arrived to interview vicar-cum-horror writer G.P. Taylor, the PRO asked me to ask my questions while the author autographed his way through piles of copies. I insisted that he put down his pen for 20 minutes, in return for which I would finish on the dot. This was agreed. Ask and you shall receive ... Entertainment journalists who allow PROs to vet the questions and the resultant copy might try being awkward. My reward for arranging for myself an interview with Bishop Richard Holloway at the 1998 Lambeth Conference, instead of going through designated channels, was the press officers' bemusement as he strolled into the press centre for the interview.

MIXED SIGNALS. Evidently no press officer was on hand to straighten out Rowan Williams's inaugural address as Archbishop of Canterbury. The congregation in Canterbury Cathedral must have been as baffled as the press corps. Next day's newspaper reports reflected this uncertainty with a variety of intros – for the speaker a public relations disaster.

PREDICTION PIECES. 'Runners and riders' articles are tricky and time-consuming, but if the predictions are wrong at least they are quickly forgotten! By good fortune my piece for the Observer syndication service about the next Pope included Cardinal Josef Ratzinger, the winner. I slipped him in among the outsiders, but at least he was there.

LENGTH LIMITS. Thompson's World Insurance News, another freelance client, had a simple but effective format for its daily electronic edition. Every issue had three items of strictly 200 words each plus a wrapping paragraph of shorts. I used a version of the idea for an entire book (*Byliners: 101 Ways to be a Freelance Journalist* – see Chapter 16), and found it a terrific way to produce disciplined writing.

PUBLICATION BY ACCIDENT. Tony Thompson, the founder of Thompson's, in his freelancing days sold the same article to rival editors by accident. This produced nuclear explosions. Tony placed the article with the Financial Times in London and also to a business publication in Chicago, forgetting that the FT might syndicate the article – which it did, to another Chicago publication. For the freelance, syndication is easy to overlook.

SPOT SALES. Freelance contributors to the Guardian used to get nothing extra when a syndication spot sale was made. Even worse, the newspaper made a profit on the article, selling it to other nationals like the Daily Mail for more than it paid the contributor. Then a freelance charter was hammered out, providing that the proceeds of spot sales were to be split 50:50 between the paper and the contributor.

FREELANCE FEES. It was no surprise to find in my long-running column for BAJ (British Association of Journalists) News that fees for articles were substantially higher in the mass circulation newspapers than in the upmarket papers. Two findings, reiterated over the years, were striking. Fees were disgracefully low in important regional daily newspapers, where a major article might command little more than £100. Fees in glossy consumer magazines were as high as in mass circulation newspapers – but editors expected more for their money. They might demand full rewrites – rarely done in newspapers.

Entrepreneur (Chapter 15)

JOINT MARKETING. In the early 1990s, I turned myself from a freelance trainer into an entrepreneur of open journalism courses. The trigger for the creation of Pulford Media Ltd was the National Council for the Training of Journalists' decision to close down its Writing for a Market course. As the lead tutor, I felt there was more mileage in the course (renamed News and Feature Writing). My colleagues and I took over the NCTJ's design course for the same reason, and added courses of our own. We had a marketing agreement with the training council. When this ended a dozen or so years later, they offered News and Feature Writing themselves – vindicating my decision to save it all those years before.

COURSE ECONOMICS. Our courses ran for one or two days. An attraction of the open course business is that fees are charged per participant. The main direct costs – tutor fees and venue hire – are essentially the same with three or 30 participants. This means that profit rises steeply after breakeven is passed. Nor do open courses incur upfront costs (subject to agreements with the tutor and the venue) if they have to be cancelled through lack of support. This was increasingly the case as the training environment became more difficult after the Millennium.

My philosophy was that if a course covered its costs it was worth doing. It was a shop window for the more dependable and profitable in-house courses. Here we worked for an organisation on a day rate, thus being assured of a profit. In practice, a training provider's reputation is damaged if it keeps announcing open courses and cancelling them. This led us sometimes to run courses for two people, at a loss.

MATURE RECRUITS. People of many ages and backgrounds, if they are motivated enough, can become successful journalists. This was clear from training projects at Fairplay shipping magazine and the Evening Post newspaper in Bristol. I found that middle-aged ex-mariners, recruited by Fairplay because of their specialist knowledge, were well able to adapt to the demands of journalism. The same was true with former printers at the Evening Post. They were retrained as sub-editors as part of a management-union deal for the introduction of computers, which made most printers redundant.

CONTROLLED CIRCULATION. When I was the design consultant for the Association of Free Newspapers, it looked as if free newspapers would become universal in the local press. Free, or 'controlled circulation', specialist magazines had been around for years. It never worked out that way. A hybrid local newspaper scene has persisted, with some titles free and others paid for. Among several factors in a complex economic calculation, it seems that many readers are prepared to pay for the larger amount of editorial that paid papers provide.

NETWORKING. There is no level of success at which business comes of its own accord. Both companies and individuals must constantly refresh the awareness of what they offer. Networking may be tedious but it's necessary. Those who aren't willing to network (like me) should lower their expectations.

WHEN TO QUIT. I've known too many trainers and journalists who went on in their seventies when clearly past their best, only they didn't realise it. We can all fool ourselves, especially when the work is precious to us. It was doubly difficult for me because I had no direct boss to tell me to go. I decided to retire from teaching when I reached 70 in 2008, hopefully before people could say I was past my work. I had retired from freelance journalism three years earlier, to clear space for book writing. I've no qualms in continuing with authorship as long as capabilities allow because that is what authors do.

OFFICES ANYWHERE. My retirement did not spell the end of Pulford Media. Liz Tayfun took over co-ordinating the courses. She was based in the Geneva area. We calculated, correctly as it turned out, that in the days of emails, wifi and Skype no one would worry about the training manager being out of the country. Liz also delivered the substantial upside of attracting clients among international NGOs.

Author (Chapter 16)

RULES FOR WRITERS. For years I failed to write a publishable book because I ignored two of the basic rules of authorship. I was not writing out of my own experience. I simply chose subjects that interested me, but in none apart from journalism was I a specialist. Secondly, I gave up after the first rejection – yet many books that became huge successes were turned down by publishers queueing up to say no.

DIRECT EXPERIENCE. Commercially, my most successful book has been *JournoLISTS*. It is also the nearest, along with *Byliners*, to my own direct experience. This demonstrates the publishing dictum in the previous paragraph. *JournoLISTS* was one of the easiest and quickest books to write – an irony that lies behind many best sellers.

FINDING IDEAS. A book may emerge from the germ of an idea encountered here, there or anywhere. In *Eating Uganda* I read about Anglican and Roman Catholic missionaries at each other's throats deep in the African interior, and thought, 'I can do something with this.' In *Air Madness* I had a eureka moment of relating the growth of the motor car a century ago to the growth of aviation now.

THEMES. Producing a 100,000-word book is tougher than writing 100 articles of 1,000 words, which experienced journalists would find easy given time. The need to maintain a theme over the length of the book, and the scale of the operation, make it a qualitatively different task.

WRITING DISCIPLINE. Books don't get written by waiting for the right mood. My philosophy was and is to get something on paper or screen, even if it seems to be rubbish. It can always be revised or rewritten, and by then the creative juices will be flowing. I work to a daily quota – around 1,200 words; not especially large. Writers' quotas are anything from 500 words a day (several famous novelists) to 4,000 words or more (Mills and Boon etc). On the other hand, I turn out more or less finished copy, needing only the occasional tweaking and tightening.

USING NOTES. Working too closely from notes tends to slow down the job of writing, and disrupt the creative flow. My method for speeding up the job is to put down the content in three stages: (1) absorb the information from notes and web searches; (2) write it up from memory; (3) check and infill by returning to the notes web transcriptions.

THROW NOTHING AWAY! Two of my books were reworkings in a different form of decades-old discarded projects (*Air Madness* and *Siren Society*) – a reminder that a writer should throw nothing away!

DOING IT ALL. After failing to find a publisher for my first book, I set up Ituri Publications to bring it out. For a writer to bring out his own book was returning publishing to its 18th century roots. None of my later books has been offered to an external publisher. I've enjoyed doing things myself, harnessing my knowledge of editing and design, and learning lots about the business side of publishing.

MARKETING. The classic difficulty for the small publisher is marketing. This was even cited as a reason for the venerable mid-size house of John Murray putting itself up for sale. Ituri lacks the marketing clout of a larger publisher. I've traded bigger sales for control (including the freedom to publish what I want) – a deal I haven't regretted.

EBOOKS. Ituri has moved into ebooks. They are practical for readers, and also attractive to publishers with their minimal typographical costs and almost zero distribution costs. They should allow smaller publishers, who lack capital, to put out more books. Even so, I'd be sad if the printed book was driven to extinction or near-extinction. I doubt that a computer file, aka an ebook, will come to be seen as a thing of beauty!

... AND AWAY

America (Chapter 5)

FILLING SPACE. In America, I discovered that brevity, that much vaunted quality in journalism, isn't always a virtue! The suburban desk of the (Cleveland) Plain Dealer was often short of copy. The first priority was to fill the space. US journalism was long-winded compared with what I was used to. The main reason was economic. Newspapers with enormous pagination to accommodate advertising also meant a large and not always wanted amount of editorial space.

SUBBING TRADITIONS. As a copy editor (sub-editor) on the Plain Dealer, I found that less was expected of me than it had been in London or Yorkshire. UK subbing has a stronger tradition of cutting, tightening and polishing copy. Yet the PD was one of the more actively subbed US papers. Copy from the Associated Press news agency was re-edited. On many papers, it was fed directly from the wire to the composing room. American news writing is usually longer than its British equivalent, but by no means more informative.

'TURNING' STORIES. I was struck by the abundance of 'turns', or 'jumps', of stories from the front page to their continuation inside. Readers like a story to be complete on the page. While inevitable for some long stories, the practice was appalling when the turn was only an inch or two (2.5 cms or so). That's where cutting should come in!

DOMINANT ADVERTISING. Advertisers often preferred a page with a tiny amount of editorial to a full page for themselves. The idea was that readers were less likely to skip the page if it contained a news story. This produced shapes that no journalist would choose: a shallow story in a strip across the broadsheet page, or a single column of editorial manner from top to bottom of the page. These unattractive layouts exemplified the dominance of advertisements.

U.S. JOURNALISM. It wasn't hard for a Briton to adapt to American journalism. The understanding of journalism in the two countries is essentially the same. Both traditions, for example, maintain the difference between news and comment. This isn't always so – for good and ill – in the journalism of other countries. In both the US and UK traditions, the media are separate from government and normally don't have overt political party affiliations.

The differences in the journalism of the two countries are superficial – a few cases of spelling, even fewer points of grammar; articles longer; legal reporting subject to fewer restrictions. One of the most striking differences for me was the pre-trial reporting of criminal cases. The media reported in detail the very allegations that a jury would later have to consider. Although complaints were heard about 'trial by the press', the US media were untroubled by a sub judice rule. In Britain, such reporting was impossible without being in contempt of court. Pre-trial publicity was held to compromise a jury's ability to decide solely on the issues presented in court. I formed the view that the answer lay somewhere in the middle – that crime reports say too much in the US and too little in the UK, particularly in cases to be decided by a judge alone.

The common law offence of libel is the same in both countries, but its working in practice is very different. It is far harder for a claimant to succeed in America because, under a US Supreme Court decision, a defendant newspaper need be not only wrong but also wrong with malice. In Britain, on the other hand, inadvertent error is no defence. Neither approach is perfect. The British approach tends to favour the individual at the expense of the public; the American approach tends to favour the public at the expense of the individual.

FREE SPEECH. A commitment to free speech is enshrined in the US constitution. One consequence is the ease with which journalists can reach public officials. These take it as part of their duty to talk to the media. During my short spell as a reporter with the Plain Dealer, the chief of police for the city of Cleveland had his home number in the phone book. When I wanted to speak with Chief Coffey, I just picked up the phone and called him.

INTERVIEWING AIDES. I regretted agreeing to interview a senator's aide, not the man himself, for an article about the Vietnam War, to be sent home. My newspaper (the Yorkshire Post) probably didn't show on the senator's radar, but why did I accept that valuation? If I'd insisted on the senator or nothing, probably I'd have got him.

FOREIGN CORRESPONDENTS. The Plain Dealer's London correspondent – a 'remittance man' from the former owning family – was a determined provider of topical backgrounders. Perhaps he took it too far, but he was right not to compete with the news agencies. The job of the foreign corr is to add value to the information provided by agencies through analysis, feature articles, colour pieces and first-hand experiences.

FREEBIES. The better American publications are strict about 'freebies'. They set limits on what a journalist may accept. Some travel writers have paid for flights and accommodation rather than accepting facility visits. The concern is justified. From a free restaurant meal for two to a complimentary stay at a Caribbean resort, freebies are buying a sense of goodwill with the journalists who benefit. That's why companies and other organisations do it.

UNIVERSAL JOURNALISM. Between them, Britain and America have moulded journalism in other English-speaking countries. This means that English-language journalism has a recognisable similarity around the world. English-speaking journalists have a unique advantage in working away from home. We have a 'ticket to ride' because English and English-language newspapers are so universal.

Thomson Foundation (Chapter 6)

MAJORITY WORLD ISSUES. My time with the Thomson Foundation was a crash course in the special issues of Majority World journalism. State control rarely meant a censor poring over copy with a blue pencil, but it was a reality all the same. Issues like government corruption and ethnic divisions typically could not be reported. The appalling wages of journalists – a reflection of economic underdevelopment – left them open to inducements or bribes.

SKILLS GAP. Europe and America's best contribution to closing the skills gap between north and south was to provide down-to-earth, practical training. The world was awash with media sociologists and mass communication specialists. The men and women who came to the Thomson Foundation had heard about nation building a thousand times: they wanted to know how to put out a better newspaper or TV programme. The skills gap has narrowed over the years, but will remain until the level of economic development in the global south catches up with that of the north. Since the north continues to pursue a path of further development, this is nowhere in sight.

TALK-DO-DISCUSS. The Thomson Foundation taught me to avoid 'talking shop' courses. It used the talk-do-discuss format, which keeps programmes active and interesting. I've followed this format ever since, normally programming a practical exercise every half-day. I try to avoid back-to-back talk sessions (lectures). I don't subscribe to the modish practice of turning every session into a discussion, an occasion to be 'facilitated'. I'm there because I know something they don't: they need to be told what it is before they can usefully discuss it! (I use the same approach with courses for British students.)

AGE ISSUES. Working with people from less privileged countries challenges many of our everyday assumptions. When I commented that the Thomson Foundation director was aged 62, the students gave a collective gasp of amazement. In many countries 62 is old, not late middle age as we like to think in the West.

SPEAKING SLOWLY. A special way of speaking is needed with people for whom English is a second language. The knack is to speak slightly more slowly than normal, but not so slow that the audience realises it. I was often praised for my clarity, so I concluded that I had acquired the knack. Zambia was an exception. There I spoke at normal speed. Zambians receive even their primary schooling in English, even though few have it as their first language.

CULTURAL CONFUSIONS. No one thought to brief me that when Indians shake their heads they are expressing agreement. I became downcast when during a lecture two Indians shook their heads ever more vigorously. This impressed me with the need to prepare for cultural and language differences when working in foreign countries and meeting foreign nationals. When Africans and some others say the meal was 'quite nice', they mean it was *very* nice, not *fairly* nice!

LONELY. The foreign assignments were the glamorous part of my work with the Thomson Foundation. Yet they came with lonely evenings in hotel rooms for a month or more. Sometimes I travelled with a fellow lecturer; at other times, I was alone. In the end, I preferred to work solo. My personal test for alcohol dependency, or the avoidance of it, was to keep a bottle of whisky in my room and have some left at the end of the month.

Africa (Chapters 7 and 9)

ECONOMICS THE KEY. My first assignments in the Majority World were in West Africa – Sierra Leone, Nigeria, Ghana and the Gambia. The situation of the press fell into a pattern that I was to find widely around Africa and Asia. Newspapers in

Nigeria and Ghana were more developed than those in Sierra Leone and the Gambia. This was nothing to do with a country's sophistication or cultural level. It was economics, pure and simple – having a big enough commercial sector to support advertising revenue and a big enough population to buy the papers.

Even in Nigeria, the press at that time (1972-73) had plenty of room to grow. Total daily newspaper circulation was around 350,000. In the UK, with a somewhat smaller population, the comparable figure was more than 20 million. This was the measure of the economic and literacy gaps needing to be closed.

PRESS VARIETY. Nigerian newspapers were numerous and exuberant, a mixture of the official, or government-controlled, and private press. They ranged from the accomplished Daily Times, which looked and felt like Britain's Daily Mirror (it was part-owned by the Mirror group), to the starving amateurism of the West African Pilot, a famous nationalist paper living on its past glories.

PRESS CONTROLS. The Nigerian news media lived and worked under the shadow of a 1964 press law, which held journalists responsible for the truth of what they wrote. This was a harsher version of what the civil law of libel provides anyway where the information is defamatory. It invited self-censorship, which I was to discover was the norm in various forms around the Majority World. One of Britain's worst legacies to its former colonies was to leave behind laws on the statute book to control the press. If the colonising power's intention was to invoke these only in emergencies, they nevertheless provided a blueprint for successor regimes.

PRACTICAL TRAINING. The impact of the Thomson Foundation in Africa, and elsewhere, was enormous. This was demonstrated when in my short visits to Ghana and Sierra Leone alumni turned out to greet me. Some came to the airport to see me off. The secret of the foundation's success lay in the practicality of its training in a world drowning in theorising.

BACKGROUND PREPARATION. Regrettably not for the last time, I failed to do enough background preparation before an in-country assignment. A group of South African journalists rightly criticised my colleague Tony Thompson and me for heading for Lesotho and having no idea who 'Mokhehle' was. The leftist Ntsu Mokhehle was the ballot-box choice as prime minister who was denied office.

PROPAGANDA. In South Africa itself, I was involved in a clandestine course that struggled to agree on the news media's role in a future, free country. Propaganda, even in a good cause, isn't the way. The media have a role and a responsibility in social justice, yet overt advocacy journalism is self-defeating. Dispassionate information is the most valuable contribution, not preaching to the converted.

In independent Zimbabwe, later to show that white regimes had no monopoly on repression, the Herald newspaper made a comfortable accommodation with the new government. The (European) senior managers seemed to be happy to fill the paper with propaganda. Maybe they really didn't mind. We can't count on media managements to go to the stake for press freedom. Many journalists in the Majority World will, but not necessarily their managers.

MORAL QUESTIONS. Ethiopia under the repressive rule of Colonel Mengistu raised awkward questions for the Thomson Foundation and consultants like me. We were engaged in a project of 'media development', but can this mean anything in a dictatorship except more effective propaganda and tools of oppression? Maybe. Even the wickedest government does some good on the ground. And yet ... Individual consultants are even more conflicted than the organisations behind them. Our perennial hunger for work risks blinding us to the rights and wrongs of what we do. But in any case we won't stop the project going ahead. I turned down a name-your-price assignment for the Reunification Church (the Moonies). With the predictability of a piranha fish taking the bait, the another consultant snapped up the project. Both organisations and consultants must rest our case, convincingly or not, on two bases: that we hope to help progressive elements mitigate the bad, and that if we refuse the project someone less appropriate will take it on.

URBAN AND RURAL. Addis Ababa, the capital of Ethiopia, showed in extreme form two sides of African cities. Cows wandered unherded past the gleaming new building where with the magic of the computer I was choosing my exact seat on a Paris to London flight. African cities have a modern sector founded by the colonisers and a traditional sector. Often overlooked is the third sector: the shantytowns that edge the cities. They are neither urban nor rural; in the city but not fully of it.

AGENDA SETTING. 'Agenda setting' was and is an issue in Africa and throughout the Majority World. Newspapers and broadcasters absorb and reflect the news values of the international, predominantly Western news agencies and other global media, at the expense of their own coverage and values. The agencies don't set out to project a jingoistic Western or specifically American news agenda, but they are naturally attuned to their primary markets. A developed country like Britain suffers a tidal wave of US material; in the Majority World it is a – largely unrecognised – tsunami.

BEING A TOURIST. Kenya in the 1980s was (relatively) rich and Tanzania was (unambiguously) poor. Yet tourists were advised not to walk about Nairobi, the Kenyan capital, after dark because of the risk of being mugged. Nobody had to worry about that in Dar es Salaam, the Tanzanian capital.

Tanzania, Nigeria and Zambia were among the many places where I was fortunate to see something of the country beyond my place of work, which was usually the capital city. Sometimes I stayed on privately for a few days at my own expense. I never understood many of my colleagues, who, in some of the world's most interesting places, could think only of rushing home at the first chance.

LANGUAGE SKILLS. The English-language press in some Commonwealth countries faced problems of finding journalists with sufficient skill in the language. I recommended that English ability should be a condition of recruitment. Remedial lessons for adults produce very uncertain results because by then difficulties are ingrained.

Zambia (Chapters 7 and 13)

LANGUAGE HANG-UPS. Zambia, where I worked regularly between 1973 and 1995, is a typical African country in having colonial-drawn boundaries that take no account of tribes or ancient kingdoms. The consequence of the many ethnic groups – the Bemba (also found across the border in Congo) are numerically dominant – is that English is used universally. It is the medium of instruction from primary school onwards, so the standard is excellent. Because the country has no practical choice of lingua franca, Zambia has none of the hang-ups over using English that have beset, for example, Tanzania and Malaysia – a great advantage in the modern world.

LITERACY. Even in the 1970s, Zambia had very favourable indicators for the printed press: national adult literacy (in English) at 73 per cent and urbanisation at 56 per cent – both high for Africa.

SELF-CENSORSHIP. The one-party state of President Kenneth Kaunda had complete dominance over the Zambian news media (although some minor private print productions were tolerated). Television and radio were state-owned. The two daily newspapers (the Zambia Daily Mail and the Times of Zambia) were either owned or controlled by the party and government. There was no formal censorship. There didn't need to be. Self-censorship did the job.

Satellite TV was on the scene only late in the period, and short-wave radio could be erratic. The internet was in the future. What international news Zambians read or heard was also controlled by the state. The output of foreign news agencies like Reuters and Agence Frence-Presse was filtered through the official Zambia News Agency (ZANA), which then passed the stories to the subscribing media. This control rarely involved altering material. The government was more concerned with stopping unsuitable stories, like anything tending to show apartheid South Africa in a favourable light.

OFF-DIARY STORIES. Zambia received a great deal of training aid over the years. This helped to drive up journalistic standards within the limits imposed by the government. The daily newspapers did an adequate job in processing domestic 'diary' news, but were weaker with the dug out, 'off diary' stories – the sort that doesn't come from press releases, press conferences or official announcements. This was a general weakness in Majority World newspapers, which remains an issue today around the world.

RURAL LITERACY. The government tried to expand literacy in the rural areas through newspapers in four or five vernacular languages. Among the several difficulties of the scheme was a lack of books and other reading matter in the indigenous language. Without fresh material, reading skills erode.

MORE FREEDOM. The Movement for Multiparty Democracy government of President Frederick Chiluba from 1991 freed up the media scene considerably. Partly this was intention; partly it was unavoidable in the era of satellite TV and the internet. The MMD, to its credit, accepted the vigorous, privately owned Weekly Post. Its political exposes and brisk comments – it described Chiluba as 'a product of Kaunda's repression', a man whose 'credibility begins and ends with Kaunda' – made it a best seller to a public that was highly literate in English.

PRESS REGISTRATION. However, the government was in no hurry to give up its dominance of daily newspapers. Many Zambians would have been satisfied if it had released one into the private sector and kept the other. The government's stance appeared to be that so long as anyone else could start a newspaper there was no reason why it should not keep the two it owned. Nor did it show signs of ending practices like the registration of publications or filtering the foreign news agencies through ZANA.

RELIGIOUS JOURNALISM. During my time in Zambia, I became an adviser to the international programme for religious media at the Mindolo Ecumenical Centre, Kitwe. It was an interesting excursion into non-secular journalism. I strongly urged on the organisers that religious media should operate to the same standards as secular media; that being a church publication wasn't a licence for lack of rigour or hard-edged news gathering. I also wanted to see the director in the classroom. An exaggerated sense of hierarchy is an African disease, but there is no place for it in the media.

BRAIN DRAIN. By the 1990s I had trained a substantial chunk of Zambia's press corps. Some of my original students occupied high positions. Sadly, however, there had been a 'brain drain' to other work. It happens in all countries big and small. Smaller, less economically developed countries have the further problem that the media sector can't pay enough, or offer enough career ladders, Many therefore don't see it as a lifelong career choice.

NEWSPAPERS A LUXURY. In later years, as economic austerity bit deep, newspapers became a luxury item. The MMD government eventually lost at a general election and, like Kaunda's government before it, handed over power (2011). This showed the strength of Zambian civil society, of which the news media are a part and to which they are contributors.

Asia/Caribbean (Chapters 10 and 11)

ECONOMICS UNDERLINED. The newspapers of Asia ranged from the size and sophistication of the South China Morning Post in Hong Kong to basic newssheets in Bangladesh. One was typeset by hand. Yet the Bengalis, the people of Bangladesh, are famous for their articulacy and intellectual interests. It demonstrated again, as I saw in Africa, that the state of a country's economy, not the cleverness of its people, determines the sophistication of its news media.

CORRUPTION. Corruption of journalists, in cash and kind, is an issue that has stalked the Majority World up to the present day. The lack of corruption in Britain and America, at least in a monetary sense, is founded on adequate salaries – again a by-product of economic development.

SLOW PROGRESS. Journalism hasn't improved as much as it might have done in Asia in the four decades or so since independence. It is wrong to blame the journalists for this. For much of the period, the news media in many countries faced political restrictions on what could be said and economic constraints on the availability of newsprint, photographic film etc. Maintaining an English-language press in the face of official policies to replace English was an uphill struggle. These remain issues in some countries.

Many times I saw journalists emerge from workshops with new skills and ideas, which were blocked by higher-ups unable to embrace new ways of doing things.

PRESS FREEDOM. Press freedom in Asia ranged from the openness of Hong Kong and the Philippines to the restrictiveness of Singapore and, to a lesser extent, Malaysia. I was ready to acknowledge that the requirements of the media were different in advanced and emerging countries. For example, sectarian and politically affiliated newspapers were common in emerging countries, and had the potential to stir up strife. This was especially so where the legal system was not sufficiently entrenched to secure post-publication responsibility through the courts (eg libel and confidentiality).

LEVELS OF DEVELOPMENT. I was equally keen to stress that the theoretical model of press control should not be prolonged after the need for it had gone. In the 21st century, the picture is rather different. The non-Communist world is not as dichotomous as it was 40 years earlier. Many countries are approaching Western levels of development, and need Western standards of press freedom. Malaysia's history of Communist insurgencies in both Malaya and Sarawak, with inevitable restrictions on information, didn't help. Nor did the colonial legacy of press regulation.

JOURNALISM WITH 'FIZZ'. Newspapers throughout the region tended to be too solemn, with the striking exception of the Philippines. The many newspapers there screamed their heads off. Filipino newspapers took to an exaggerated degree the American practice of turning front-page stories to inside pages. Sometimes every story turned. Obviously, this allows for more stories on the front – but readers dislike turns, and many stop at the point where the story jumps inside. The practice of frequent turns has spread to Britain with equally baleful results. In my early days, the broadsheet dictum was one turn only from the front page.

Elsewhere in the region, the press was full of politics, but where were the features, the human interest stories – the items that give the fizz?

MORAL BALANCE SHEET. A course in the Philippines posed the dilemma of working with an organisation that did bad things for good reasons. Despite the Roman Catholic Church's sincerity, the consequences of its sexual doctrines were runaway population growth, Aids, unwanted children and family poverty. Our workshop on journalism for church media helped the priests and nuns to spread the message more effectively. Are we to draw up a balance sheet of good consequences – like schools and hospitals, in this case – and bad consequences before accepting an assignment? I failed to confront the dilemma.

CONSULTANT'S ROLE. In Trinidad I agreed to a plan at the Express newspaper to work in with the staff and help them by example. It appealed to me as a way to get my hands dirty with some real journalism. The trouble was it tended to make me just another sub-editor, albeit an expensive one and a sluggard on the computer system. Consultants should use their time to best effect, not indulge personal whims.

COVERT FUNDING. Press freedom seemed to flourish in the Commonwealth Caribbean. Guyana (South American by geography but Caribbean by culture) was an exception. Local man David de Caries received openly stated funding for an independent newspaper from the National Endowment for Democracy, a US government agency that also engaged in covert funding elsewhere. I was convinced that money could be raised by other means. I argued that it would be better not to publish than to be beholden to a compromised source, which was capable of destroying the credibility of the publication. This was an example of the universal problem of whether the end (an independent voice) can justify the means (acceptance of bad money).

MEDICAL SUPPORT. Sponsors of training programmes don't always look after their people on the ground. When I was seriously injured in a street attack in Guyana, the Overseas Development Administration soon lost interest. They arranged an appointment at a London hospital, then sent me a letter reminding me that under the contract they weren't responsible. I never heard from them again. It took me nine months to recover fully. Lost in the bureaucratic maze perhaps?

China (Chapter 10)

REOPENING TO THE WORLD. China in 1981, the year of my assignment there, seemed utterly remote. Western visitors were rare. As I arrived in a bitter midwinter, I felt as if I were on another planet. The masses of blue-suited men and women, the thousands of bicycles and few cars, the monumental buildings and wide streets, the political slogans shouting from billboards – all were barely less strange. But the country was reopening to the world after decades of seclusion.

CONSULTANTS' DILEMMA. Two Thomson Foundation colleagues and I were helping to launch a newspaper for foreigners, the China Daily. We felt we were part of the liberalisation of the country, but were naive to expect that political freedom, including the media, would march in step with economic freedom. In reality, we were working with the Chinese on how to make better propaganda. This is the familiar consultants' dilemma – to stay out, or to join in and hope to be a moderating influence? Perhaps we can argue that the cause of press freedom was better served by us being there rather than a team of East Germany or Hungary (see also Ethiopia, above).

Tiananmen Square – several years after we had done our work – was an extreme test of this theory. The shots that made headlines around the world were 'buried' as a tiny item in the China Daily. It wasn't the paper I thought I was helping to launch and yet, for all I know, the editorial staff had to argue with the censor to include even that. At least the item was there.

BLUE PENCIL. Self-censorship was the norm in the Majority World, but in China an actual censor – a blue-pencil person – sat somewhere in the back. This was an extra production layer beyond the editorial staff. It was to make assurance doubly sure, even though the journalists knew what was expected of them.

'POLISHERS'. The China Daily had a commendable system to ensure that the English was correct and idiomatic. Elderly British and American expatriates, true believers who had chosen to live in China rather than their own countries, acted as 'polishers', knocking the English into shape. The system of polishing was not a million miles away from the American concept of the rewrite man, and was worth copying elsewhere.

BACKING BRITAIN. The Thomson Foundation team leader on several occasions made disparaging public comments about Britain, apparently in the belief that this was what the Chinese wanted to hear. His other colleague and I stressed to him that it wasn't appropriate to run down his own country, and nor did our hosts expect it.

B.B.C. WORLD SERVICE. Short-wave radio was my information lifeline in the days before satellite TV and the internet. I was dissatisfied with news from the BBC World Service. Too few items about Britain were included in the main bulletins. The argument that stories were played on merit and that day after day nothing from London made the cut was unconvincing. News shouldn't be manufactured, but it can be actively sought and found. Listeners to a London station were entitled to hear more about Britain than the theme tune, Lillibullero.

Borneo (Chapters 10, 11 and 17)

ETHNIC VARIETY. With five assignments between 1980 and 2010, Malaysian Borneo is the place along with Zambia that I can claim to know best. I was struck as much by the continuities of life as by the economic development over the three decades. Sarawak and Sabah remain fascinating places with three distinctive ethnic communities – Dayaks, Chinese and Malays – each with its well established language press. Nor does English have a monopoly of readers among the elites. The Chinese press is strong, and widely read among the leaders of that community.

PERMIT SYSTEM. The government's permit system for newspapers was still in place in 2010. Yet Malaysia was no longer an underdeveloped economy in need of united efforts at nation building – the situation customarily held to justify measures of press control. Yet the controls remained. This suggests that Malaysian politicians, like those everywhere, aren't keen to give up the powers they enjoy. The country has a difficult and potentially explosive mixture of races, which the news media ought not to stoke.

PRIOR RESTRAINT. My students were keen to hear of alternatives to 'prior restraint', a form of censorship that includes permits. Defamation (libel), privacy, confidentiality, contempt of court and national security are examples of laws that limit the media, but after the fact of publication. I was aware that, among other things, Malaysia's international standing was damaged by the blunt instrument of continuing censorship.

MUHAMAD CARTOONS. The Sarawak Tribune in 2006 republished Danish cartoons lampooning the prophet Muhamad. Although Muslims are a minority in Sarawak, uproar followed. The newspaper decided to beat the axe, and shut itself down.

LASTING LESSONS. My friend and colleague in Sarawak, Ashari (Nash) Manis, was an example of the Thomson Foundation's impact on journalists in the sometimes isolated settings of the Majority World. He had kept his study material and used it in his own teaching more than three decades later.

DUTY OF SUPPORT. Colleagues should support each other on overseas assignments. I was doubly depressed after I admitted to an elderly travelling companion that I'd had a bad session. He replied insensitively, 'Oh, I've had an absolutely splendid session,' and listed why it was so splendid.

BETTER FEATURES. Like almost every newspaper outside the developed West at that time and since, the Sarawak Tribune in 1984 needed more and better feature articles. I compared a newspaper without features to a meal without desserts or fruit to follow the meat and fish – incomplete!

PROOF CORRECTION. My unwise assumption that every typesetter understood proof-correction marks with the facility of a London printer led to an important article appearing as nonsense in parts. This underlined the importance of ensuring that everyone spoke the same language – in this case, the language of print.

AGENDAS FOR IMPROVEMENT. The simplest of changes gave the Sunday Tribune a welcome different look from that of its weekday counterpart. I altered the headlines to sans serif types, while the daily paper retained serif types.

I worked for the Tribune's competitor, the Borneo Post, three years later (1987), finding that it had comparable issues for improvement. Once again, I preached the need for feature articles and active news stories – ie news that the paper had found for itself to complement stock sources like listed events and press releases. This was a key Thomson Foundation message, which it had found applied widely around the Majority World.

EDITORIAL COLOUR. At this time the Borneo Post published its first editorial colour. This was mainly cartoons, with some spot (individual) colours for headlines, rules and panels. It was right for the newspaper to do it small and get it right rather than do it big and fail. The printing department was able to develop its colour expertise from there.

LINKED EDITIONS. Being reunited with the BP after more than 20 years (2009) gave me an unusual perspective on the progress of the newspaper. I found an assured production. Its original ability in producing editions in three towns (Kuching, Sibu and Miri) had evolved into delivering separate but linked issues in two states (Sarawak and Sabah).

ENGLISH THRESHOLD. One of the main issues was the language level of the editorial staff. The standard of English was thought to be falling in the society as a whole because of increasing official, and educational, emphasis on Malay (known as Bahasa Malaysia). I recommended that a minimum standard of English should be a requirement for recruitment to the paper, and that existing staff who needed them should take English classes. Sessions of one or two hours once a week over a prolonged period would be the most effective format.

TOO MUCH POLITICS. I called attention to a characteristic of the entire Malaysian press: too much politics and too few lighter, 'human interest' stories. Political set pieces were an easy way to fill space, and additionally both national newspapers, the New Straits Times and the Star, were owned by political parties. As a newspaper not controlled by politicians, the Borneo Post had a potential advantage in a restrictive political environment.

COMPETITION. In Sarawak, new competition arose when the Star started a local edition in the state. The Borneo Post was well placed to meet this competition. It was already strong on national and international news – vital if a regional paper is to hold its own with the nationals. I stressed to the staff that the paper must stand up as the only one a reader takes or at least needs to take. When it is seen as a second or supplementary paper, it is potentially finished.

SUNDOWNER TIME. Now another sun goes down. This one is not over the bay at Kota Kinabalu or above the cataract of the Victoria Falls. It is across the Devon hilltops. But Devon is part of my story, too. There are lessons to be learnt, as well as enjoyments to be had, in journalism everywhere.

APPENDIX ONE
E-JOURNALISM AND THE FUTURE

Website posting (ituri.co.uk), November 2012

When a newspaper can be read on a website or delivered to a mobile phone, tablet computer or ebook reader, clearly we are into a new era. How different is that era, beyond the hype?

Portable electronic devices are a powerful force for decentralising the media. The Arab spring of 2011 showed the power of words and images relayed in this way. Similarly, we have the power of news stories hoovered up by Google, Yahoo and other search engines.

Even so, electronics looks likely to change newspapers more than it will change journalism. The internet, the mobile phone and the rest are delivery systems. They have limited implications for what is delivered, mainly in the direction of greater brevity. For many news items that is no great loss.

When Kindle readers like their journalism in bite-sized chunks – 100 words at a time – who wants to read a well worked 1,500-word feature? The answer may continue to be plenty of people. I don't believe electronics invalidates the Northcliffe dictum of journalism needing both news and features to hold readers. And features often require length. It's uncomfortable to read a long piece on a smartphone, but on a website it's no harder than on paper.

Printed newspapers aren't necessarily heading for extinction. Forecasting fallacy no1 is to extrapolate present trends, in this case the growth of electronically delivered newspapers, in a straight line. As older readers die off, maybe people who have known the internet from infancy will drive print to extinction. Maybe they won't. Some will still prefer to read on paper, but will they be numerous enough for this format to remain financially viable?

A straw in the wind is how paid-for print sales have held up relatively well even though the same content has been available free for years on the websites of newspapers like the Guardian and the Telegraph. Paid circulations are declining, but why haven't they gone through the floor already?

Reading on screen can be very efficient. We can use a small device more easily than a newspaper in crowded situations. The news is available when we want it without waiting for the newspaper to be delivered or going out to get it. Abroad, we no longer have to pay a ransom for printed newspapers to get the news from home. Efficient, but how enjoyable? What value will new generations of readers put on the pleasure of turning pristine pages or the impact of bold pictures and type displays?

It probably makes no long term sense to provide electronic content free and expect people to pay for the same stuff in printed form. The justification for free newspaper websites is to develop solid user bases. The Guardian, for example, has spent many millions on its free web newspaper, destabilising the company's financial position. It's seen as an investment in a future whose outlines are unclear.

Advertising may never be enough to support this free delivery. Matters may look different when people are asked to pay to access content on screen. The *electronic telegraph* is known to make millions – but not enough millions. In UK terms, the Financial Times is the key example. It has a niche market and stories that no other papers provide. Therefore it can sell them profitably, and does so. This points us in the direction of generating unique content that people want to pay for, rather than all drinking from the same pool.

While electronics may come to have a limited impact on *journalism*, it is already adding layers, largely unwelcome, to the work of the *journalist*. New skills must join the skills described in this book. For example, the demands of the net change the way we think about headlines. Well wrought lines and well made puns are at a discount. As long as the headline has the key words – the person, the place, the product – that will enable it to be picked up by search engines, you're OK.

Websites take an inordinate amount of journalistic time and effort. They are like furnaces that need constant feeding. Reporters and feature writers write the stories – then have to upload them onto the net; often find pictures. All time consuming. They're doing two jobs and are effectively chained to the office, with less time to get out and meet people. Quality drops: stories are ripped out of other papers' websites to feed the furnace. The pursuit of 'hits' becomes all important.

Journalists write to be read. Where a paywall is in place, they get fewer readers and their names are no longer fully in the public domain. 'Paywall refugees' will seek out papers that continue to offer free access.

The fashion for putting a reporter's email address with the story is another addition to the writer's workload. Most journalists are chronically poor at administration (and many seem to take a perverse pleasure in ignoring correspondence). One wonders then how many of these contacts from readers get answered, and by whom. This is a potential public relations disaster.

While these are all problems for journalists, the web also offers us the opportunities of its own limitations. Amateur output on the web – that is, many blogs and campaigning sites – merely underlines the importance of classic journalism. It needs a professional journalist to deliver reliable and tolerably even-handed accounts of the news. The blogosphere is about opinions. As this book has suggested, facts drive the news enterprise. Few blogs have the resources, or the inclination, to gather hard information by 'pounding a beat'; nor do most bloggers maintain (or even know about) the distinction between news and comment. These are the jobs of regular journalism (in printed or electronic form) for which there is a continuing need. Paradoxically, the more blogs, the more the need for newspapers and magazines.

APPENDIX TWO
PRESS FREEDOM IN THE MAJORITY WORLD

Article in the Times of Zambia, 1993

The liberalisation of the news media in Zambia is part of a global process that is sweeping vast areas including Africa, Eastern Europe and South America into democracy. Even before this rush of political pluralism, the idea of State control of the media was losing its grip in Zambia and other countries because of its deficiencies in practice.

Whatever the myth of everyone pulling together for the Great Upward Heave, people in the modern sector of Third World countries have always been just as keen on an independent press as their counterparts in the advanced countries. Want it and need it, for muzzled media do not allow the elites – the entrepreneurs, professionals, academics, civil servants, managers and teachers – to communicate properly, and nor do governments get vital feedback.

The state control model of the press devised by developmental theorists in the '50s and '60s had a respectable pedigree, but it never delivered. As countries like Kenya, Singapore and South Korea have shown over the years, increasing economic development does not necessarily produce the predicted easing of shackles on the press.

So by now a free press is the only credible model in the market place. What does it say, and what might it mean for Zambia?

In a pluralistic democracy the news media and the government are seen as separate pillars of the free society. The whole edifice is weakened if the pillars are joined together. This means there can be no proper place for the registration or licensing of publications, or for a state-controlled news agency monopolising incoming wire services and redistributing a selected file to the media organisations.

New publications still have to be registered in Zambia and Zana [the national news agency] continues to redistribute

Reuters, Agence-France Presse and the other external agencies. Because media and government are separate pillars of democracy there is a presupposition against the state controlling newspapers (I will come to broadcasting in a moment). This does not mean that the government cannot own a paper, but in the Zambian situation the government would surely lose credibility with international donors and investors if it continues to own both daily newspapers.

People buy newspapers for three main reasons: To make money, for social prestige (you are seen as a more interesting person if you own a newspaper than a textile mill) and to make propaganda. The last point can clearly be a problem: If government is not to regulate the content of news media, that does not mean no-one else should.

A press council operating a code of conduct is the best way to maintain acceptable standards of independent media. A fundamental issue is whether such an ethical body is to be government-created with statutory powers, or operated by the media industry and journalistic profession based on voluntary compliance. The former is more potent but risks state control by the back-door. If Zambia introduces a code of conduct for news media, I hope the voluntary route will he tried first.

Ethical codes are not solely about control, however. They also permit journalists to do things. For instance, Britain's Press Complaints Commission operates a code that gives reporters wide latitude to use subterfuge if the information sought is:

• In the public interest; and
• Not obtainable by open methods.

This permissive philosophy has produced many worthwhile investigative disclosures. One of the most ingenious came in the aftermath of Lockerbie [when Libyan terrorists destroyed a PanAm airliner in flight] when a newspaper and a TV station – separately – had staff obtain jobs as cleaners at London's Heathrow Airport. In that guise each was able to place a dummy bomb in parked jumbo jets – proving that security had not been made as foolproof as the authorities claimed.

When everybody else can have their say in print, there seems no reason why the government shouldn't too. But there is a far stronger case for a democratic government in a developing country to keep a presence in radio and television than in newspapers. This is partly because broadcasting has a vital development communication role, and it is uncertain that commercial interests would carry this out properly.

Also, alternative ownership models have their problems. The BBC model of non-commercial broadcasting is based on viewers' legal requirement to pay a licence fee. This means adequate arrangements to collect the fee, detect evaders and avoid corruption by those enforcing the system – a tall order in an advanced country and probably an impossible one here.

The commercial model as in the main US networks raises extreme problems of low standards of programming as channels fall over themselves to win the ratings war as well as over-obtrusive advertising as channels chase the dollars.

Zana [the Zambian news agency] could be sold to the Zambian news organisations, perhaps with some outside involvement, each organisation having an equity share in proportion to the capital provided. A socially more attractive solution, since it would tend to preserve jobs, is for the news organisations to be given Zana in exchange for a pledge to keep it going for a specified time.

It would take a stronger privatisation stomach than mine to accept the selling off of ZIS. Government information services continue to have a role all over the world. For developing countries they have a development communication function and also supply news from rural areas that the user media do not reach.

Yet the winds of change have reached even here. British government departments do much of their own information and public relations work rather than putting it through the Central Office of Information (equivalent to a ministry of information). They are also free to contract out work so COI must sometimes compete for the job against private- companies.

So far, the liberalisation of the news media in Zambia has been encouraging if slow. The existence of the Weekly Post – vigorous, annoying and stimulating – is a fine advertisement for democracy here. Privatisation of media is being watched with interest in Africa and beyond. Because state control of information was never total (National Mirror etc.), so hopes now for an independent media are correspondingly higher.

SELECTIVE NAMES INDEX